THE $7 A MEAL QUICK & EASY COOKBOOK

FEED A FAMILY FOR $7 OR LESS

301 DELICIOUS MEALS YOU CAN MAKE IN 30 MINUTES OR LESS

Chef Susan Irby

Aadamsmedia
Avon, Massachusetts

D0111617

Copyright © 2009 by F+W Media, Inc. All rights reserved.
This book, or parts thereof, may not be reproduced in any form without permission from the
publisher; exceptions are made for brief excerpts used in published reviews.

CobornsDelivers.com and CalorieKing.com were used for nutrition and costing analysis.

Contains material adapted and abridged from *The Everything® College Cookbook* by Rhonda Lauret Parkinson, copyright © 2005 by F+W Media, Inc., ISBN 10: 1-59337-303-1, ISBN 13: 978-1-59337-303-0; *The
Everything® Flat Belly Cookbook* by Fitz Koehler, MSESS and Mabelissa Acevedo, LDN, copyright © 2009
by F+W Media, Inc., ISBN 10: 1-60550-676-1, ISBN 13: 978-1-60550-676-0; *The Everything® Gluten-Free
Cookbook* by Nancy T. Maar and Rick Marx, copyright © 2005 by F+W Media, Inc., ISBN 10: 1-59337-394-
5, ISBN 13: 978-1-59337-394-8; *The Everything® Healthy Meals in Minutes* by Patricia M. Butkus, copyright
© 2005 by F+W Media, Inc., ISBN 10: 1-59337-302-3, ISBN 13: 978-1-59337-302-3; *The Everything® Italian
Cookbook* by Dawn Altomari, BPS, copyright © 2005 by F+W Media, Inc., ISBN 10: 1-59337-420-8, ISBN
13: 978-1-59337-420-4; *The Everything® Mediterranean Cookbook* by Dawn Altomari-Rathjen and Jennifer
Bendelius, copyright © 2003 by F+W Media, Inc., ISBN 10: 1-58062-869-9, ISBN 13: 978-1-58062-869-3;
The Everything® No Trans Fat Cookbook by Linda Larsen, copyright © 2007 by F+W Media, Inc., ISBN 10:
1-59869-533-9, ISBN 13: 978-1-59869-533-5; *The Everything® One-Pot Cookbook, 2nd Edition* by Pamela
Rice Hahn, copyright © 2009 by F+W Media, Inc., ISBN 10: 1-59869-836-2, ISBN 13: 978-1-59869-836-7;
The Everything® Quick and Easy 30-Minute, 5-Ingredient Cookbook by Linda Larsen, copyright © 2006
by F+W Media, Inc., ISBN 10: 1-59337-692-8, ISBN 13: 978-1-59337-692-5; *The Everything® Quick Meals
Cookbook, 2nd Edition* by Rhonda Lauret Parkinson, copyright © 2008 by F+W Media, Inc., ISBN 10: 1-
59869-605-X, ISBN 13: 978-1-59869-605-9; and *The Everything® Vegetarian Cookbook* by Jay Weinstein,
copyright © 2002 by F+W Media, Inc., ISBN 10: 1-58062-640-8, ISBN 13: 978-1-58062-640-8.

Published by
Adams Media, a division of F+W Media, Inc.
57 Littlefield Street, Avon, MA 02322. U.S.A.
www.adamsmedia.com

ISBN 10: 1-4405-0223-4
ISBN 13: 978-1-4405-0223-1

Printed in the United States of America.

J I H G F E D C B A

Library of Congress Cataloging-in-Publication Data
is available from the publisher.

This publication is designed to provide accurate and authoritative information with regard to the subject
matter covered. It is sold with the understanding that the publisher is not engaged in rendering legal,
accounting, or other professional advice. If legal advice or other expert assistance is required, the ser-
vices of a competent professional person should be sought.
—From a *Declaration of Principles* jointly adopted by a Committee of the
American Bar Association and a Committee of Publishers and Associations

Many of the designations used by manufacturers and sellers to distinguish their product are claimed as
trademarks. Where those designations appear in this book and Adams Media was aware of a trademark
claim, the designations have been printed with initial capital letters.

This book is available at quantity discounts for bulk purchases.
For information, please call 1-800-289-0963.

CONTENTS

INTRODUCTION

Today's families are busier than ever—parents are working, children are in school, and it seems children's activities grow in number and scope every day. Kids today seem to have more homework, more involved projects, more afterschool activities, more competitions, and more friend playdates and birthday parties. There is always something to do, and that doesn't include keeping the house clean and putting healthy meals on the table. Where does all the time go? And where does all the money go? A simple lunch at a restaurant for a family of four can cost up to $60, if not more. Why not cook at home, enjoy a delicious and most likely more nutritious meal and more family time, and save money?

In this book, I will share with you much of what I teach in my cooking classes. You will learn some fundamentals for smart shopping and basic cooking. Don't be intimidated by either one. Smart shopping is easier and less time-consuming than you think. You will learn what shopping on a budget really means, how to manage your food budget, how to shop for it, and how to properly store it. That's the preparation part. Then, we'll go over basic cooking terms and techniques so you, too, can cook healthy, tasty recipes for your family. Get your family to help you cook so the burden isn't all yours. Families who cook together are more apt to try new foods, spices, and dishes than they would if it were just served to them. When you make cooking a family event and not a chore, it is more fun for everyone and you have helping hands to chop, stir, and, best of all, clean up!

The recipes in this book are both quick and easy. That doesn't mean that each recipe only takes five minutes to make, but it does mean that they only require a very reasonable amount of preparation (prep) time, and, in most cases, less cooking time. Plus, you'll find that the recipe instructions are as simple and easy as possible. You'll also find nutritional information so you know what you're giving your family. Nutrition information is listed on a per serving basis, while cost information is listed per recipe.

This book is designed to help you become the top chef for your household—in short order and with short money! Now let's get cookin'!

CHAPTER 1

GETTING STARTED

Whether you are a beginner cook or have been cooking your whole life, this book provides you with tips for making your dollar go farther in the grocery store and ideas for making the most of the foods, spices, and other ingredients you already have (or should have) in your pantry. With a little help, you will soon be on your way to serving your family delicious meals and putting a few extra bucks into your savings account!

GROW A LITTLE PATIENCE

No matter how rushed you are in your busy life, take a few minutes every week to plan out your family's meals. That's right—slow down and plan more because planning helps you relax! The better the plan you lay out, the less worry you have when you're flying in the house at dinnertime with a boatload of hungry kids. Yes, planning takes patience, but it's worth it.

Why? Without planning, you are going to spend more time in the grocery store, spend more money than you budgeted for, and you are most likely going to cook too much food and therefore, waste more. That is all in addition to how frustrated you'll be when you're in a hurry and don't know exactly what your shopping goals are. So, grow a little patience and recognize that planning your family meals is a good thing!

HOW TO PLAN

Don't be intimidated by the thought of planning out your family's meals. It may take some getting used to at first, but before you know it, it'll be second nature. Here's how to start.

What Should I Do First?

First, keep a family calendar. Each person in your family has his or her own schedule of events, and the better you keep track of these schedules, the better you can plan. No sense making a three-course turkey dinner if Tommy is eating at a Boy Scouts get-together, Susie has a soccer game, and your husband has a late business meeting! Write every major activity on the calendar, including out-of-town guests' arrivals and departure dates, and special events like birthday parties. This way, for family meal planning, you know who you are cooking for, how many you are cooking for, and when you need to cook it!

Decide on Your Menu

Now take a few minutes to think about what you want to make. Let's say it is Saturday morning and you are looking at the calendar before making your big trip to the grocery store. Your thought process might go something like this: *I know I need basic breakfast stuff, a few things for lunch during the week, and what do we want to have for dinner this week? Monday is spaghetti night, Tuesday we'll do chicken, Wednesday I'll make something with my leftover meatballs from Monday, Thursday sounds like a good soup night, and Friday, let's make our own pizza! Then Saturday I can roast a chicken, and Sunday we'll do a beef roast, and then I'll have some great leftovers for next week. Sounds good!*

See how easy that was? That's your initial plan. Now take out a pen and write it down. This way you sort of sketch it out for yourself to see how it looks. Once you get it settled in your mind and on the page, you are ready for your next step, choosing your recipes.

Choose Your Recipes

If your menu plan looks good to you, grab your cookbook and select some recipes that sound good to you. Based on your menu plan, you are specifically looking for interesting recipes that use, in the example above, meatballs, chicken, and beef as they work into your plan for this week. If you have leftovers on Saturday and Sunday, great, you can use those for next week and can keep that in mind for later. However, you don't need to select those recipes for next week right now. The goal now is to select only recipes for this week because this is the week you are shopping for today.

Make a Grocery List

Once you have decided on what you want to make, write down all the ingredients you need whether you know you have them or not. Write down every ingredient, then worry about whether you have it or not. This way you have a comprehensive list of every single item you will need to have on hand to complete your recipes.

Check Your Pantry

Now that you have listed all your ingredients, open your cabinets, refrigerator, and freezer, and see what you have and what you are missing. If you already have an item, then check it off your list! If you don't check it off, then you know you need to buy some. There is nothing more frustrating when you are cooking and you discover halfway through the recipe that you are missing a key ingredient. That is a surefire way to take the fun out of cooking and add to your stress. So, check your cabinets, and make any adjustments to your shopping list. What is not checked off your list should be what you are buying at the store. The next chapter, Shopping on a Budget, helps you with the actual shopping process.

DON'T BE AFRAID TO COOK AT HOME

Now is the time to take the plunge and get over any fears you have of cooking and give it a try. Most recipes are guidelines, not hard, fast rules. Yes, there are a few rules to cooking, but honestly, those mostly apply to baking, where precision is required. That means that you are free to experiment, and perhaps make some not-so-perfect dishes. But you'll also wind up with tons of delicious foods your family can enjoy using some very simple cooking techniques.

Don't be afraid to make mistakes! You might accidentally make a delicious recipe by leaving out an ingredient or using too much of another.

This book is filled with recipes that are easy to follow and have instructions that are not too complicated. So, you have no excuses.

WHAT'S IN YOUR PANTRY?

Even the most experienced chefs need to keep inventory of what is in their pantry. It is essential to cooking efficiently and can save you tons of time, money, and frustration. Following are suggestions for a few items to keep stocked in your pantry. As you prepare your grocery shopping list each week, you will discover which items you use more or less of, and this whole process of cooking at home will become easier and easier and therefore, more fun! If you are a beginner cook, stock your pantry over time, as needed for the recipe, in order to stay within your budget. These are the essentials for a well-stocked pantry:

- apple cider vinegar
- baking powder
- baking soda
- balsamic vinegar
- basil leaves, dried
- bay leaves
- beef broth, keep at least two cans on hand at all times
- black pepper (freshly ground) or whole black peppercorns for refilling pepper grinder
- butter (unsalted)
- canola oil
- cayenne pepper
- celery seeds
- Champagne vinegar
- chicken bouillon cubes

- chicken broth, keep at least three cans on hand at all times
- cinnamon, ground
- cocoa powder
- confectioner's sugar (powdered)
- cumin, ground
- curry powder
- diced tomatoes, canned
- Dijon mustard
- dry mustard, ground
- evaporated milk
- extra virgin olive oil
- flour (all-purpose)
- garlic powder
- ginger, ground
- granulated sugar, light brown
- granulated sugar, white
- honey
- lemon pepper
- long grain, white rice, uncooked
- marjoram, dried
- Marsala wine
- nutmeg, ground
- Old Bay seasoning
- olive oil
- oregano, dried
- paprika
- parsley flakes, dried
- red pepper flakes
- sea salt
- sesame seeds
- Sherry vinegar
- sweetened condensed milk
- tomato paste, canned
- tomato sauce, canned

- tomatoes with green chilies, canned
- unflavored gelatin
- vanilla extract (pure only—do not buy imitation vanilla)
- white pepper
- white wine, for cooking
- whole tomatoes, canned
- yeast, dry

BASIC COOKING UTENSILS AND EQUIPMENT

Here's a list of some tools you'll want to have on hand for at-home cooking.

The Big-Ticket Items
- **chef knife set:** Invest in a good, simple set of chef knives. These do not have to be top-of-the-line, expensive knives. Look for knives made of molded steel, not knives with handles attached by screws, as these knives are not as sturdy when chopping or slicing and the handles tend to fall off over time.
- **hand mixer or standing mixer:** Hand mixers are less expensive and can be just as effective as standing mixers.
- **food processor or blender:** Optional; chopping by hand works for most items. The food processor is preferable for purées and making certain dips and sauces. Food processors are easier to clean and tend to chop and combine the food products better than blenders.

- **basic set of pots and pans:** Your pots and pans do not have to be high-end lines such as All-Clad or Viking to be good and useful. Costco, Sam's Club, and Wal-Mart all sell pots and pans that work just fine for everyday use.

Everything Else
- aluminum foil
- baking sheets (formerly called cookie sheets)
- cutting board
- grater
- larger strainers (or colanders) for draining pasta
- lemon reamer or juicer
- parchment paper
- plastic wrap
- sharpening steel for knife set
- small strainers
- spatulas, rubber and metal
- tongs
- vegetable peeler
- whisk, wire
- wooden spoons
- zester (also called a microplane)

WHAT'S IN YOUR FREEZER?

Keep a few basic foods on hand in your freezer for making quick and easy cooking just that much faster and that much easier. A few of the foods you should keep in your freezer are:

- 1 or 2 pounds ground beef
- 1or 2 pounds ground turkey
- 1 whole chicken
- 2 to 3 pounds chicken breasts, boneless, skin on
- 2 to 3 pounds fish such as halibut
- 2 to 3 pounds shrimp
- 1 large package frozen peas
- 1 large package frozen mixed vegetables

IS FRESH ALWAYS BEST?

As a general rule, yes, fresh is best. However, as with anything in life, there are lots of exceptions. Most of those exceptions fall into two categories with the first category being, what are you cooking? And the second category being, what is the price differential?

The "fresh is always best" approach mainly refers to fresh herbs. As a single person, unless you have an herb garden and grow your own herbs, you will typically end up paying premium prices for fresh herbs that you may not use. However, when cooking for a family, you tend to require more of an ingredient and you most likely cook more often. Given that fact, use fresh herbs whenever possible. However, dried herbs are fine for cooking soups, stews, and any recipe that requires a cooking time of over 1 hour. For recipes with shorter cooking times, strive to use fresh herbs whenever possible. Their flavors are more crisp; they have a beautiful, natural aroma; and they are, well, fresh!

The recipes in this book usually state when to use fresh and when to use canned, frozen, or packaged food products. One factor to consider when using fresh or packaged products is price point. Frozen and canned food products can often be much less expensive yet still maintain good nutritional value and flavor.

CHAPTER 2

SHOPPING ON A BUDGET

Shopping on a budget can mean lots of different things as there are as many different budget sizes as there are families! No matter what your budget, two common ingredients that we should all share are the desire to enjoy good nutrition and save money. When you shop more efficiently, no matter what your budget, you can provide the proper nutrition your children and family need.

DON'T BE DISCOURAGED

If you are shopping on a small budget right now, don't get discouraged. Shopping on a large budget does not necessarily guarantee your family will enjoy healthy, nutritious, delicious meals. In fact, it can mean quite the opposite. Many families with a larger budget tend to buy more preprocessed and packaged foods. These types of foods often have a high sodium content, high fat content, and most always a high price tag. So, in the long run, you pay a high price for convenience while sacrificing nutrition, often flavor, and definitely your pocketbook.

You just have to shop a little smarter, and you will find you have more money than you think you do. Although shopping on a smaller budget requires a few more guidelines, the same basic principals apply to any budget size.

LESSON #1: ADJUST YOUR THINKING

First, think of shopping on a budget as a game. How much money can you take back from the store? Seriously, grocery stores have sales just like every other store. Don't you love a bargain at the department store? Love the bargains at the grocery store, too! Remember, every dollar, or penny, you save can go toward something else, be it a splurge on a family dinner out or saving toward your dream trip to Hawaii. Every penny counts, and that's the attitude you want to have whether you are buying handbags or hamburger. This applies to big budgets and small ones.

LESSON #2: TAKE THE TIME TO COMPARE PRICES

Even if you don't feel that you have any time to take, you do. And when you start planning your family meals for the week, and writing out your shopping list, you will find you have lots more time to compare prices. It's a game, remember? Comparing prices is fun, and it is not as hard as you think it is.

Different grocery stores have different prices. Of course, high-end grocery market chains cost more than the lower-end stores. But you also need to compare prices at similar stores. It is not important to know why a store's prices are consistently higher, you just need to know that they are and know that you don't need to shop there unless you see a true price special advertised in the local paper. (More on that later.)

If the store around the corner is on average $1.00 more on every single item you purchase, if you purchase twelve items, that's $12.00! Do you know what you could do with $12.00? A lot! With $12.00, you can buy enough chicken for four or more meals! With $12.00, you can buy fresh produce for the week! Or, if you buy chicken for two meals, you will have enough leftover to rent a movie for your family to enjoy. The point is that saving $1.00 here or there may not seem like much, but saving a little here or there adds up to substantial savings even in one trip to the grocery store! Compare prices at your local stores. You can be pretty sure you will find a significant difference between the two or three.

LESSON #3: BUY CERTAIN ITEMS IN BULK

There is no question you should buy certain items in bulk, such as ground beef, whole chickens, chicken breasts or pieces, ground turkey, steaks, and sometimes fish. They are generally priced cheaper because they are sold in bulk, and for the most part they are items you can keep in your freezer for quick and easy access for meals. Many stores sell these items in family packs at extreme discounts. Stock up, if you can, and then separate the bulk items into family-size servings before freezing. This way, when you do need to thaw out some chicken, you will have the perfect amount you need for this one meal without having to thaw the entire package and risk surplus contents going bad.

Ideally, you want to stock up on these items when the store runs a special on them. Look for specials in your local newspaper or in the standalone advertisements that come in the mail. Pay close attention to the dates the special prices are being offered so you don't go to the store a day early or a day late, and check for allowable purchase quantities. Many times the store will run a coupon in the paper in that section providing an additional discount storewide. Apply those additional savings to your current purchase, or save those coupons for future use. Just be sure to keep them organized and use before the expiration date.

Also pay close attention to the product label and make sure you really are getting the best deal of the day. It can be very confusing—different brands have different prices, different ways of packaging, and different cuts. In the end, however, you can score a great deal. For example, instead of purchasing boneless, skinless chicken breasts for $3.99 per pound, you can buy boneless chicken breasts with skin on for $.99 per pound. Sure, you have to pull the skin off the chicken, but you saved yourself approximately $2.50 per pound. So pay attention, read the labels, and compare the price tags. If you have a question about the price on something, don't be too shy to ask. Also, when buying items such as cooking oil or ketchup, check the price per ounce as sometimes the largest container is not the cheapest. You can locate the price per ounce on the front of the grocery store shelf, under the product. Remember, it's your money, and the object of this game is for you to keep as much of your money as possible.

LESSON #4: BUY PERISHABLE ITEMS MORE FREQUENTLY

In this regard, shop like the Europeans! In countries such as France and Italy, people typically shop for fresh bread and produce every day. In the United States, we may not go to that extreme, but the point is, don't buy a bunch of perishable ingredients only to have them ruined because you did not have time to eat them. It is an awful feeling to know that good, nutritious food went to waste simply because it rotted! When it comes to buying produce, bread, and deli meats, buy in smaller quantities and eliminate waste.

Also, when you buy these items, be aware of which items can be frozen for safe keeping and which items could be ingredients for other recipes if you don't use them as originally intended. For example, if your family does not eat a lot of sandwiches, buy your bread at Costco or another large store that sells wholesale to the public, and keep the loaves in the freezer. When you want a sandwich, simply remove the number of bread slices you need, thaw them in the microwave for 15 seconds, and then make your sandwiches. Or, let's say you buy a bunch of bananas and the last few are becoming overripe. Use them to make banana bread or banana muffins.

Likewise, if you have overripening apples, before they get too ripe, core them, slice them, and cook them in a little bit of butter and sugar, then freeze them to make apple turnovers or apple pie at a later date. This leads to the next lesson.

LESSON #5: BE CREATIVE IN THE KITCHEN

Don't be afraid to experiment in the kitchen. That statement is never more true than when it comes to making good use of the items you have on hand. It's all about seeing the items in your kitchen as resources for a good meal. If you have a few basics—like a starch such as potatoes, rice, or pasta; some fresh vegetables; and a little olive oil or butter—you have the makings of a meal. Remember, recipes are guidelines. You don't have to follow a recipe exactly unless you are doing some serious baking. So don't let those vegetables and fruits go to waste—look up a few recipes, get some ideas, and then create your own dish. Just write down the ingredients you use so when you create a new masterpiece, you will know how to repeat it!

LESSON #6: FREEZE AND THAW PROPERLY

Freezing foods properly is important as you don't want to open up your ground beef or chicken and find it is inedible because it has freezer burn. Freeze foods in individual or family-size servings because freezing, thawing, and refreezing can cause bacteria to grow and can often change the consistency of your foods.

If you have freezer-safe containers, freeze leftovers in those. Just be aware they take up more space so you may need to get creative in organizing your freezer. Ziploc bags are effective for freezing foods. Be sure to clearly label any containers with the contents and the date frozen.

For thawing, plan ahead and write a note to yourself to take the needed product out of the freezer the night before. Thawing any kind of protein product is best if done overnight in the refrigerator. Any chef will tell you this is the best and proper thawing technique. If you forget to thaw out your protein product ahead of time, try not to defrost it in the microwave. And never defrost any product in plastic or plastic wrap in the microwave as it is believed the toxins from the plastic will seep into the food. Microwaving usually ends up cooking the product as opposed to thawing the product, and it changes the consistency of the product as well. You can thaw in cold water in the sink in an emergency situation; however, you increase the risk of the protein sitting out too long and bacteria beginning to grow. So leave yourself a note!

LESSON #7: NEVER SHOP HUNGRY

This is a very basic principal for grocery shopping, yet it is one of the most important. If you shop on an empty stomach, your grocery cart will be overly full at the checkout counter. Eat a snack before you shop to ensure you stick to your budget.

LESSON #8: SEND THE RIGHT PERSON TO THE STORE

Last but not least, when it comes to grocery shopping, send the right person to the store. If another family member is not as experienced as you are in shopping for bargains, don't send them to the store to do the bulk of the grocery shopping for that week. This may sound silly, but sending an inexperienced shopper to the store can cost you lots of money, and you will most likely end up with several items you don't need or perhaps the wrong quantities or products of the items you do need. For all their well-intentioned efforts, inexperienced shoppers are just that—inexperienced—and can blow your budget even if it's by accident.

CHAPTER 3

BREAKFASTS

Basic Pancakes

Serves 5

Prep time: 10 minutes
Cook time: 6 minutes
Total cost: $2.42
Calories: 180
Fat: 7g
Protein: 5g
Cholesterol: 33mg
Sodium: 36mg

1 cup plain flour

1 tablespoon granulated sugar

2½ teaspoons baking powder

¼ teaspoon sea salt

1 egg

1 cup low-fat milk

2 tablespoons canola oil

Pancakes are very inexpensive and also filling. For maximum health benefit, buy low-cal syrup if possible and be sure to check your local paper for the weekly special. Next time syrup is on special, buy two and set one aside in your pantry!

1. Combine the flour, sugar, baking powder, and salt in a bowl by stirring. Then, make a well in the middle of the mixture. In a separate bowl, beat the egg using a fork and thoroughly combine with the milk and oil. Add the liquid to the flour mixture and stir quickly until moistened; the batter will have some lumps.
2. Preheat a greased or buttered griddle or skillet over medium-high heat. Cook pancakes on the hot griddle, using about ¼ cup batter per cake. Cook about 2 or 3 minutes on each side; pancakes are ready to turn when the tops have broken bubbles on the surface and the edges appear dry.

Buttermilk Pancakes

Serves 5

Prep time: 10 minutes
Cook time: 6 minutes
Total cost: $2.51
Calories: 178
Fat: 7g
Protein: 5g
Cholesterol: 33mg
Sodium: 62mg

1 cup plain flour

1 tablespoon granulated sugar

2½ teaspoons baking powder

¼ teaspoon sea salt

1 egg

1 cup buttermilk

2 tablespoons canola oil

The distinctive flavor of buttermilk adds depth to ordinary pancakes.

1. Combine the flour, sugar, baking powder, and salt in bowl by stirring. Then, make a well in the middle of the mixture. In a separate bowl, beat the egg using a fork and thoroughly combine with the milk and oil. Add the liquid to the flour mixture and stir quickly until moistened; the batter will have some lumps.
2. Preheat a greased or buttered griddle or skillet over medium-high heat. Cook pancakes on the hot griddle, using about ¼ cup batter per cake. Cook about 2 or 3 minutes on each side; pancakes are ready to turn when the tops have broken bubbles on the surface and the edges appear dry.

Quick and Easy Tip

If you don't have a pancake griddle, use an iron skillet. Iron skillets can be used to cook almost anything and add iron nutrients to your foods.

High-Protein Pancakes

Serves 4

- Prep time: 8 minutes
- Cook time: 10 minutes
- Total cost: $2.96
- Calories: 185
- Fat: 4g
- Protein: 14g
- Cholesterol: 124mg
- Sodium: 382mg

3 eggs, separated

¾ cup small-curd cottage cheese, low-fat

½ teaspoon sea salt

½ cup plain flour

1 tablespoon granulated sugar

These protein-packed pancakes are a calorie-efficient way to start your day. Skip the syrup completely or go with ½ tablespoon of butter. Tastes terrific, keeps calories down, and saves on costs!

Combine the eggs, cottage cheese, and salt in a blender (or food processor) and blend until smooth. Add the flour and sugar and blend again. Pour onto a hot, well-greased griddle, keeping pancakes no larger than 4 inches in diameter. Cook until golden brown, turning once. These pancakes will take longer to cook through than Basic Pancakes.

Quick and Easy Tip
Extra calories can add up at the end of the day leading to extra, unwanted pounds. Use nonfat or low-fat cottage cheese here to help balance out heavier meals at the end of the day.

Basic Omelet

Serves 1

Prep time: 4 minutes
Cook time: 8 minutes
Total cost: $1.04
Calories: 108
Fat: 8g
Protein: 6g
Cholesterol: 316mg
Sodium: 104mg

2 eggs per omelet

Cooking spray if using non-stick skillet or omelet pan

2 teaspoons butter if using uncoated skillet or omelet pan

Don't worry if you don't have a traditional omelet pan. A small 6- to 8-inch skillet works fine. Nonstick is preferred; however, if you don't have a nonstick pan, make sure your entire pan is coated with the butter. Use 2 teaspoons butter for each omelet.

1. Beat the eggs well in a bowl, but do not allow them to become frothy. Spray the nonstick skillet and heat slightly over medium heat, or if using an uncoated skillet, melt the butter over medium heat, tilting the skillet to coat the bottom. Pour in the eggs; stir gently with a fork while they thicken to distribute the eggs from top to bottom. Stop stirring when the eggs begin to set. As the eggs thicken, lift the edges of the omelet and allow the uncooked eggs to flow underneath.

2. Allow to cook until the bottom is golden and the top is set but shiny. With a long, flat spatula, gently loosen the edge of the omelet and fold the omelet in half toward you. With the help of the spatula, slide the omelet out of the pan and onto a plate. If making multiple omelets, cover them with foil to keep warm.

Roasted Red Pepper Omelet

Serves 1

Prep time: 8 minutes

Cook time: 10 minutes

Total cost: $1.94

Calories: 222

Fat: 11g

Protein: 32g

Cholesterol: 336mg

Sodium: 73mg

2 eggs

Sea salt and black pepper to taste

¼ cup cooked spinach, drained (frozen is okay)

2 tablespoons grated Parmesan cheese

2 tablespoons red roasted peppers (from can or jar), chopped

Omelets are perfect for customizing—make yours and add your favorite touches, then have the rest of your family choose their own additions.

1. In a small mixing bowl, beat eggs until well combined using wire whisk or fork. Coat a nonstick skillet with nonstick spray (see Basic Omelet, page 16, for uncoated skillet directions) and heat slightly over medium heat.
2. Add eggs to skillet and salt and pepper to taste. Cook on medium until eggs are just setting. Add spinach, cheese, and red peppers to center of eggs. Fold omelet over and cook for 2 minutes.
3. Flip omelet and cook for an additional 2 minutes.

Quick and Easy Tip
Be sure to use a spatula to lift edges of omelet and tilt skillet to drain off excess egg in the center of the omelet. This helps prevent burning your omelet while waiting for the center to finish cooking.

Vegetarian Omelet

Serves 1

Prep time: 10 minutes
Cook time: 5 minutes
Total cost: $1.67
Calories: 123
Fat: 9g
Protein: 11g
Cholesterol: 316mg
Sodium: 104mg

2 eggs

Sea salt and black pepper to taste

2 tablespoons diced tomatoes, canned okay if drained

2 tablespoons mushrooms, chopped

1 tablespoon green onion, chopped

Add any combination of vegetables or cheeses to customize your omelet. Part of the fun of cooking is to try new creations, just be sure to remember what you did so you can repeat it!

1. In a small mixing bowl, beat eggs until well combined using wire whisk or fork. Coat a nonstick skillet with nonstick spray (see Basic Omelet, page 16, for uncoated skillet directions) and heat slightly over medium heat.
2. Add eggs to skillet and salt and pepper to taste. Cook on medium until eggs are just setting. Add tomatoes, mushrooms, and onions to center of eggs. Fold omelet over and cook for 2 minutes.
3. Flip omelet and cook for an additional 2 minutes or until done.

Quick and Easy Tip
Prepare vegetables the day before to save time in the morning.

The $7 a Meal Quick & Easy Cookbook

Golden Apple Omelet with Cheese

Serves 2

Prep time: 15 minutes

Cook time: 6 minutes

Total cost: $3.28

Calories: 175

Fat: 22g

Protein: 15g

Cholesterol: 322mg

Sodium: 250mg

4 eggs

1 Golden Delicious apple, pared (peeled), cored, and sliced

2 tablespoons butter, divided

1 tablespoon water

Sea salt and black pepper to taste

2 tablespoons crumbled blue cheese

2 tablespoons grated Parmesan cheese

Pears also taste great with this recipe. For a lighter omelet, leave out the blue cheese and save on calories and your pocketbook!

1. In a small mixing bowl, beat eggs using wire whisk or fork until combined.
2. Sauté the apple in 1 tablespoon butter until barely tender; remove from the pan.
3. Combine eggs, water, salt, and pepper until blended. Heat the remaining butter in an omelet pan or skillet; add the egg mixture. Cook slowly, lifting the edges to allow the uncooked portion to flow under. Arrange the apple slices on half of the omelet. Sprinkle with the cheeses; fold in half. Cook an additional 2 minutes or until done. Transfer to plate for serving.

Quick and Easy Tip
Pears are also great with this recipe. Cook the same way as the apples!

Breakfasts

19

Italian-Style Frittata

Serves 4

Prep time: 15 minutes
Cook time: 7 minutes
Total cost: $6.35
Calories: 163
Fat: 11g
Protein: 14g
Cholesterol: 328mg
Sodium: 267mg

8 eggs

1 tablespoon white or yellow onion, chopped

1 tablespoon green or red bell peppers, chopped

1 ounce ham or turkey, chopped

⅓ cup grated Cheddar cheese

A frittata is an open-faced omelet that originated in Italy. Frittatas taste delicious and are easier to cook than an omelet because you don't have to fold them.

1. In a medium mixing bowl, beat eggs using wire whisk or fork until combined.
2. Coat an ovenproof, nonstick skillet with nonstick spray (see Basic Omelet instructions for uncoated skillets). On medium-high heat, add onions, peppers, and ham to skillet. Sauté for 2 minutes.
3. Add eggs to skillet and cook for 2 to 3 minutes. Place cheese on top of frittata, then place skillet in oven under the broiler and broil for 2 to 3 minutes or until cheese melts and eggs are set. Remove from pan and serve.

Quick and Easy Tip
As with omelets, be sure to lift the edges of the frittata with a spatula to help prevent sticking. This recipe serves 4, so it's faster than making individual omelets and you don't have to fold it!

Parmesan Frittata

Serves 4

Prep time: 10 minutes
Cook time: 5 minutes
Total cost: $4.44
Calories: 258
Fat: 15g
Protein: 11g
Cholesterol: 315mg
Sodium: 680mg

8 eggs

5 slices day-old toast

2 tablespoons butter

1 small white or yellow onion, chopped

Sea salt and black pepper to taste

1 tablespoon grated Parmesan cheese

If you prefer, substitute your favorite cheese or, better yet, whatever you have in your refrigerator.

1. In a small mixing bowl, beat eggs using wire whisk or fork. Set aside.
2. Place toast in plastic bag and roll over it with a rolling pin to crush. In ovenproof skillet, melt butter over medium heat and add onions and crushed bread crumbs. Sauté 3 minutes. Add eggs, salt and pepper, and cheese. Cook until eggs are setting. Turn on broiler and place skillet under broiler. Broil for 1 minute or until eggs are cooked.

Quick and Easy Tip
Anytime you have leftover toast, save in a plastic bag and keep in freezer if not using within a day or two. Toast can be used not only for this recipe but as croutons for salad or in meatloaf or hamburgers. Add veggies into this recipe and serve for dinner as a meal!

Sausage Bake

Serves 4

Prep time: 15 minutes
Cook time: 20 minutes
Total cost: $6.93
Calories: 447
Fat: 30
Protein: 18g
Cholesterol: 59mg
Sodium: 918mg

¾ pound ground sausage, mild or medium

1 puff pastry sheet, Pepperidge Farm preferred

2 tablespoons grated Cheddar cheese

2 tablespoons grated Parmesan cheese

Pinch sea salt

Puff pastry is available at most grocery stores and is located near the frozen pie shells. Pepperridge Farm is usually the only brand available and is a good quality product. The package contains 2 puff pastry sheets, so use one for this recipe and save the other one for another quick meal!

1. Preheat oven to 400°F. Line a baking sheet with parchment paper and set aside. In a heavy skillet, cook sausage over medium heat until golden brown and cooked, about 5 to 7 minutes. Drain off grease.
2. Unfold puff pastry sheet and place on parchment or wax paper. In a small bowl, combine cheeses and mix well. Sprinkle cheese mixture over the puff pastry and gently press cheese mixture into pastry; roll to a 12" x 18" rectangle. Spread cooked sausage over pastry and roll up like a log. Press edges of pastry to seal.
3. Place pastry on lined baking sheet and bake for 12 to 18 minutes until puffed and golden brown. Slice "loaf" and serve hot.

Traditional French Toast

Serves 6

* Prep time: 12 minutes
* Cook time: 10 minutes
* Total cost: $2.13
* Calories: 186
* Fat: 6g
* Protein: 5g
* Cholesterol: 27mg
* Sodium: 209mg

1 cup milk

1 egg, beaten

½ teaspoon cinnamon

Small pinch nutmeg

3 tablespoons butter

6 slices Texas toast or other thickly sliced bread

Top French toast with any pancake topping, usually syrup. Dust with powdered sugar for a pretty presentation.

1. Preheat griddle over medium heat. In a shallow casserole dish, combine milk, egg, cinnamon, and nutmeg and beat until combined.
2. Melt butter on preheated griddle, then dip bread into egg mixture, coating both sides. Let the bread sit in the egg mixture for 30 seconds. Immediately place onto sizzling butter on griddle. Cook over medium heat for 6 to 9 minutes, turning once, until golden brown.

Quick and Easy Tip
If you are cooking for a crowd on a weekend, save any leftovers and use them for Amaretto Bread Pudding, (page 317).

Basic Muffins

Serves 6

Prep time: 12 minutes
Cook time: 20 minutes
Total cost: $1.43
Calories: 307
Fat: 7g
Protein: 6g
Cholesterol: 28mg
Sodium: 31mg

2 cups plain flour

¼ cup granulated sugar

1 tablespoon baking powder

½ teaspoon sea salt

1 large egg

1 cup low-fat milk

⅓ cup canola oil

Add blueberries, nuts, or smashed ripe bananas to this basic mix for fresh, tasty muffins in a pinch.

1. Preheat the oven to 400°F. Grease well a 12-cup muffin tin, or line with paper cups. Sift together the flour, sugar, baking powder, and salt. Place the sifted dry ingredients into a bowl and make a well in the center. In a second bowl, beat the egg lightly. Add the milk and oil and combine. Pour the egg mixture into the well in the dry ingredients and combine quickly, until dry ingredients are just moistened. Some lumps will remain in the batter.
2. Fill the muffin cups about ⅔ full. Bake about 20 minutes, or until the center tests done when toothpick inserted comes out clean.

Quick and Easy Tip

Muffins are a great snack for kids to stave off afterschool but before-dinner hunger pangs. When making, make two batches and keep some in the freezer for quick access.

The $7 a Meal Quick & Easy Cookbook

Cherry-Oat Muffins

Serves 12

Prep time: 15 minutes
Cook time: 20 minutes
Total cost: $3.51
Calories: 131
Fat: 10g
Protein: 4g
Cholesterol: 27mg
Sodium: 44mg

1½ cups oatmeal

1½ cups plain flour

1 teaspoon baking powder

½ teaspoon baking soda

⅔ cup brown sugar

1 cup buttermilk

½ cup canola oil

2 eggs

1½ cups halved, pitted cherries or frozen cherries, unthawed

There are several ways to pit cherries. You can cut the cherry in half and pry the pit out with your fingers. Cherry pitters work well; be sure that you see the pit come out each time. Or you can push a straw through the center of the cherry, removing the pit and stem at the same time.

1. Preheat oven to 375°F. Line 24 muffin cups with paper liners and set aside. In a large bowl, combine oatmeal, flour, baking powder, baking soda, and brown sugar. In a small bowl, combine buttermilk, oil, and eggs and beat well. Add to oatmeal mixture and stir just until combined. Stir in cherries.
2. Fill prepared muffin cups two-thirds full with batter. Bake for 17 to 22 minutes or until muffins are rounded and tops are golden brown.

Quick and Easy Tip
Use quick-cooking oatmeal for best results in these tender and flavorful muffins. You can use either Bing cherries or sour cherries, or use dried cherries to save some more time and juicy mess!

Raspberry–Cream Cheese Biscuits

Serves 7

Prep time: 15 minutes

Cook time: 10 minutes

Total cost: $2.48

Calories: 279

Fat: 7g

Protein: 7g

Cholesterol: 6mg

Sodium: 33mg

3 cups plain flour

2 tablespoons baking powder

¾ teaspoon sea salt

3 tablespoons shortening

¾ cup orange juice or low-fat milk

1 3-ounce package cream cheese

2 tablespoons raspberry all-fruit spread or jam

2 tablespoons sugar for sprinkling tops

Raspberries are both pretty and delicious. When cooking with fresh raspberries, be sure to stir them gently as they are very delicate!

1. Preheat the oven to 450°F. Sift together the flour, baking powder, and salt. Cut in the shortening until the mixture resembles coarse crumbs. Add the orange juice and beat to form a soft dough. Turn the dough onto a surface well dusted with flour and knead 10 times. Roll or pat the dough till it's ½-inch thick. Cut rounds with a biscuit cutter or a 2½-inch round cutter (a drinking glass can be used). Place the rounds on an ungreased cookie sheet.
2. Soften the cream cheese. Add the jam and mix until marbled but not thoroughly combined. Spoon about 1 teaspoon onto the center of each round. Sprinkle with sugar. Bake 8 to 10 minutes, or until golden brown.

Quick and Easy Tip
To save time and possibly money, replace flour, baking powder, salt, and shortening by using 3 cups of biscuit mix such as Bisquick. This will only save money if your pantry is lacking in all of the ingredients.

Scrambled Eggs

Serves 3

Prep time: 10 minutes
Cook time: 8 minutes
Total cost: $2.43
Calories: 159
Fat: 13g
Protein: 11
Cholesterol: 315mg
Sodium: 66mg

6 eggs

⅓ cup low-fat milk

Sea salt and black pepper
to taste

1 tablespoon butter

Scrambled eggs are easy, tasty, and nutritious. Use them as a base and add your favorite things such as cheese or spice up with a salsa for added flavor with few calories.

Beat the eggs, milk, and seasonings together lightly (with white and yellow streaks still visible) or well (until a uniform color) as preferred, using a fork or whisk. Heat the butter in a skillet and pour the egg mixture in. After the eggs begin to thicken, stir gently with a wooden spoon until eggs are thick but still moist.

Quick and Easy Tip
Add a splash of club soda for extra fluffy eggs, or for added protein, add 2 tablespoons of cottage cheese.

Vegetable Egg Scramble

Serves 6

Prep time: 12 minutes
Cook time: 10 minutes
Total cost: $5.42
Calories: 67
Fat: 5g
Protein: 6g
Cholesterol: 157mg
Sodium: 53mg

1 teaspoon olive oil

3 scallions (green onions), minced

2 cloves garlic, minced

½ pound mushrooms, sliced

1 green bell pepper, chopped

1 8-ounce can kernel corn, drained

6 eggs

Sea salt and black pepper to taste

Vegetables are a great way to include extra flavor and nutrients to a dish without adding fat!

1. In a large skillet, heat the oil over medium heat. Add the scallions, garlic, mushrooms, bell pepper, and corn. Sauté, stirring occasionally, until the vegetables are tender, about 5 minutes.
2. Meanwhile, beat the eggs lightly in a bowl. Add the eggs to the vegetables, season with salt and pepper, and scramble until thoroughly cooked. Serve at once.

Quick and Easy Tip
Precook your vegetables the day before or use canned vegetables; just make sure they are drained really well or they will make your eggs soggy.

Quiche Lorraine

Serves 5

Prep time: 15 minutes
Cook time: 25 minutes
Total cost: $4.35
Calories: 207
Fat: 16g
Protein: 15g
Cholesterol: 209mg
Sodium: 447mg

2 slices bacon

1 medium onion, chopped

1½ tablespoons canola oil

6 eggs

1½ cups shredded Swiss cheese

1 small pinch nutmeg

Sea salt and black pepper to taste

Quiche is delicious and not something you think of every day. You can also make mini-quiche and serve as an appetizer!

1. Preheat the broiler. Cook the bacon in a skillet until hard. Drain well, crumble, and reserve. In a 10-inch ovenproof skillet, heat the oil and sauté the onion for about 2 minutes.
2. Beat the eggs well. Stir in the cheese, nutmeg, salt and pepper, and bacon. When the onions have finished cooking, stir to distribute evenly (do not drain), and pour the egg mixture over them. Reduce the heat to medium low and cook until set but still moist on top, about 8 minutes. Immediately put the skillet in the broiler, about 5 inches from the flame or element, and cook until the top is done but not browned.

Quick and Easy Meals

Prepare quiche ahead of time and keep in the freezer securely wrapped. Then pull it out and serve as a quick and easy appetizer or meal for breakfast, lunch, or dinner.

Breakfasts

29

Chilled Swiss Oatmeal (Muesli)

Serves 6

Prep time: 15 minutes

Chill: 8 hours

Total cost: $5.60

Calories: 183

Fat: 10g

Protein: 6g

Cholesterol: 2mg

Sodium: 61mg

2 cups quick-cooking rolled oats

½ cup orange juice

¾ cup chopped prunes, raisins, or currants

⅓ cup chopped nuts or wheat germ

¼ teaspoon salt

¼ cup honey

1¼ cups low-fat milk

Most muesli has to be cooked, and that's why this one is so great to have on hand for breakfast or snacks.

Place the oats in a bowl and pour the juice over them; toss till it is evenly absorbed. Stir in the fruit, nuts, and salt. Pour the honey over the mixture and toss until evenly combined. Stir in the milk. Cover and refrigerate at least 8 hours. Do not cook; serve cold with brown sugar and additional milk or cream if desired.

Quick and Easy Meals
Try making two batches of this recipe, as you can make it ahead and hold it in the refrigerator for up to one week. Or, because it's freezer friendly, seal it in a Ziploc and enjoy in a month!

Mini Pastry Puffs

Serves 12

Prep time: 15 minutes
Cook time: 20 minutes
Total cost: $1.22
Calories: 52
Fat: 2g
Protein: 2g
Cholesterol: 26mg
Sodium: 16mg

2 eggs

⅔ cup low-fat milk

⅔ cup plain flour

1 tablespoon canola oil

This recipe is a favorite with adults and kids alike!

1. Preheat oven to 425°F. Spray mini-muffin pans with baking spray and set aside.
2. Combine all ingredients in a medium bowl and beat well with wire whisk until batter is blended and smooth. Pour 1 tablespoon of batter into each prepared muffin cup. Bake for 15 to 22 minutes or until puffs are deep golden brown and are puffed. Serve immediately.

Quick and Easy Tip

Puffs "puff up" without any leavening in the batter because it contains lots of gluten and liquid. When the popovers are placed in the hot oven, the batter almost explodes with steam, and the gluten keeps the shell together.

Basic Waffles

Serves 3

Prep time: 10 minutes
Cook time: 5 minutes
Total cost: $1.84
Calories: 401
Fat: 41g
Protein: 17g
Cholesterol: 110mg
Sodium: 110mg

2 cups plain flour

4 teaspoons baking powder

¼ teaspoon sea salt

2 eggs

1¾ cups low-fat milk

½ cup canola oil

If your family loves waffles, consider investing in a waffle iron. They are not too expensive and will bring joy to your family for years to come.

Preheat waffle iron following manufacturer's instructions. Stir together the flour, baking powder, and salt, and make a well in the middle of the mixture. Beat the eggs lightly, then beat in the milk and oil until well combined. Add all at once to the dry ingredients and combine until just moistened. Batter will have a few lumps.

Quick and Easy Tip
Use the manufacturer's directions to determine how much batter to use per waffle; use about 1 cup for a standard 7-inch circular waffle. Do not open the iron while the waffle is cooking! Remove with a fork to avoid burning your fingers.

CHAPTER 4

APPETIZERS

Grilled Vegetable Kebabs

Serves 8

Prep time: 18 minutes
Cook time: 10 minutes
Total cost: $5.25
Calories: 49
Fat: 0g
Protein: 1g
Cholesterol: 0mg
Sodium: 1mg

1 large yellow onion, cut into eighths

1 red bell pepper, cut into 2-inch squares

1 green bell pepper, cut into 2-inch squares

1 yellow bell pepper, cut into 2-inch squares

8 cremini or button mushrooms, stems removed and halved

2 tablespoons olive oil

Sea salt and black pepper to taste

8 wooden skewers about 5 to 6 inches long

Presoak wooden skewers for about 45 minutes. If 5- to 6-inch skewers are not available, purchase the long ones and cut them with kitchen scissors to the desired length.

1. Preheat grill or broiler. Place all vegetables in a bowl. Pour in olive oil, add sea salt and pepper to taste. Toss vegetables to coat.
2. Skewer vegetables in random order such as red bell pepper slice, onion slice, mushroom slice, green bell pepper slice, onion slice, mushroom slice, and yellow bell pepper slice.
3. Place the skewers on the grill or under the broiler, paying close attention as they cook as they can easily burn. Try to turn the vegetables only once or twice as the vegetables become tender while cooking and can fall off the skewer. Cook until the vegetables are fork tender, about 6 minutes.

Quick and Easy Tip
This is definitely a recipe you want to make ahead of time. Do all the preparation the day before up until the point of cooking. When you are ready to grill, just heat up the grill and throw them on!

Roasted Red Pepper Bruschetta

Serves 6

Prep time: 15 minutes
Cook time: 12 minutes
Total cost: $6.81
Calories: 157
Fat: 5g
Protein: 5g
Cholesterol: 2mg
Sodium: 904mg

1 sourdough baguette,
  cut into ½-inch slices

1 jar roasted red bell peppers,
  drained and chopped

¼ cup fresh basil leaves,
  chopped

2 tablespoons grated
  Parmesan cheese

1 garlic clove, chopped

2 tablespoons extra virgin
  olive oil

1 tablespoon balsamic
  vinegar

Sea salt and black pepper
  to taste

Roasted red bell peppers add depth to the most basic of ingredients like the recipe here. If you have time, roast your own—but be aware, they do make a little mess. If not, these marinated ones work just fine!

1. Line a baking sheet with parchment paper. Preheat oven to 250°F. Place baguette slices on baking sheet and place in oven. Let baguette slices rest in oven while you prepare the bruschetta. The low temperature of the oven will not burn the baguette, and for this appetizer, the crunchier the baguette the better!
2. In a medium mixing bowl, place peppers, basil, cheese, garlic, olive oil, and balsamic vinegar. Toss well. Season with salt and pepper as desired.
3. Remove baguette slices from oven. Place on serving tray and top with bruschetta. Serve immediately.

Traditional Hummus

Serves 6

Prep time: 7 minutes
Cook time: none
Total cost: $2.44
Calories: 61
Fat: 2g
Protein: 12g
Cholesterol: 0mg
Sodium: 718mg

1 cup garbanzo beans, drained

2 garlic cloves

1 lemon, zested and juiced

2 teaspoons extra virgin olive oil

Sea salt and black pepper to taste

¼ cup fresh Italian parsley, chopped, or 2 teaspoons dried parsley

Hummus is always a crowd pleaser. Add tomato wedges to the serving platter for added color.

In a food processor or blender, purée the garbanzo beans, garlic, and lemon zest and juice. While puréeing, drizzle in the olive oil until well combined. Remove the mixture and season to taste with salt and pepper. Sprinkle with parsley when serving. Serve with crackers or Melba toast.

Quick and Easy Tip
Serve with celery stalks for a low-fat, low-cost appetizer that your friends and guests will love.

Dip of Eggplant and Herbs

Serves 6

Prep time: 15 minutes
Cook time: 10 minutes
Total cost: $4.40
Calories: 88
Fat: 6
Protein: 4
Cholesterol: 4mg
Sodium: 16mg

1 large eggplant

1 tablespoon olive oil

3 cloves garlic, minced

½ cup yogurt, low-fat or nonfat is okay

½ cup sour cream, low-fat or nonfat is okay

1 tablespoon fresh rosemary, chopped

1 tablespoon fresh basil, chopped

1 tablespoon fresh Italian parsley, chopped

Sea salt and black pepper to taste

A lot of people don't get that excited when they hear the word eggplant, but it makes for a tasty appetizer and is almost always a hit at parties.

1. Preheat oven to 375°F and line a baking sheet with parchment paper.
2. Slice eggplant lengthwise and drizzle with olive oil and garlic. Cover with foil and place on baking sheet. Bake in oven for 10 minutes. Remove from oven and place in plastic bag to sweat.
3. Spoon the eggplant pulp into a food processor or blender, and pulse. Add the yogurt and sour cream ¼ cup at a time, and blend until it reaches the consistency of thick sauce. Add the herbs and blend well. Season with salt and pepper to taste. Refrigerate until ready to use.

Quick and Easy Tip
Preroast the eggplant whenever possible and then throw everything together for a spur-of-the-moment party.

Roasted Roma Tomatoes
with Herbs

Serves 4

Prep time: 8 minutes

Cook time: 11 minutes

Total cost: $2.52

Calories: 32

Fat: 2g

Protein: 1g

Cholesterol: 0mg

Sodium: 3mg

4 Roma or plum tomatoes

3 cloves garlic

¼ cup fresh thyme, leaves removed from stems

Sea salt and black pepper to taste

Extra virgin olive oil for drizzling after baked

This appetizer was a favorite at the restaurant I worked for in Florence, Italy. We would bake hundreds of tomatoes each day and serve as an appetizer on our regular menu.

1. Preheat oven to 385°F.
2. Cut the tomatoes into quarters and remove seeds. Lay out each quarter in a single layer on a baking sheet lined with parchment paper. Mince the garlic, and chop the thyme slightly to open up the flavors. Sprinkle the tomatoes with the garlic, thyme, sea salt, and black pepper.
3. Bake in the oven for approximately 10 to 12 minutes. Then remove and serve on top of crackers, Melba rounds, and drizzle with olive oil. Or, skip the carbs and calories and enjoy the Italian way with olive oil!

Quick and Easy Tip

If you are making several appetizers for a party, roast (or bake) these tomatoes at 275°F for 25 minutes while you prep other appetizers or set your tables.

The $7 a Meal Quick & Easy Cookbook

Chicken Herb Meatballs

Serves 6

- Prep time: 20 minutes
- Cook time: 20 minutes
- Total cost: $5.83
- Calories: 190
- Fat: 18g
- Protein: 23g
- Cholesterol: 85mg
- Sodium: 221mg

2 slices bread, toasted

1 pound ground chicken

¼ cup dried cranberries

½ cup pecans, chopped, or pecan pieces, chopped

1 egg

¼ teaspoon cinnamon

¼ teaspoon curry powder

½ teaspoon fresh thyme leaves or dried thyme

Sea salt and black pepper

1 jar mango chutney or other favorite jam or chutney

Meatballs are always great for appetizer parties as they are filling for guests who arrive super hungry. You could also serve these as a meal with rice and vegetables for your family.

1. Preheat oven to 350°F. Line a baking sheet with parchment paper. In a small bowl, soak the bread in water for 1 minute or until wet. Squeeze out liquid and set aside.
2. In a larger mixing bowl, combine bread with remaining ingredients. Shape the mixture into balls. Place balls on a baking sheet and cover with foil. Bake about 20 minutes. Serve with jam or chutney.

Quick and Easy Tip

This recipe tastes good with or without the pecans, or substitute walnuts if you prefer. Meatballs can also be made ahead of time and kept frozen either uncooked or cooked. If cooking from frozen, thaw in refrigerator overnight.

Roasted Garlic Spread

Serves 6

Prep time: 3 minutes
Cook time: 30 minutes
Total cost: $5.25
Calories: 160
Fat: 7g
Protein: 3g
Cholesterol: 0mg
Sodium: 233mg

2 heads garlic

¼ cup extra virgin olive oil

1 bunch fresh Italian parsley

1 sourdough baguette, sliced into ½-inch slices and toasted

Eating parsley immediately after eating a lot of garlic really does help calm down intense garlic breath. Make sure you have plenty around for your guests after they savor this simple yet tasty dish.

1. Preheat oven to 400°F. Slice tops off each garlic head (or bulb) revealing the cloves inside. Place both bulbs on aluminum foil and pour olive oil over each. Wrap foil around garlic and place in center of oven rack and bake for 30 minutes.
2. Remove garlic from oven, place in center of serving platter, and arrange parsley and baguette slices around garlic and serve.

Quick and Easy
The best way to toast baguettes is to place them on a baking sheet in a 225°F oven and let them slowly toast in the oven for about 20 to 25 minutes. Make ahead and keep in an airtight container.

The $7 a Meal Quick & Easy Cookbook

Creamy Crab Wontons

Serves 10

Prep time: 20 minutes
Cook time: 7 minutes
Total cost: $7.00
Calories: 126
Fat: 9g
Protein: 4g
Cholesterol: 22mg
Sodium: 182mg

3 fresh basil leaves, chopped or ½ teaspoon dried basil

¾ pound canned lump crabmeat

¾ cup sour cream, low-fat okay

Black pepper to taste

1 package square or round wontons

2 cups canola oil

These appetizers are best served warm or hot. Prepare them ahead of time and fry just before guests arrive, but be sure to wear an apron so you don't get dirty!

1. Combine basil, crab, sour cream, and pepper. Mix well.
2. Remove wontons from wrapper and place ½ to 1 tablespoon crab mixture in center of wonton. Using your fingertip, spread a little water around the edges. Pinch edges of wonton together to seal.
3. In a medium skillet, heat oil. When oil is hot, add crab wontons and fry until golden brown. Remove from skillet and drain on paper towels.

Quick and Easy Tip
Wonton wrappers come in handy for lots of dishes, including ravioli. The key is not to overfill them so they stay sealed when cooking. Fry, as they are here, or bake them for a crispy cracker.

Baked Cheese Loaf

Serves 8

Prep time: 8 minutes
Cook time: 12 minutes
Total cost: $6.96
Calories: 313
Fat: 22g
Protein: 6g
Cholesterol: 20mg
Sodium: 391mg

1½ cups sour cream

¼ cup gorgonzola cheese

¼ cup shredded fontina cheese

1 package Pepperridge Farm puff pastry sheets

2 tablespoons olive oil

Appetizers usually indicate someone's having a party or get-together, and there is nothing better than cheese to make guests happy.

1. Preheat oven to 350°F. Line a baking sheet with parchment paper. In a mixing bowl, combine sour cream and cheeses. Blend well.
2. Roll out pastry sheet and coat with olive oil. Spread cheese mixture on top. Roll up dough like a jelly-roll into a log. Slice the log into 1-inch slices.
3. Place on baking sheet and bake for 12 minutes or until pastry is puffed and golden. Serve warm.

Quick and Easy Tip
Prepare log ahead of time and keep in the refrigerator. Do not freeze as sour cream and cheese tend not to freeze well.

The $7 a Meal Quick & Easy Cookbook

Citrus-Glazed Shrimp

Serves 4

Prep time: 8 minutes

Cook time: 3 minutes

Total cost: $6.85

Calories: 150

Fat: 5g

Protein: 23g

Cholesterol: 172mg

Sodium: 168mg

1 orange, zested and juiced

1 shallot, diced

½ teaspoon capers, drained

black pepper to taste

1 tablespoon olive oil

¾ pound large shrimp, peeled, tails on

Try this recipe in place of the traditional shrimp cocktail.

1. In a bowl, combine orange zest and juice, shallots, capers, and oil.
2. In a skillet over medium heat, heat orange mixture. When heated, add shrimp and black pepper, and cook until just done, about 2 to 3 minutes. Remove from heat and serve with toothpicks.

Quick and Easy Tip

Reserve any leftover citrus sauce as a side dipping sauce for the shrimp. Frozen, cooked shrimp also work well for this recipe. Just make sure they are thawed before cooking and only cook for 30 to 45 seconds to heat and coat with citrus mixture.

Grilled Beef Skewers

Serves 4

Prep time: 16 minutes
Cook time: 15 minutes
Total cost: $6.99
Calories: 235
Fat: 27g
Protein: 27g
Cholesterol: 56mg
Sodium: 53mg

¾ pound sirloin beef

¼ cup walnuts, chopped

2 garlic cloves

1 tablespoon olive oil

½ cup dry red wine

Sea salt and black pepper

Sirloin is a quality cut of beef and is much less expensive than filet. Marinades also tenderize beef, allowing you to use less choice cuts for certain recipes such as this one.

1. Thinly slice and skewer the beef; skewers do not need to be presoaked. Place beef skewers in a large rectangular baking dish.
2. In food processor or blender, finely grind the walnuts and add garlic, oil, wine, and pinch of salt and pepper. Blend well. Pour mixture over beef skewers, coating well. Cover and refrigerate for 15 minutes or up to 2 hours.
3. Preheat oven to 400°F. Bake skewers, covered, for 15 minutes. Serve hot.

Quick and Easy Tip
Sharp knives are essential to slicing beef; however, before slicing, place beef in freezer for about 15 minutes and beef will become more firm making it easier to slice.

Citrus-Broiled Pears with Gorgonzola

Serves 10

Prep time: 10 minutes
Cook time: 5 minutes
Total cost: $5.75
Calories: 71
Fat: 2g
Protein: 1g
Cholesterol: 2mg
Sodium: 40mg

2½ teaspoons olive oil

5 Anjou or Bartlett pears, quartered but not peeled

½ cup gorgonzola cheese, crumbled

1 teaspoon honey

2 oranges, zested and juiced

Pinch black pepper

Pears were a staple at Beccofino Ristorante & Wine Bar, Florence, Italy, where I worked for then Executive Chef Francesco Berardinelli. There I learned cheeses go well with pears as with this recipe. In Italy, we also served mascarpone (Italian cream cheese) with our pears.

1. Preheat broiler. Lightly grease baking sheet with 1 teaspoon of oil. Toss pears with remaining oil and place skin side down on the baking sheet. Sprinkle cheese over the pears and drizzle with honey. Sprinkle with zest and a little pepper.
2. Place under broiler and cook until browned. Serve warm.

Quick and Easy Tip
Serve any leftovers for breakfast the next day with waffles or use cooked pears as an addition to the Basic Muffins (page 24).

Herbed Sour Cream Dip

Serves 8

Prep time: 8 minutes
Chill: 1 hour
Total cost: $3.75
Calories: 128
Fat: 12g
Protein: 2g
Cholesterol: 22mg
Sodium: 51mg

2 cups sour cream, low-fat okay

¼ cup mayonnaise

2 tablespoons fresh dill, chopped, or 1 tablespoon dried dill

2 tablespoons green onion, chopped

2 tablespoons chives, chopped

1 tablespoon fresh Italian parsley, chopped

Sea salt and black pepper to taste

Although in the onion family, chives are not the same as green onions. Chives are smaller and therefore more pungent in flavor. Used here with the green onion, this dip takes on a crisp, refreshing flavor. If you have a lemon on hand, add a squeeze of lemon juice or pinch of lemon zest for an extra flavor punch without adding fat or calories.

Mix all ingredients together, cover and chill. Serve with vegetables such as celery, carrots, or broccoli florets.

Quick and Easy Tip
Recipes don't get much easier than this. When out-of-town guests arrive for a weekend, have some of this on hand for an easy, inexpensive snack.

The $7 a Meal Quick & Easy Cookbook

Parmesan-Spinach Croquettes

Serves 10

Prep time: 15 minutes
Cook time: 20 minutes
Total cost: $6.99
Calories: 201
Fat: 11g
Protein: 7g
Cholesterol: 107mg
Sodium: 432mg

2 packages frozen spinach, thawed and well drained

½ cups dry herb-seasoned bread stuffing mix

5 eggs

1 cup yellow onion, finely chopped

¾ cup butter, melted

½ cup Parmesan cheese, grated

¾ cup fresh Italian parsley, chopped

1½ teaspoons garlic powder

½ teaspoon dried thyme

½ teaspoon black pepper

½ teaspoon sea salt

This dish is traditional to Italy; however, the Italians usually use ricotta cheese instead of the Parmesan chosen here.

Preheat oven to 375°F. In a large bowl, combine all ingredients and mix well. Form into 1- to 1¼-inch balls (croquettes) and place on a baking sheet lined with parchment paper. Bake for 15 to 20 minutes. Serve warm.

Quick and Easy Tip
Croquettes may be frozen and stored until needed. When cooking straight from freezer, do not thaw. Place directly on a baking sheet and bake for 20 to 25 minutes.

Celery Crisps with Cheese

Serves 12

Prep time: 10 minutes

Chill: 1 hour

Total cost: $4.58

Calories: 76

Fat: 6g

Protein: 3g

Cholesterol: 8mg

Sodium: 82mg

12 long celery stalks with leaves attached, if possible

6 ounces cream cheese, room temperature

½ cup nonfat cottage cheese

¼ cup yellow onion, chopped

2 tablespoons nonfat milk

12 large pimento-stuffed green olives, cut into ¼-inch-thick slices

Paprika for garnish

Stuffed celery is also a great snack for in-between meals. When watching your calorie intake, substitute low-fat cream cheese.

1. Cut celery sticks in half, crosswise, to create 24 sticks. In food processor, combine cream cheese, cottage cheese, and onion. Process at high speed for 4 minutes until smooth. If the texture is very thick, add the milk a little at time to reach desired spreading consistency.
2. Using a knife, spread the mixture into the hollows of the celery stalk, dividing it evenly among the stalks. Push the olive slices into the spread along the entire length of stalk. Wrap in plastic wrap and chill well. Just before serving, unwrap and sprinkle with paprika.

Quick and Easy Tip
Make 1 or 2 days ahead of time to save time on day of party. However, do not freeze. Cheeses do not freeze well because of the moisture they contain.

The $7 a Meal Quick & Easy Cookbook

Taco Dip

Serves 8

Prep time: 8 minutes
Cook time: none
Total cost: $6.98
Calories: 375
Fat: 17g
Protein: 8g
Cholesterol: 24mg
Sodium: 312mg

1 8-ounce container sour cream

½ teaspoon chili powder

2 cups shredded iceberg lettuce

1 tablespoon fresh cilantro, leaves chopped

1 tablespoon fresh Italian parsley, chopped

1 tablespoon fresh chives, chopped

8 ounces sharp Cheddar cheese, shredded

2 medium ripe tomatoes, seeded and chopped

1 bag tortilla chips

Serve this with extra hot sauce on the side for those who really like the spice!

Blend sour cream and chili powder together and spread mixture into a 13" x 9" inch baking dish or other deep serving platter. Sprinkle lettuce, herbs, cheese, and tomatoes on top. Serve with nacho chips.

Quick and Easy Tip
Add a can of refried beans to the bottom of the baking dish before putting sour cream for a more traditional taco dip. They are inexpensive and taste good!

Spicy Jalapeño Black Bean Dip

Serves 8

Prep time: 15 minutes
Cook time: none
Total cost: $2.28
Calories: 112
Fat: 1g
Protein: 6g
Cholesterol: 0mg
Sodium: 413mg

2 15-ounce cans black beans, drained

2 jalapeño peppers, seeded and chopped

2 cloves garlic, chopped

1 tomato, seeded and chopped

2 tablespoons fresh cilantro, minced

Pinch sea salt and black pepper

For a spicier dip, leave in the jalapeño seeds. Just beware—those seeds can be pretty hot. Also, if you overspice your mouth, drink milk to calm the heat. Water will only flare it!

Combine the beans, jalapeños, and garlic in a food processor. Purée until smooth. Transfer to a bowl. Add the tomato, cilantro, salt, and pepper. Mix well and serve with raw vegetables or pita slices.

Quick and Easy Tip

Food processors are great. If you don't have one, save up and invest in one as they are easier to use and easier to clean than blenders!

Roasted Red Pepper Aioli

Serves 6

Prep time: 8 minutes
Cook time: none
Total cost: $3.99
Calories: 83
Fat: 5g
Protein: 3g
Cholesterol: 7mg
Sodium: 796mg

1 7-ounce jar roasted red peppers, drained

1 tablespoon balsamic vinegar

½ tablespoon fresh mint leaves, chopped

⅓ cup low-fat cottage cheese

⅓ cup mayonnaise

2 cloves garlic

Sea salt and black pepper to taste

Aioli is a traditional Mediterranean dip that can also be used as a sauce for fish or chicken.

Combine the roasted red peppers and vinegar in a food processor. Purée until smooth. Add the mint, cottage cheese, mayonnaise, garlic, salt, and pepper. Process until smooth. Serve with raw vegetables, crostini, or pita wedges.

Quick and Easy Tip
Usually aioli is made by combining eggs and oil in a food processor; however, using mayonnaise saves time and reduces the health risk that comes with consuming raw eggs.

Traditional Spinach Dip

Serves 6

Prep time: 15 minutes

Cook time: none

Total cost: $4.08

Calories: 345

Fat: 27g

Protein: 3g

Cholesterol: 40mg

Sodium: 765g

1 10-ounce package frozen spinach, thawed and drained

2 cups sour cream

1 cup mayonnaise

1 packet Knorr vegetable soup mix

1 yellow onion, chopped

1 8-ounce can water chestnuts, drained and chopped

2 tablespoons Parmesan cheese, grated

Try heating up this dip and using it to top baked chicken or halibut.

In a mixing bowl, combine spinach will all other ingredients. Cover and refrigerate until ready to serve. Serve with raw vegetables, sourdough rounds, or crackers.

Spicy Beef Empanadas

Serves 8

Prep time: 15 minutes
Cook time: 12 minutes
Total cost: $6.14
Calories: 150
Fat: 5g
Protein: 7g
Cholesterol: 21mg
Sodium: 110mg

1 tablespoon extra virgin olive oil

½ cup yellow onion, finely chopped

2 teaspoons curry powder

8 ounces ground beef

Sea salt and black pepper

1 small can kernel corn, drained

1 red bell pepper, seeded and finely diced

¼ teaspoon cayenne pepper

1 package square wonton wrappers

Empanadas are traditional to Spain, and you can find them served in any tapas bar, which is Spanish for "little plates" bar.

1. Preheat oven to 375°F. In heavy saucepan, heat olive oil over medium heat. Add onion and curry powder and sauté for 4 minutes until onions are tender. Add ground beef, salt, and pepper and cook 2 minutes. Add bell pepper, corn, and cayenne pepper and cook an additional 3 minutes. Beef should be cooked through.
2. Line a baking sheet with parchment paper. Place 1 wonton wrapper on baking sheet. Spoon approximately ½ to 1 tablespoon of beef filling onto center of wonton. Use your fingertip to coat edges of wonton with water. Fold wonton over to form a triangle and press the edges together to seal. Bake for 8 to 12 minutes or until empanadas are light golden brown. Serve warm.

Quick and Easy Tip

Traditionally empanadas are made with a pastry. If you like, you can use puff pastry instead of wonton wrappers; however, wonton wrappers are inexpensive, easy to work with, and save lots of time.

Antipasto Platter

Serves 8

Prep time: 15 minutes
Cook time: none
Total cost: $6.80
Calories: 187
Fat: 19g
Protein: 15g
Cholesterol: 42mg
Sodium: 1,304mg

2 4-ounce jars mushrooms, undrained

1 8-ounce package frozen artichoke hearts, thawed

¾ cup Italian salad dressing

1 bunch asparagus spears, stalks trimmed

1 jar roasted red bell peppers, drained

8 ounces Cheddar cheese, cubed or sliced

8 ounces Swiss or provolone cheese, cubed or sliced

½ pound thinly sliced salami

An antipasto platter is essentially a platter filled with a variety of cold vegetables, cheeses, and salamis to nibble on before a meal. Traditionally they are not served with crackers, but feel free to serve as you wish. Use your favorite cheeses and salamis, and you can even add olives if you like.

In a bowl, combine mushrooms, artichoke hearts, and salad dressing. Toss well. On a serving platter, arrange asparagus, red peppers, cheeses, and salami. Place artichoke hearts and mushrooms in a decorative bowl for serving and place on the platter. Serve chilled or room temperature using toothpicks.

Quick and Easy Tip
If you have leftover roasted or grilled vegetables from a previous meal, substitute those here. It will save you time and money.

The $7 a Meal Quick & Easy Cookbook

Marinated Boneless Chicken Wings

Serves 8

Prep time: 10 minutes
Cook time: 20 minutes
Total cost: $6.89
Calories: 95
Fat: 1g
Protein: 10g
Cholesterol: 29mg
Sodium: 223mg

2 pounds chicken tenders

⅓ cup soy sauce

¼ cup apple cider vinegar

2 tablespoons Dijon mustard

¼ cup honey

¼ cup brown sugar

1 teaspoon salt

1 teaspoon hot sauce

4 cloves garlic, chopped

½ cup yellow onion, minced

Buffalo chicken wings are a must for any party, especially Super Bowl! Using chicken tenders here saves on calories and cleanup!

1. Cut chicken tenders in half crosswise. In a mixing bowl, combine all ingredients except chicken and mix well. Pour into sealable bag. Add chicken tenders, seal bag, and marinate in refrigerator for 2 hours or overnight.
2. In a large saucepan, drizzle in some of the marinade and heat over medium heat. Add chicken and remaining marinade. Cover sauce pan with lid and cook for 10 minutes or until chicken is cooked through. Remove from pan and serve!

Quick and Easy Tip

The acid in the soy sauce and vinegar helps cook the chicken while infusing flavors. If you can, make the marinade the day before and marinate the chicken overnight for easy cooking and cleanup the day of your party. Here, the marinade cooks along with the chicken so even if you are in a hurry and don't have time to marinate the chicken for 2 hours or overnight, your chicken will still have nice flavor to it.

Spiced Nuts

Serves 8

Prep time: 8 minutes
Cook time: 25 minutes
Total cost: $6.48
Calories: 456
Fat: 43g
Protein: 5g
Cholesterol: 11mg
Sodium: 15mg

2 cups walnuts, whole or halved

2 cups pecan halves

3 tablespoons butter

¼ cup honey

⅓ cup brown sugar

1 teaspoon cinnamon

1 teaspoon ground ginger

½ teaspoon cardamom

⅛ teaspoon cayenne pepper

Spices add flavor to foods without adding fat and calories. Cardamom is actually known to enhance your mood. You can't go wrong with that!

1. Preheat oven to 375°F. Spread walnuts and pecans on a baking sheet lined with parchment paper and toast for 8 minutes or until you can smell the fragrance of the nuts. Remove from oven and set aside. Reduce oven temperature to 325°F.
2. Meanwhile, in a small saucepan, combine butter, honey, and remaining ingredients. Heat over medium heat, stirring frequently so the sugars don't burn, just until mixture comes to a boil. Drizzle mixture over nuts and toss to coat. Return nuts to oven and bake for 15 to 20 minutes, stirring every 5 minutes. Remove from oven and cool completely. Store in airtight container.

Quick and Easy Tip
If you know you are having guests, make these the week before and keep stored. Just be sure your family doesn't eat them all before your big day!

The $7 a Meal Quick & Easy Cookbook

Caprese Salad

Serves 8

Prep time: 10 minutes
Cook time: none
Total cost: $6.92
Calories: 88
Fat: 6g
Protein: 5g
Cholesterol: 10mg
Sodium: 20mg

8 ounces buffalo mozzarella

6 Roma tomatoes, sliced

1 bunch fresh basil leaves, stems removed

Extra virgin olive oil

Sea salt and black pepper

This simple salad comes from the island of Capri, Italy.

Slice mozzarella into small 2-inch slices. Arrange platter with tomato slice first, then basil leaf, then cheese. When finished, drizzle with olive oil, and sprinkle with just a pinch of salt and pepper. Enjoy!

Quick and Easy Tip

If you have the choice of buying the large mozzarella balls or the small ones, opt for the small ones and save the juice for any leftover cheese. Buffalo mozzarella is a fresh cheese and can be stored in the refrigerator for up to one week, but it must be stored in its juices. The smaller balls make for prettier, more even slices for this dish.

CHAPTER 5

SALADS

Tomato Crostini Salad

Serves 4

Prep time: 8 minutes
Cook time: none
Total cost: $2.85
Calories: 124
Fat: 5g
Protein: 2g
Cholesterol: 0mg
Sodium: 175mg

2 cups diced red tomatoes

¼ cup red onion, finely chopped

Sea salt and black pepper to taste

1½ tablespoons extra virgin olive oil

Juice of one lemon

2 cups day-old country bread, cut into ½-inch cubes and air dried overnight

¼ cup fresh Italian parsley, chopped

Italians keep pretty much everything simple. I think that's why the world is so attracted to everything Italian. The simplicity is the beauty of this recipe.

In a medium mixing bowl, toss tomatoes with onion, salt, pepper, olive oil, and lemon juice. Throw in bread cubes and parsley and toss again. Serve immediately.

Quick and Easy Tip

This is a great recipe for those bread pieces you have no idea what to do with. Save the end pieces or other bits of leftover bread and let them air dry overnight or toast them in a 225°F oven for 25 minutes and store them in an airtight container for later use.

Spinach Salad with Broiled Salmon

🥄 Serves 2

Prep time: 10 minutes
Cook time: 10 minutes
Total cost: $6.43
Calories: 405
Fat: 24g
Protein: 19g
Cholesterol: 47mg
Sodium: 121mg

5 ounces salmon filet, skin on, cut into 4 pieces

¼ cup extra virgin olive oil plus 2 tablespoons

¼ cup balsamic vinegar

Sea salt and black pepper to taste

2 cups fresh spinach, washed and dried, stems trimmed

1½ cups red grapes, halved

2 tablespoons dried cranberries

This recipe is packed with all sorts of amazing nutrients!

1. Preheat broiler. Coat unskinned salmon side with 2 tablespoons olive oil, salt, and pepper. Place on aluminum foil and put under broiler, skin side up. Broil for 3 minutes and turn over. Broil for another 3 to 4 minutes or until cooked through. Remove from broiler and set aside.
2. In a mixing bowl, combine all ingredients except salmon. Toss well. Place in 4 serving bowls, top with broiled salmon, and enjoy!

Quick and Easy Tip

Salmon is very healthy for you. The omega-3 fatty acid in salmon makes your skin glow and your hair healthy. If on a tight budget, buy in bulk when on sale and cut into individual servings and freeze.

Honey-Roasted Turkey
Salad with Balsamic Vinaigrette

Serves 2

Prep time: 12 minutes
Cook time: none
Total cost: $6.32
Calorie: 379
Fat: 22g
Protein: 19g
Cholesterol: 48mg
Sodium: 32mg

¼ cup balsamic vinegar

¼ cup extra virgin olive oil

2 cups fresh spinach leaves, washed, dried, and stems trimmed

4 ounces honey-roasted turkey breast, sliced

1 medium tomato, sliced

2 tablespoons shredded low-fat mozzarella

1 apple, cored and sliced

Honey-roasted turkey is slightly sweet and is a perfect combination to the slightly sour balsamic vinegar.

In a large mixing bowl, whisk together vinegar and oil. Add all other ingredients and toss well to coat.

Quick and Easy Tip
Simple extra virgin olive oil and balsamic vinegar is a regular staple at my house and in cooking for parties. The combination adds a zesty flavor without heavy fat and calories.

Romaine Lettuce Leaf Salad
with Buffalo-Style Chicken Wings

Serves 4

Prep time: 10 minutes
Cook time: 7 minutes
Total cost: $6.52
Calories: 185
Fat: 3g
Protein: 25g
Cholesterol: 62mg
Sodium: 119mg

¼ cup water

1 pound chicken tenders

2 tablespoons Crystal Wing
   Sauce or other favorite
   sauce

6 cups romaine lettuce

2 Roma tomatoes, sliced

½ cup mushrooms, sliced

4 tablespoons celery, chopped

2 tablespoons yellow onion,
   diced

2 tablespoons Cheddar
   cheese, grated

Chicken wings go great on almost everything, but this boneless version is perfect for a salad. Use your favorite wing sauce or substitute barbeque sauce if you like.

1. Heat medium saucepan over medium heat. Add water and chicken tenders. Cover and cook until almost cooked through, about 4 minutes. Add wing sauce and toss to coat well. Continue cooking until done, about 3 minutes.
2. Separately, combine all other ingredients in a large mixing bowl. Toss together. Add chicken tenders and drizzle in any remaining sauce from pan.

Quick and Easy Tip
Chicken tenders thaw quickly and are therefore great to have on hand in the freezer at all times. Buy in bulk, separate into meal-size servings, and freeze.

Cobb Salad

Serves 4

Prep time: 7 minutes
Cook time: 20 minutes
Total cost: $6.92
Calories: 224
Fat: 18g
Protein: 19g
Cholesterol: 51mg
Sodium: 563mg

¼ cup water

⅔ cup honey Dijon dressing

8 ounces boneless chicken breast, skin removed

6 cups romaine lettuce

4 ounces sliced deli ham

4 Roma tomatoes, sliced

½ cup cremini mushrooms, sliced

2 tablespoons Swiss or provolone cheese, chopped

This recipe is packed with protein and flavor. Enjoy as a side salad or as a meal.

1. In a medium saucepan over medium heat, add water and ⅓ cup honey Dijon dressing. Use a wooden spoon to mix the two together. Add chicken and cover. Cook until chicken is cooked through, adding water if needed to prevent burning, about 20 minutes depending upon thickness of chicken.
2. Separately, in a large mixing bowl, combine all other ingredients except remaining dressing. Pour remaining dressing over ingredients and toss well to coat. When chicken is cooked, place salad in serving bowls and top with equal portions of chicken. Drizzle any remaining sauce over salad, if desired.

Quick and Easy Tip
Premade salad dressings can be used as marinades or to make sauces, as done here. Use them to make pasta salads or marinate other proteins such as turkey or pork.

Asian Chicken Salad

Serves 4

Prep time: 15 minutes
Cook time: 20 minutes
Total cost: $6.89
Calories: 114
Fat: 8g
Protein: 11g
Cholesterol: 30mg
Sodium: 204mg

1½ tablespoons canola oil or olive oil

1 pound boneless chicken breast, skin removed

6 cups green leaf lettuce

4 Roma tomatoes, sliced

1 cucumber, sliced (removing seeds, optional)

¼ cup shredded carrots

2 teaspoons sesame seeds

½ cup mandarin oranges or tangerines

¼ cup sesame ginger dressing

Natural citric acid enhances the flavors of the other foods it surrounds, and citrus fruits are packed with vitamin C.

1. Heat grill pan or sauté pan to medium heat and add oil. Add chicken breast and cook slowly for about 15 minutes or until cooked through. If using sauté pan, cover with lid to hold in juices.
2. Separately, in a large mixing bowl, combine remaining ingredients except dressing. Toss together, then pour dressing over salad and toss to coat. When chicken is cooked, serve salad in serving bowls and top with chicken.

Quick and Easy Tip
Try to plan your meals for the week. When you do, if you know you are going to have chicken on Monday, Wednesday, and Friday, precook the quantity you need and keep in the refrigerator. You'll be glad you did when it comes time to cook!

Pecan-Crusted Chicken Salad

Serves 4

Prep time: 15 minutes
Cook time: 20 minutes
Total cost: $6.48
Calories: 349
Fat: 22g
Protein: 23g
Cholesterol: 59mg
Sodium: 54mg

1 pound boneless chicken breasts, skin removed

¼ cup plus 1 tablespoon extra virgin olive oil

Sea salt and pepper to taste

½ cup pecans, finely chopped

¼ cup balsamic vinegar

6 cups romaine lettuce

2 tablespoons raisins

4 Roma tomatoes, diced

¼ cup carrots, chopped

Pecans add both flavor and a crunchy texture to chicken, turkey, even fish. And nuts contain healthy oils and proteins that are good for your skin.

1. Preheat oven to 380°F. Line a baking sheet with parchment paper. Coat chicken with 1 tablespoon of olive oil. Season with salt and pepper. Press pecans gently onto chicken. Place chicken on baking sheet, cover with foil, and bake for 20 minutes or until done.
2. Separately, in a large mixing bowl, whisk together remaining oil and vinegar. Toss in all other ingredients and coat well. When chicken is cooked, allow to cool slightly. Serve salad in bowls and top with chicken.

Quick and Easy Tip
If you enjoy cooking with pecans, buy a large bag when on sale and keep in the freezer. They stay fresh for at least three months.

Pear-Feta Salad

Serves 4

Prep time: 10 minutes
Cook time: none
Total cost: $5.01
Calories: 201
Fat: 18g
Protein: 3g
Cholesterol: 10mg
Sodium: 23mg

¼ cup extra virgin olive oil

¼ cup champagne or apple cider vinegar

6 cups romaine lettuce

1 Bartlett pear, seeded and diced

2 tomatoes, diced

2 tablespoons toasted pine nuts

¼ cup feta cheese, crumbled

The sweetness of the fruit, nuttiness of the pine nuts, and the creamy sharpness of the cheese blend together for mouth-watering goodness in this recipe.

In a large mixing bowl, whisk together oil and vinegar until well combined. Add all other ingredients and toss well.

Quick and Easy Tip
Buy feta cheese in blocks and crumble yourself. If you can refrain from eating it while cooking, you may just have enough left for your salad!

Classic Greek Salad

Serves 4

Prep time: 15 minutes
Cook time: none
Total cost: $6.36
Calories: 181
Fat: 18g
Protein: 1g
Cholesterol: 5mg
Sodium: 704mg

¼ cup extra virgin olive oil

¼ cup balsamic vinegar

1 tablespoon prepared mustard

6 cups romaine lettuce

2 tomatoes, diced

1 cucumber, diced

½ cup kalamata olives, pitted, chopped

2 pepperoncini, diced

¼ cup red onions, diced

1 red bell pepper, seeded and diced

½ cup feta cheese, crumbled

Mediterranean-style diets consists of eating olives, fruit, beans, and fish on a regular basis.

In a large mixing bowl, whisk together oil, vinegar, and mustard until well combined. Add remaining ingredients and toss well to coat.

Quick and Easy Tip

Try making your own vinaigrettes; they are easy to make and healthier because they contain less sodium and fewer processed ingredients. However, you can substitute your favorite dressing if you like.

Caesar Salad with Grilled Steak

Serves 4

Prep time: 10 minutes
Cook time: 10 minutes
Total cost: $6.93
Calories: 282
Fat: 17g
Protein: 21g
Cholesterol: 52mg
Sodium: 708mg

6 cups romaine lettuce

2 tablespoons Parmesan cheese, grated

¼ cup Caesar dressing

8 ounces grilled, lean steak

A classic Caesar is always good. Add grilled steak for a new twist and extra protein for a complete meal.

In a large mixing bowl, combine lettuce, cheese, and dressing and toss well to coat. Add steak on top of salad when serving.

Quick and Easy Tip
Sirloin cut into strips or flank steak works well for this salad and is less expensive than filet.

Taco Salad

Serves 4

Prep time: 8 minutes
Cook time: none
Total cost: $5.36
Calories: 233
Fat: 2g
Protein: 4g
Cholesterol: 5mg
Sodium: 251mg

6 cups iceberg lettuce, washed, dried, and largely chopped

2 tomatoes, diced

½ cup black beans, drained

1 medium yellow onion, chopped

½ cup kernel corn, drained

½ cup cheddar cheese, grated

1 jalapeño pepper, sliced

½ packet taco seasoning or ¼ cup salsa

Tortilla chips (optional)

You can make this dish spicy by adding hot sauce, or cool it down by adding a dollop of sour cream. Either way, this recipe is a family pleaser!

Place all ingredients in a large mixing bowl except tortilla chips. Toss well and serve with chips, if desired.

Quick and Easy Tip

With a well-stocked pantry, this salad can be made using canned foods such as diced tomatoes, green chilis, even sliced jalapeños come canned. Just be sure to drain them well. Also, if you have some leftover cooked chicken, dice it up and throw it in for extra flavor and protein!

Grilled Chicken Caesar Salad with Pepper Jack Cheese

Serves 4

Prep time: 8 minutes
Cook time: 10 minutes
Total cost: $5.48
Calories: 283
Fat: 13g
Protein: 22g
Cholesterol: 68mg
Sodium: 213mg

1 pound boneless chicken breasts, skin removed

Sea salt and pepper to taste

3 tablespoons olive oil

¼ cup Caesar dressing

1 teaspoon green pepper sauce

6 cups romaine lettuce

¼ cup pepper jack cheese, grated

Caesar salads are easily customizable depending on your family's tastes. Try grilled chicken, as here, or barbeque chicken, or blackened salmon. It's a great way to make this salad a meal and not just a side dish.

1. Cut chicken into cubes, toss in a mixing bowl and add salt, pepper, and oil and toss to coat. Heat a medium skillet over medium heat. Add chicken and cover with lid. Cook until done, about 8 to 10 minutes. Turn off heat and set aside.
2. Separately, in a mixing bowl, add remaining ingredients and toss well. When serving, serve in bowls and add chicken on top.

Quick and Easy Tip
For a variety of flavors, coat chicken with 2 tablespoons of blackened seasoning or dried herbes de Provence (a blend of herbs).

Mixed Green Salad with
Vegetables and Cranberries

Serves 4

Prep time: 10 minutes

Cook time: none

Total cost: $6.84

Calories: 171

Fat: 12g

Protein: 3g

Cholesterol: 29mg

Sodium: 175mg

¼ cup balsamic vinegar

¼ cup extra virgin olive oil

Sea salt and pepper to taste

6 cups mixed greens, see below

1 red bell pepper, seeded and diced

1 medium red onion, diced

1 large tomato, diced

1 cucumber, diced

2 tablespoons dried cranberries

1 large carrot, finely chopped

¼ cup Cheddar cheese, grated

Mixed greens can be purchased in bulk at most grocery stores. Measure by allowing for a heaping handful per person. Before using, be sure to wash and dry the leaves.

In a large mixing bowl, whisk together vinegar, oil, salt, and pepper. Add remaining ingredients and toss well to coat.

Quick and Easy Tip
As with most salads, add cooked chicken, fish, or turkey for a heartier meal, extra protein, and a new twist on perhaps a favorite salad.

Red and Green Leaf Salad with Spiced Nuts

Serves 4

- Prep time: 8 minutes
- Cook time: none
- Total cost: $6.98
- Calories: 341
- Fat: 27g
- Protein: 5g
- Cholesterol: 10mg
- Sodium: 22mg

¼ cup extra virgin olive oil

¼ cup balsamic vinegar

3 cups red leaf lettuce

3 cups green leaf lettuce

½ cup mandarin oranges, canned okay, just drain well

¼ to ½ cup Spiced Nuts (page 56)

¼ cup feta cheese, crumbled

Leftover nuts add a delicious and nutritious twist on salad. Try the Spiced Nuts (page 56) from Chapter 4.

In a mixing bowl, whisk together oil and vinegar. Add remaining ingredients and toss to coat.

Quick and Easy Tip
Red and green leaf lettuce is more nutritious than iceberg, so use whenever possible.

Chopped Grilled Vegetable Salad

Serves 4

Prep time: 10 minutes
Cook time: 10 minutes
Total cost: $5.52
Calories: 175
Fat: 18g
Protein: 1g
Cholesterol: 0mg
Sodium: 3mg

¼ cup plus 2 tablespoons olive oil

1 red bell pepper, seeded and chopped

1 shallot, peeled and diced

1 cup broccoli florets

6 cups romaine lettuce, chopped

1 zucchini, chopped

1 small can kernel corn, drained

Salt and pepper to taste

¼ cup balsamic vinegar

One of my favorite restaurants in Los Angeles serves the best chopped grilled vegetable salad, and it better be good because they charge about $20 for it! Save on money but not taste when you make your own at home.

1. Heat 2 tablespoons of oil over medium to medium-high heat on a grill pan or in a sauté skillet. Add vegetables (except lettuce) and sprinkle with a pinch of salt and pepper. Cook until all vegetables are tender, about 5 minutes. Don't worry if some of the vegetables blister. This makes them taste even better!
2. In a mixing bowl, whisk together remaining oil and vinegar. Add lettuce and other ingredients. Toss well and serve.

Quick and Easy Tip
When making salad, always whisk the dressing together in the bottom of the mixing bowl and then add the greens and other ingredients. To toss, take two wooden spoons and follow down the sides of the bowl, meeting the tips of the spoons in the middle underneath the salad. Gently lift up to toss. Turn the bowl and repeat until all ingredients are coated.

Tuna Salad

Serves 4

Prep time: 15 minutes
Cook time: none
Total cost: $4.56
Calories: 200
Fat: 11g
Protein: 21g
Cholesterol: 36mg
Sodium: 374mg

2 cans tuna fish in water, drained

1 stalk celery, chopped

1 tablespoon yellow onion, diced

Sea salt and pepper to taste

½ cup mayonnaise, low-fat if desired

1 teaspoon prepared mustard

⅓ cup red seedless grapes, halved, optional

1 hard-boiled egg, chopped

6 cups spring mix lettuce

1 tomato, sliced

Tuna salad is perfect as a snack, on sandwiches or, as here, on a bed of lettuce with tomatoes. My favorite way to eat it is right out of the mixing bowl with saltine crackers!

In a mixing bowl, combine all ingredients except lettuce and tomato and mix well. Place lettuce on a plate. Top with scoops of tuna and sliced tomatoes.

Quick and Easy Tip

A surefire way to save money is to make this easy tuna salad recipe yourself. Don't waste money on premade, packaged tuna salad, which is more expensive and doesn't taste near as good! Substitute chicken if you prefer.

BBQ Chicken Salad

Serves 4

Prep time: 10 minutes
Cook time: 20 minutes
Total cost: $6.36
Calories: 256
Fat: 13g
Protein: 22g
Cholesterol: 62mg
Sodium: 1,176mg

1 pound boneless chicken breast, skin removed

2 tablespoons olive oil

1 cup barbeque sauce (try Bull's-Eye or Chris and Pits)

¼ cup ranch dressing

1 head iceberg or boston leaf lettuce, washed, dried, and chopped

1 large tomato, diced

1 cucumber, diced

½ medium red onion, diced

There are a thousand ways to make BBQ chicken salad; this is only one way that's quick, easy, and delicious.

1. Chop chicken into 1- to 2-inch cubes. In a mixing bowl, coat chicken with olive oil. Preheat skillet to medium heat. Add chicken and ⅓ cup water. This helps prevent burning. Cover with lid and let chicken cook, about 8 to 10 minutes, adding water if needed. When cooked, remove from heat and toss with barbeque sauce. Set aside.
2. In a separate mixing bowl, pour in dressing. Add remaining ingredients and toss to coat. Add chicken and serve.

Quick and Easy Tip

You can make your own barbeque sauce at home, but to do it right, it takes time and lots of ingredients. Use store bought as a base, and then doctor it up as you wish.

Fruit and Vegetable Salad
with Apple Cider Vinaigrette

Serves 4

Prep time: 10 minutes

Cook time: none

Total cost: $5.68

Calories: 149

Fat: 11g

Protein: 1g

Cholesterol: 0mg

Sodium: 1mg

⅓ cup olive oil

⅓ cup apple cider vinegar

Pinch of granulated sugar

6 cups shredded romaine lettuce

8 cherry tomatoes, halved

1 apple, such as Gala, seeded and cubed

½ cup golden raisins

1 cup mandarin oranges

Fruit salad doesn't always have to mean only fruit. The key, however, is to use fresh fruit, not canned cocktail fruit, which is overly mushy because it has been sitting in syrup for a long time.

In a mixing bowl, whisk together oil, vinegar, and sugar. Add remaining ingredients and toss to coat.

Quick and Easy Tip
Substitute your favorite fruits in this recipe. For added flavor, texture, and protein, add in toasted nuts if you have them on hand.

Broccoli Medley

Serves 5

Prep time: 8 minutes
Cook time: 5 minutes
Total cost: $5.38
Calories: 128
Fat: 8g
Protein: 2g
Cholesterol: 8mg
Sodium: 161mg

4 cups fresh broccoli florets

½ cup mayonnaise

2 tablespoons balsamic vinegar

2 tablespoons granulated sugar

⅓ cup raisins

¼ cup sunflower seeds

¼ cup red onion, chopped

1 cup frozen peas, thawed

This recipe gives broccoli a new twist.

1. Fill a large-quart boiler ¾ with water, bring to a boil, and add 1 teaspoon salt. Add broccoli florets and let boil for 10 seconds. Quickly remove and transfer to a bowl filled with ice or ice water. Drain well.
2. In a separate bowl, combine mayonnaise, vinegar, and sugar. Whisk together well. Add remaining ingredients and toss to coat.

Quick and Easy Tip

Ever wonder why the vegetables at nice restaurants look so beautiful? It's not because they are special vegetables that cost more. They bring out the colors by blanching, as this recipe does with the broccoli. The ice bath stops the cooking process so vegetables don't get overcooked and limp.

Chinese Chicken Salad

Serves 4

Prep time: 15 minutes
Cook time: none
Total cost: $6.88
Calories: 535
Fat: 40g
Protein: 21g
Cholesterol: 0mg
Sodium: 73mg

¼ cup bean sprouts

⅓ cup rice vinegar

¼ cup peanut oil

1 tablespoon soy sauce

3 tablespoons hoisin sauce

1 tablespoon fresh ginger, minced

½ pound boneless chicken, skin removed, cooked, and cubed

2 cups Napa cabbage (Asian cabbage), sliced crosswise

¼ cup green onions, chopped

¼ cup sliced water chestnuts, drained

¼ cup roasted,unsalted peanuts, chopped

Chinese chicken salad is always fun to eat. Serve on additional mixed greens if you like, and add mandarin oranges if you have some leftover from another recipe.

1. Place the bean sprouts in a bowl of ice water to cover. Combine the vinegar, oil, soy sauce, hoisin sauce, and ginger in a large bowl and whisk to combine. Remove ½ cup dressing from bowl and set aside. Add the chicken, cabbage, green onions, and water chestnuts to bowl and mix to combine. Add more dressing as needed and toss.
2. Drain bean sprouts. Serve salad in bowls and top with sprouts and peanuts.

Cucumber Salad with Chicken

Serves 4

Prep time: 10 minutes
Cook time: none
Total cost: $5.48
Calories: 111
Fat: 11g
Protein: 6g
Cholesterol: 15mg
Sodium: 31mg

1 tablespoon peanut butter

2 tablespoons rice wine vinegar

2 tablespoons sesame oil

½ teaspoon ground cayenne pepper

Sea salt as needed

½ red onion, chopped

2 cups cucumber, diced

½ pound cooked chicken, chopped

2 tablespoons toasted sesame seeds

Peanut butter and rice wine vinegar give this recipe a rich flavor without breaking your budget.

1. Combine the peanut butter, vinegar, oil, cayenne, and salt in a medium mixing bowl. Adjust seasoning as desired. Add the red onion and cucumber and toss well.
2. To serve, place the cucumber salad on serving plate. Top with cooked chicken and garnish with sesame seeds.

Quick and Easy Tip
If you don't have sesame oil, substitute canola or olive oil.

Smoked Turkey Salad with Yogurt Dressing and Sunflower Seeds

Serves 4

Prep time: 12 minutes
Cook time: none
Total cost: $6.99
Calories: 341
Fat: 14g
Protein: 27g
Cholesterol: 84mg
Sodium: 276mg

3 cups sliced smoked turkey breast

¼ cup sunflower seeds, without husk

1 cup celery, chopped

½ cup green seedless grapes, halved

½ cup red seedless grapes, halved

½ cup low-fat mayonnaise

¼ cup plain yogurt

1 tablespoon honey

Juice of 1 lemon

½ teaspoon ground ginger

The smoked flavor of the turkey balances well with the lemon juice and honey to make this salad one not to miss.

1. In a large mixing bowl, combine turkey, half the sunflower seeds, celery, and grapes. Set aside.
2. In a separate mixing bowl, combine remaining ingredients except remaining sunflower seeds. Add the dressing mixture to the turkey and lightly toss to coat. Serve and top with remaining sunflower seeds.

Quick and Easy Tip
If you have fresh ginger, substitute that here instead of ground. Just be sure you chop it really fine so the flavor gets distributed throughout the dressing.

The $7 a Meal Quick & Easy Cookbook

Arugula Greens with Goat Cheese and Yellow Squash

Serves 6

Prep time: 12 minutes
Cook time: none
Total cost: $6.93
Calories: 129
Fat: 12g
Protein: 5g
Cholesterol: 16mg
Sodium: 39mg

¼ cup extra virgin olive oil

2 tablespoons lemon juice

1 tablespoon shallot, minced

Sea salt and pepper to taste

½ pound zucchini, chopped

½ pound yellow (summer) squash, chopped

5 cups loosely packed arugula greens

¼ cup tightly packed fresh basil leaves, chopped

5 ounces goat cheese, crumbled

Shallots are in the onion family, and their flavors are more condensed. Use them in any recipe that calls for onions!

Combine the oil, lemon juice, shallot, salt, and pepper in a large mixing bowl and whisk together. Add the zucchini and squash, toss to coat, and let rest for 3 minutes. Add the arugula greens and basil and toss to combine. When serving, sprinkle with goat cheese.

Quick and Easy Tip
If you can't find arugula greens, substitute fresh spinach for this recipe. Either way, it's yummy!

SOUPS

Mushroom Soup
with Parmesan

Serves 2

Prep time: 10 minutes
Cook time: 15 minutes
Total cost: $4.50
Calories: 256
Fat: 17g
Protein: 4g
Cholesterol: 26mg
Sodium: 1,223mg

3 tablespoons butter

6 ounces assorted mushrooms

1 yellow onion, chopped

4 cups beef broth, canned

¼ cup dry Sherry wine or Merlot

Sea salt and pepper to taste

4 tablespoons Parmesan cheese, grated

½ tablespoon fresh thyme, leaves only

Cooking with fresh herbs is a great way to enhance the flavor of foods without adding fat and calories.

1. Melt the butter in a medium skillet over medium heat. Add the mushrooms and onions. Cook, stirring frequently, until soft, about 8 minutes.
2. Add the beef broth, sherry, salt, and pepper. Simmer for 5 to 7 minutes. Taste and adjust the seasoning (add salt or pepper to taste). If too "winey", cook 5 minutes longer. To serve, ladle soup into bowls and garnish with fresh thyme leaves and Parmesan.

Quick and Easy Tip

Thyme is a very versatile herb. Thyme blends well with other herbs such as rosemary and pairs nicely with beef, chicken, and fish.

Mushroom Soup of Beef and Sour Cream

Serves 6

Prep time: 10 minutes
Cook time: 20 minutes
Total cost: $6.36
Calories: 162
Fat: 7g
Protein: 17g
Cholesterol: 49mg
Sodium: 365mg

¾ pound top sirloin steak, cut into ½-inch cubes

Sea salt and pepper to taste

4 tablespoons plain flour

4 tablespoons butter

2 tablespoons olive oil

1 yellow onion, chopped

3 cups cremini mushrooms, stems removed, sliced

2 tablespoons garlic, minced

¼ cup dry white wine

2 cups beef broth, canned

2 tablespoons fresh Italian parsley, chopped

2 teaspoons Worcestershire sauce

½ cup sour cream

Top sirloin is a quality cut of beef that is also affordable. It is high in protein, has zero carbs, and adds protein and flavor to your foods.

1. Pat the meat dry with paper towels and season with salt and pepper. Place the flour in a shallow bowl. Dredge the meat in the flour, shaking off excess. Reserve remaining flour.
2. Melt butter in a large skillet over medium-high heat until bubbling. Add the meat and brown on all sides, stirring occasionally to cook evenly, about 6 minutes. Use a slotted spoon to transfer meat to plate, cover with foil to keep warm.
3. In same skillet, heat oil and add the onions, mushrooms, and garlic. Cook until soft, about 6 minutes, stirring occasionally.
4. Sprinkle reserved flour over cooking vegetables. Cook and stir until thick. Add the white wine and cook until thick and reduced, about 4 minutes. Add the broth, parsley, Worcerstershire, bring to a simmer, and cook an additional 6 minutes.
5. Add the meat and any juices and simmer uncovered for about 10 minutes. Stir in sour cream and serve.

Cheese and Onion Soup

Serves 4

Prep time: 8 minutes
Cook time: 15 minutes
Total cost: $5.76
Calories: 315
Fat: 27g
Protein: 16g
Cholesterol: 77mg
Sodium: 497mg

2 tablespoons butter

¼ cup yellow onion, chopped

½ cup celery, chopped

2 tablespoons plain flour

½ teaspoon ground cayenne pepper

¼ teaspoon dry mustard

½ tablespoon Worcestershire sauce

1 cup whole milk

1½ cups chicken broth, canned

2 cups cheddar cheese, grated

Sea salt and black pepper to taste

Paprika for garnish

If you love cheese, you will love this recipe. Be sure to keep an eye on it while cooking as cheese and milk tend to burn if not stirred constantly and supervised.

1. Melt butter in a medium saucepan over medium heat. Add the onion and celery and cook until tender, about 4 minutes. Add the flour, cayenne, mustard, and Worcestershire, and mix to combine.
2. Add the milk and chicken broth and bring to a boil. Cook for 1 minute, stirring constantly. Reduce heat to low, add cheese, and stir frequently just until the cheese is melted. Add salt and pepper. When serving, sprinkle with paprika.

Quick and Easy Tip
The milk makes this soup creamy. Use low-fat if you prefer and add ½ cup of light sour cream.

Chicken Vegetable Soup

Serves 4

Prep time: 10 minutes

Cook time: 20 minutes

Total cost: $6.56

Calories: 135

Fat: 2g

Protein: 23g

Cholesterol: 59mg

Sodium: 591mg

2 tablespoons olive oil

1 cup yellow onions, chopped

2 cups broccoli, chopped

1 cup carrots, peeled and chopped

1 cup green bell pepper, seeded and chopped

Sea salt and black pepper to taste

4 cups chicken broth

2 cups cooked chicken, diced

2 tablespoons Italian parsley, chopped

Soup can be very soothing after a stressful day.

1. Heat oil in a large-quart boiler over medium heat. Add the onions and cook until soft, about 5 minutes. Add broccoli, carrots, and peppers. Cook about 4 minutes. Add salt, pepper, and broth and bring to a simmer. Cook until vegetables are tender, about 8 minutes.
2. Add the chicken and parsley, return to a simmer. Serve hot.

Quick and Easy Tip

This is a great recipe to make double batches of and freeze in family-size servings in your freezer. Need a quick meal? Just pull it out of the freezer and you are set!

The $7 a Meal Quick & Easy Cookbook

Soup of Pasta and Red Beans

Serves 8

Prep time: 8 minutes
Cook time: 20 minutes
Total cost: $5.28
Calories: 169
Fat: 3g
Protein: 9g
Cholesterol: 4mg
Sodium: 392mg

3 tablespoons olive oil

1 medium onion, chopped

3 cloves garlic, chopped

1 teaspoon dried oregano

2 bay leaves

1 large can (16 ounce) tomato sauce

2 teaspoons sea salt

1 tablespoon soy sauce

2 large cans red beans, undrained

1 small bunch Italian parsley, chopped

6 cups vegetable broth

2 cups cooked pasta such as fusilli

Pasta soup is native to Italy where winters are cold and soups are hearty! Enjoy this one here during the winter or anytime.

1. In a large pot, heat olive oil over medium heat, then add onions and garlic, and sauté for 5 minutes or until onions are tender. Add oregano, bay leaves, tomato sauce, salt, and soy sauce. Bring to a simmer and add beans, parsley, and broth.
2. Bring to a boil. Add cooked pasta and bring back to boil for 1 minute. Serve hot.

Quick and Easy Tip
You can use dried beans if you like, but the canned ones here are inexpensive and already tender! Use the liquid from the beans for that true hearty flavor and consistency.

Cream of Asparagus Soup

Serves 6

Prep time: 10 minutes
Cook time: 30 minutes
Total cost: $6.48
Calories: 269
Fat: 14g
Protein: 4g
Cholesterol: 27mg
Sodium: 432mg

2 tablespoons olive oil

1 medium onion, chopped

4 cloves garlic, chopped

1 bunch fresh asparagus, including stalks, chopped

Sea salt and black pepper to taste

¼ cup white wine or Sherry

3 cups vegetable broth

1 10-ounce package frozen peas

2 cups sour cream

1 teaspoon dried basil

The alcohol in the wine cooks off, but before it cooks off, the alcohol extracts flavors from the other ingredients surrounding it to make a very tasty dish.

1. In a large-quart boiler, heat olive oil over medium heat until fragrant, about 1 minute. Add onion, garlic, asparagus, and salt. Cook 8 minutes, until onions are translucent but not browned. Add wine or Sherry and cook 1 minute. Add the broth. Simmer for 20 minutes, until asparagus is very tender. Remove from heat and stir in frozen peas.
2. Purée in food processor, in batches, until smooth. Transfer back to pot and heat to a simmer. Add sour cream, season with salt, pepper, and basil. Serve hot or cold.

Quick and Easy Tip
Not many soups afford you the choice between serving hot or cold. Prepare this one ahead of time and keep in the refrigerator. When ready to serve, your soup is well chilled.

Tomato Soup

Serves 6

- Prep time: 5 minutes
- Cook time: 25 minutes
- Total cost: $4.90
- Calories: 120
- Fat: 2g
- Protein: 4g
- Cholesterol: 1mg
- Sodium: 110mg

2 tablespoons olive oil

1 medium chopped onion

2 cloves garlic, finely chopped

4 32-ounce cans whole, peeled tomatoes with juice

Sea salt and black pepper to taste

Tomato soup and grilled cheese sandwiches are as American as baseball and apple pie. This tomato soup recipe is so simple there is simply no excuse not to make it.

In a large-quart boiler over medium heat, heat olive oil until fragrant, about 1 minute. Add onion and garlic and cook for 8 minutes. Stir in tomatoes, with juice, and simmer about 20 minutes. Purée in a food processor, in batches, until smooth. Add salt and pepper to taste. Serve hot or cold.

Quick and Easy Tip
Using canned tomatoes saves on time and money in this recipe.

Chilled Gazpacho

Serves 6

Prep time: 15 minutes
Cook time: none
Total cost: $5.36
Calories: 112
Fat: 4g
Protein: 2g
Cholesterol: 0mg
Sodium: 350mg

8 tomatoes, seeded and finely diced

2 cucumbers, peeled and finely diced

2 green bell peppers, seeded and finely diced

1 clove garlic, finely diced

2 tablespoons extra virgin olive oil

1½ teaspoons red wine vinegar

1 teaspoon sea salt

2 cups tomato juice

Dash hot sauce or more as desired

It may take a few extra minutes to chop the vegetables in this dish, but then throw it all together, put it in the refrigerator, and boom, you are done!

Combine all ingredients and mix well, adding additional hot sauce as your tastes allow. Serve immediately or chill, covered, in the refrigerator for up to two days.

Quick and Easy Tip
Make a day ahead. This is one recipe that gets better with age!

The $7 a Meal Quick & Easy Cookbook

Tuscan Cannellini Bean (White Bean) Soup

Serves 8

Prep time: 5 minutes
Cook time: 25 minutes
Total cost: $5.76
Calories: 276
Fat: 5g
Protein: 14g
Cholesterol: 16mg
Sodium: 717mg

4 tablespoons extra virgin olive oil

1 bunch green onion, chopped

3 cloves garlic, finely chopped

1 tablespoon fresh rosemary, stems removed, finely chopped

4 cups vegetable broth

2 32-ounce cans white Northern beans with juice

½ cup diced ham or whole ham bone

Sea salt and black pepper to taste

Drizzle a little extra virgin olive oil on top when serving.

In a large-quart boiler over medium heat, heat 1 tablespoon olive oil until fragrant, about 1 minute. Add onion and garlic and cook for 8 minutes. Add rosemary, broth, beans, and ham (or ham bone). Bring to a boil. Stir, cover, and reduce heat to simmer. Simmer 25 minutes. Adjust seasoning as desired. Serve and drizzle remaining olive oil over individual servings for extra flavor.

Quick and Easy Tip

Use canned cannellini (white Northern) beans as a base for this recipe. You can start from dried beans, but that requires soaking overnight and cooking for 1½ hours. Save yourself some time and use the canned beans. Your family will love it and you can relax a little longer.

Corn and Potato Chowder

Serves 6

Prep time: 10 minutes
Cook time: 25 minutes
Total cost: $6.89
Calories: 370
Fat: 9g
Protein: 15g
Cholesterol: 30mg
Sodium: 817mg

4 ears sweet corn, shucked, kernels cut, cobs reserved

1 tablespoon olive oil

1 large onion, chopped

2 stalks celery, chopped

6 red potatoes, cut into 1-inch chunks

3 sprigs fresh thyme or 1 teaspoon dried thyme

1 bay leaf

3 teaspoons sea salt

1 teaspoon chili powder

4 ounces (1 stick) unsalted butter

8 cups vegetable broth or water

4 teaspoons cornstarch mixed in ¼ cup water

8 cups low-fat milk

White pepper to taste

2 tablespoons chopped fresh chives

Don't let a long list of ingredients intimidate you. Sometimes those recipes are the easiest ones because it's just a bunch of flavors all mixed together!

1. Cut corn kernels from the cob using a slicing motion, going down the cob, with a large chef knife. Reserve the cobs and set kernels aside. In a large-quart boiler over medium heat, heat olive oil until fragrant, about 1 minute. Add corn cobs, onion, celery, potatoes, thyme, bay leaf, salt, and chili powder. Cook for 8 minutes. Add butter and cook gently, allowing vegetables to stew in the butter, about 5 minutes.

2. Add the vegetable broth and corn kernels. Increase heat to high and bring to a full boil, allow to boil for 1 minute, reduce heat to simmer, and cook for 10 minutes. Remove the corn cobs, add cornstarch mixture, and simmer 5 minutes more. Stir in the milk, and adjust seasoning with salt and white pepper to taste. Serve sprinkle with chives.

The $7 a Meal Quick & Easy Cookbook

Miso Soup

Serves 4

- Prep time: 15 minutes
- Cook time: 10 minutes
- Total cost: $4.44
- Calories: 61
- Fat: 2g
- Protein: 3g
- Cholesterol: 0mg
- Sodium: 750mg

¼ cup miso paste

3½ cups chicken broth

8 ounces medium to firm tofu, cubed

4 sprigs Italian parsley, chopped

2 shitake mushrooms, sliced

Sea salt and black pepper to taste

Miso soup is traditional at Japanese restaurants. It is so easy to make—save yourself the expense of eating out by making it at home.

In a large-quart boiler, whisk the miso into 2 tablespoons of slightly warmed broth and blend well. Gradually add the miso liquid into the remaining broth. Bring the soup to a simmer. Add the tofu cubes, parsley, and mushrooms. Maintain a simmer until the mushrooms and tofu are heated. Do not boil or the soup will become bitter and cloudy. Serve soup in bowls and serve immediately.

Quick and Easy Tip

Miso is a fermented soybean paste that can be found in most well-stocked supermarkets. Red miso is pungent and quite salty, while white miso is mellow and slightly sweet. Miso paste can be left at room temperature for a year or more, since its flavor improves with age. It should not be frozen.

Creamy Pea Soup

Serves 4

Prep time: 15 minutes
Cook time: 12 minutes
Total cost: $3.48
Calories: 149
Fat: 2g
Protein: 19g
Cholesterol: 2mg
Sodium: 47mg

2 10-ounce packages frozen green peas

2 cups water

3½ cups chicken broth

Juice of 1 lemon

1 clove garlic, minced

1 small yellow onion, chopped

Sea salt and black pepper to taste

¼ cup mint leaves, chopped

¼ cup plain yogurt

Add little crispy bacon bits on top for a smoky flavor that complements the peas.

Cook the peas in 2 cups of boiling water for just a few minutes. Drain, reserving water for use later in the recipe. Purée peas in a food processor. Mix 2 cups of the cooking water, broth, and lemon juice in a saucepan. Add the puréed peas and bring to a simmer. Add garlic, onion, salt, and pepper. Turn off heat. Add the mint and stir to combine. Serve with a dollop of yogurt.

Quick and Easy Tip
Keep a large bag of frozen peas in your freezer at all times. They are great as a snack right out of the freezer, or add some to rice for Italian risi e bisi!

The $7 a Meal Quick & Easy Cookbook

Simple Gumbo

Serves 4

Prep time: 15 minutes
Cook time: 20 minutes
Total cost: $6.88
Calories: 378
Fat: 7g
Protein: 34g
Cholesterol: 56mg
Sodium: 955mg

1 14½-ounce can beef broth

1 14½-ounce can Italian stewed tomatoes

2 cups water

2 cups frozen hash brown potatoes

1 10-ounce package frozen mixed vegetables

8 ounces smoked sausage, sliced

⅛ teaspoon black pepper

2 tablespoons Parmesan cheese, grated

Sea salt and black pepper to taste

Gumbo is a popular dish made famous by New Orleans chefs. Traditional gumbo includes okra, which can be hard to find. If you happen to find it at your local grocery store, add a cup along with the stewed tomatoes for extra flavor and a thicker consistency.

Combine beef broth, undrained stewed tomatoes, and water in a large-quart boiler. Bring to a boil. Stir in hash brown potatoes, mixed vegetables, sausage, and pepper. Return to boiling. Reduce heat and simmer, covered, for 5 to 10 minutes. Serve soup in bowls and sprinkle with Parmesan cheese and salt and pepper to taste.

Tomato Bisque

Serves 4

Prep time: 15 minutes
Cook time: 12 minutes
Total cost: $6.74
Calories: 261
Fat: 18g
Protein: 8g
Cholesterol: 44mg
Sodium: 397mg

1 tablespoon olive oil

1 yellow onion, finely chopped

1 10-ounce container refrigerated Alfredo sauce

1½ cups chicken broth

1½ cups whole milk

2 14-ounce cans diced tomatoes, undrained

½ teaspoon dried basil leaves

¼ teaspoon dried marjoram leaves

Sea salt and black pepper to taste

Bisque is any kind of thick, creamy soup usually made with cream. Use this recipe as a base for seafood bisque and just add your favorite cooked seafood.

1. In a heavy saucepan, heat olive oil over medium heat and add onion. Cook and stir until onion is tender, about 4 minutes. Add Alfredo sauce and chicken broth; cook and stir with wire whisk until mixture is smooth. Add milk and stir; cook over medium heat for 2 to 3 minutes.
2. Meanwhile, purée undrained tomatoes in food processor or blender until smooth. Add to saucepan along with remaining ingredients and stir well. Heat soup over medium heat, stirring frequently, until mixture just comes to a simmer. Serve immediately.

Quick and Easy Tip
When a recipe calls for yellow or white onion, I always opt for the yellow onion as the flavors are somewhat similar and yellow onions can be substantially cheaper. Also, Alfredo sauce is a white creamy sauce that is found in the refrigerated dairy and cheese section of your grocery store.

Vegetable Beef Stew

Serves 6

Prep time: 10 minutes
Cook time: 25 minutes
Total cost: $6.54
Calories: 175
Fat: 9g
Protein: 18g
Cholesterol: 51mg
Sodium: 465mg

3 tablespoons olive oil

1 yellow onion, chopped

3 garlic cloves, minced

1 pound deli roast beef, thick sliced, chopped

1 large can brown gravy

1 16-ounce package frozen mixed vegetables

1 10-ounce can cream of mushroom soup

2 cups water

½ teaspoon dried thyme leaves

Sea salt and black pepper to taste

Stews are similar to soups only with thicker liquid, and stews are made with heartier ingredients such as potatoes and use thickeners such as flour or cornstarch.

1. In a heavy large saucepan, heat olive oil over medium heat. Add onion and garlic; cook and stir until tender, 4 to 5 minutes. Add beef, gravy, mixed vegetables, soup, water, and thyme leaves.
2. Cook over medium-high heat until soup comes to a boil, about 8 minutes. Reduce heat to low and simmer for 7 minutes longer, until vegetables and beef are hot and tender. Serve immediately.

Quick and Easy Tip
This recipe is the perfect remedy for leftover roast beef. Watch your budget go farther by using leftover beef for this stew the next day or freeze the beef for later!

Tortellini Soup

Serves 6

Prep time: 10 minutes
Cook time: 18 minutes
Total cost: $6.72
Calories: 302
Fat: 28g
Protein: 29g
Cholesterol: 91mg
Sodium: 1,062mg

1 pound sweet Italian bulk sausage

1 8-ounce jar sliced mushrooms

4 cloves garlic, minced

3 14-ounce cans beef broth

1½ cups water

1 teaspoon dried Italian seasoning

½ teaspoon black pepper

1 24-ounce package frozen cheese tortellini

Tortellini are available both fresh or frozen. Frozen tend to be less expensive than fresh but are not lacking in flavor!

1. In a large saucepan over medium heat, brown sausage with mushrooms and garlic, stirring to break up sausage. When sausage is cooked, drain thoroughly. Add broth, water, Italian seasoning, and pepper to saucepan and bring to a boil over high heat. Reduce heat to low and simmer for 8 to 10 minutes.
2. Stir in frozen tortellini and cook, stirring frequently, over medium-high heat for 7 minutes or until tortellini are hot and tender. Serve immediately.

Quick and Easy Tip
Get tired of having plain pasta? This recipe is an easy and affordable way to enjoy pasta.

Hearty Minestrone

Serves 6

Prep time: 10 minutes
Cook time: 18 minutes
Total cost: $6.60
Calories: 243
Fat: 3g
Protein: 6g
Cholesterol: 0g
Sodium: 583mg

4 cups chicken broth

1 16-ounce package frozen mixed vegetables

1 15-ounce can cannellini beans, drained

½ teaspoon dried basil leaves

½ teaspoon dried oregano leaves

1 14-ounce can diced tomatoes, undrained

3 cloves fresh garlic

1½ cups elbow macaroni

Oregano is an herb frequently used in cooking; however, be cautious not to use too much as its flavor is distinctive and often overpowering.

In a large saucepan over medium heat, combine chicken broth and vegetables; bring to a boil. Add beans, basil, oregano, garlic, and tomatoes. Bring to a simmer, lower heat, and cook for 5 minutes. Add macaroni; stir and simmer for 8 to 9 minutes until pasta is tender.

Quick and Easy Tip
Canned beans are inexpensive and also time saving. However, they can often be packed full of sodium. To minimize sodium content, drain beans when possible and rinse before using.

Mexican Beef Stew

Serves 6

Prep time: 10 minutes
Cook time: 22 minutes
Total cost: $6.12
Calories: 162
Fat: 8g
Protein: 17g
Cholesterol: 49mg
Sodium: 365mg

2 tablespoons olive oil

1 yellow onion, chopped

1 pound ground beef

1 package taco seasoning

2 15-ounce cans chili beans, undrained

2 cups frozen corn

1 14-ounce can tomatoes with green chiles, undrained

2 cups water

1 tablespoon chili powder

½ teaspoon cumin

½ teaspoon cayenne pepper

The spice cumin is a member of the parsley family and actually is a good source of iron! Cumin is widely used in Indian, Mexican, and Cuban dishes as it brings out the sweetness of the other ingredients and is a good balance to spicy foods.

In a large saucepan over medium heat, heat olive oil. Add in onions and sauté until tender, about 5 minutes. Add ground beef and cook until browned, about 5 minutes. Add remaining ingredients, stir, cover, and simmer for about 20 minutes, until flavors are combined.

French Onion Soup

● Serves 6

Prep time: 15 minutes
Cook time: 25 minutes
Total cost: $6.72
Calories: 498
Fat: 10g
Protein: 28g
Cholesterol: 20mg
Sodium: 132mg

2 tablespoons olive oil

2 tablespoons butter plus
¼ cup butter softened

2 large yellow onions, chopped

2 tablespoons plain flour

1 quart beef broth

6 slices French bread

2 cups Gruyère cheese, shredded

This recipe is really simple, so don't be intimidated.

1. In a large saucepan, combine olive oil and 2 tablespoons butter over medium heat until butter is foamy. Add onions; cook over medium heat for 10 minutes, stirring frequently, until onions brown around edges. Sprinkle flour over onions; cook and stir for 2 to 3 minutes.

2. Stir in broth, bring to a simmer, and cook for 10 minutes. Meanwhile, spread French bread slices with ¼ cup butter. Toast bread until browned and crisp. Sprinkle with 1 cup of cheese and toast until cheese melts. When serving soup, divide soup among bowls and top with remaining cheese. Float toasted cheese bread on top.

Quick and Easy Tip

The onions take a little extra time to chop, but buying prechopped onions is more expensive. So try to prechop the day before to save time and stress! Also, if Gruyère cheese is out of your budget, substitute provolone.

Vegetable Soup with Meatballs

Serves 6

Prep time: 10 minutes
Cook time: 20 minutes
Total cost: $6.96
Calories: 237
Fat: 4g
Protein: 27g
Cholesterol: 92mg
Sodium: 506mg

1 pound frozen meatballs

2 cups V8 juice or other tomato juice blend

2 cups frozen mixed vegetables

1½ cups beef broth

3 cups water

½ teaspoon dried Italian seasoning

½ teaspoon black pepper

1½ cups mini penne pasta

This recipe is similar to Italian wedding soup. The meatballs here are traditionally larger than the ones in Italian wedding soup.

In a large-quart boiler, combine all ingredients except pasta and mix gently. Bring to a boil over high heat, then stir in pasta. Reduce heat to medium high and cook for 10 minutes or until pasta is al dente (cooked but slightly firm to bite, not mushy).

Quick and Easy Tip

Frozen meatballs are the way to go for this recipe. Most taste delicious, are affordable, and save loads of time! If you see meatballs discounted on a special sale, buy several pounds and keep them in the freezer for later use.

Spiced Corn and Cheese Soup

Serves 6

Prep time: 10 minutes
Cook time: 15 minutes
Total cost: $5.40
Calories: 370
Fat: 9g
Protein: 6g
Cholesterol: 31mg
Sodium: 871mg

2 tablespoons olive oil

1 yellow onion, chopped

1 package taco seasoning mix

2 cups canned creamed corn

2 10-ounce cans chicken broth

1½ cups water

2 cups shredded pepper jack cheese

2 tablespoons plain flour

Serve this soup with salsa, sour cream, chopped avocado, and tortilla chips.

1. In a large-quart boiler, heat olive oil over medium heat. Add onion and sauté until crisp-tender, about 4 minutes. Sprinkle taco seasoning mix over the onions and stir. Then add corn, chicken broth, and water. Bring to a simmer and cook for 10 minutes, stirring occasionally.
2. Meanwhile, in a medium bowl, toss cheese with flour. Add to soup and lower heat; cook and stir for 2 to 3 minutes, until cheese is melted and soup is thickened. Serve hot.

Quick and Easy Tip
Make sure you stir the cheese almost constantly. If you allow the cheese to sit and melt, it tends to burn.

Black Bean Soup

Serves 6

Prep time: 10 minutes
Cook time: 18 minutes
Total cost: $478
Calories: 171
Fat: 2g
Protein: 9g
Cholesterol: 3mg
Sodium: 549mg

2 tablespoons olive oil

1 yellow onion, chopped

3 cloves garlic, minced

2 15-ounce cans black beans, drained and rinsed

1 14-ounce can tomatoes with green chiles, undrained

4 cups chicken broth

½ teaspoon cumin

½ teaspoon white pepper

White pepper has more heat than black pepper so use more sparingly. Chefs use white pepper often when making cream sauces or other dishes that are white so as not to ruin the color of the dish with black pepper flakes.

In a large saucepan over medium heat, heat olive oil. Add onion and garlic. Cook for 2 to 3 minutes, stirring occasionally. Add beans to saucepan along with other ingredients. Bring to a simmer and cook for 12 minutes. Stir to combine and serve.

Quick and Easy Tip

For added color and flavor, add a dollop of sour cream. And, if not cooking for kids, add a splash of sherry wine when serving. The sweetness of the sherry and the alcohol in the wine really pull all the flavors together for a big WOW in your mouth!

The $7 a Meal Quick & Easy Cookbook

No-Peel Potato Soup

Serves 6

Prep time: 10 minutes
Cook time: 20 minutes
Total cost: $5.64
Calories: 325
Fat: 12g
Protein: 11g
Cholesterol: 35mg
Sodium: 683mg

4 slices bacon

1 yellow onion, chopped

1 cup package cheesy scalloped potato mix

3 cups water

1 15-ounce can evaporated milk

2 cups frozen hash brown potatoes

½ teaspoon dried dill

½ teaspoon white pepper

Evaporated milk, not to be confused with sweetened condensed milk, is milk from which 60 percent of the water has been removed. The result is a more concentrated flavor. Because the milk comes in a can, it has a shelf life of months or sometimes years.

In heavy saucepan, cook bacon until crisp. Remove bacon, drain on paper towels, crumble, and set aside. Cook onion in bacon drippings until tender, about 5 minutes. Add potato mix and seasoning packet from potato mix along with remaining ingredients. Bring to a boil and simmer for 17 to 20 minutes, until potatoes are tender. Sprinkle with bacon and serve.

Quick and Easy Tip
Dehydrated potatoes, used here, are not expensive and you don't have to peel them. Plus, they save on cooking time.

Simplest Ever Chili

Serves 6

Prep time: 10 minutes
Cook time: 18 minutes
Total cost: $5.28
Calories: 362
Fat: 4g
Protein: 19g
Cholesterol: 3mg
Sodium: 1,049mg

2 tablespoons olive oil

1 yellow onion, chopped

1 package taco seasoning

2 15-ounce cans black beans, drained

2 15-ounce cans kidney beans, drained

2 14-ounce canned diced tomatoes with green chiles, undrained

1 cup water

Add ground beef or ground turkey to this recipe, if you wish, for extra protein and flavor.

In heavy saucepan over medium heat, add olive oil and sauté onion until tender, about 4 to 5 minutes. Sprinkle taco seasoning mix over onions; cook and stir for 1 minute. Add drained but not rinsed beans, tomatoes, and water. Bring to a simmer; cook for 10 to 12 minutes, until thickened and blended.

Quick and Easy Tip
Make your own taco seasoning mix by combining 2 tablespoons chili powder, 2 teaspoons onion powder, 2 tablespoons cornstarch, 1 teaspoon dried oregano, 1 teaspoon dried red pepper flakes, 2 teaspoons salt, and ½ teaspoon cumin. Blend well and store in a cool dry place: 2 tablespoons equals one envelope mix.

Bean Soup with Bacon and Cheese

Serves 4

Prep time: 10 minutes
Cook time: 15 minutes
Total cost: $6.84
Calories: 326
Fat: 16g
Protein: 22g
Cholesterol: 49mg
Sodium: 704mg

2 slices bacon

1 yellow onion, chopped

1 14-ounce can diced tomatoes, undrained

2 15-ounce cans pinto beans, drained

2 cups chicken broth

1½ cups Cheddar cheese, shredded

Most kids love anything with cheese—that's why this soup is perfect for kids' lunches.

In a large saucepan, cook bacon until crisp. Drain bacon on paper towels, crumble, and set aside. Drain off all but 2 table-spoons bacon drippings. Cook onion in drippings over medium heat for 3 to 4 minutes. Add tomatoes, beans, and broth and bring to a simmer. Simmer for 10 to 12 minutes, then use a potato masher to mash some of the beans. Add reserved bacon, stir, and simmer for 5 minutes longer. Serve immediately and top with cheese. Or pour into warmed insulated thermoses for kids' lunches or picnics.

Quick and Easy Tip
When buying bacon, the leanest cuts have the least amount of white marble. Some is okay, but just make sure there is more meat than fat!

CHAPTER 7

CHICKEN AND TURKEY

Potato Chip Crusted Chicken

Serves 4

Prep time: 10 minutes

Cook time: 25 minutes

Total cost: $6.60

Calories: 470

Fat: 18g

Protein: 33g

Cholesterol: 63mg

Sodium: 378mg

12 ounces potato chips

1 teaspoon freshly ground black pepper

2 tablespoons fresh chives, chopped

1 teaspoon dried thyme

4 boneless chicken breasts, skin removed

⅔ cup sour cream

The potato chips give a crunchy coating to this chicken, but don't add salt—there is enough on the potato chips.

1. In a food processor, chop potato chips until you have 1 cup crumbs. Mix crumbs together with pepper, chives, and thyme.
2. Preheat oven to 350°F. Coat baking dish with butter or spray with nonstick cooking spray. Lay chicken in dish and coat with sour cream, then sprinkle with potato chip mixture. Bake in oven for 25 minutes or until browned and crispy.

Quick and Easy Tip
Substitute chicken tenders for a quick and easy appetizer. Serve with barbeque sauce.

Spicy Cornbread Chicken Tenders

Serves 4

Prep time: 10 minutes
Cook time: 6 minutes
Total cost: $3.85
Calories: 380
Fat: 9g
Protein: 28g
Cholesterol: 71mg
Sodium: 73mg

1 cup plain flour

1 teaspoon sea salt

Red pepper flakes to taste

1 teaspoon baking powder

1 cup cornbread crumbs

1 egg, beaten

2 tablespoons milk

1 pound chicken tenders, cut into bite-sized pieces

Canola oil as needed, about 2 to 3 cups

Sea salt is a natural salt from the sea. It is more flavorful than iodized salt and is better for you because it is natural.

1. In a mixing bowl, combine flour, salt, pepper, and baking powder, then spread it on to parchment paper or wax paper.
2. On a separate sheet of parchment or wax paper, spread out cornbread crumbs. In a mixing bowl, beat egg and milk together using fork or wire whisk. Dredge the tenders in the flour mixture, then dip them in the egg mixture, and, lastly, coat them with breadcrumbs.
3. In a heavy-bottomed frying pan, heat ½ inch of oil to 365°F or until hot. Fry chicken tenders until golden, about 3 to 4 minutes. Drain on paper towels.

Quick and Easy Tip
To see if oil is hot enough for frying, insert spoon end of wooden spoon into oil. If the oil bubbles around the spoon, oil is ready.

The $7 a Meal Quick & Easy Cookbook

Southern Fried Chicken

Serves 4

Prep time: 10 minutes
Cook time: 20 minutes
Total cost: $6.92
Calories: 395
Fat: 14g
Protein: 35g
Cholesterol: 131mg
Sodium: 82mg

1 whole chicken, cut into 8 pieces, or buy whole chicken pieces

1 cup buttermilk

1½ cups corn flour

1 teaspoon sea salt

1 teaspoon black pepper

1 teaspoon baking powder

1 egg, beaten

½ cup beer

1½ cups cornmeal

Canola oil for frying

If you don't have beer, don't worry, leave it out.

1. Place chicken in ziploc bag with buttermilk and let rest in refrigerator while you prepare other ingredients.
2. In a large paper bag, mix together corn flour, salt, pepper, and baking powder. Add the chicken pieces to the corn flour mixture one at a time. Close the bag and shake until the chicken is well coated.
3. Separately, whisk together the egg and beer (if using, otherwise, just the egg). Spread the cornmeal on a large piece of parchment or waxed paper.
4. Bring 1 inch of oil to 365°F in a skillet or fryer. Fry the chicken for 20 to 25 minutes, turn every 4 or 5 minutes. Watch the chicken carefully to make sure it doesn't burn.

Quick and Easy Tip
Another tip for frying chicken is to preheat oven to 400°F. Fry chicken in a skillet until outer coating is crisp and browned, about 5 to 10 minutes. Then place chicken in a baking dish in oven to finish cooking, about 10 to 15 minutes.

Chicken Cacciatore

Serves 4

Prep time: 10 minutes
Cook time: 50 minutes
Total cost: $6.94
Calories: 346
Fat: 6g
Protein: 32g
Cholesterol: 95mg
Sodium: 451mg

1 cup plain flour

Sea salt and black pepper

1 teaspoon oregano, crumbled

¼ cup olive oil

1 teaspoon butter

1 yellow onion, diced

2 to 3 cloves garlic, minced

2 tablespoons fresh rosemary, chopped

2 cups mushrooms, brushed and chopped

2-pound chicken, cut into pieces

1 16-ounce jar marinara sauce

½ cup red wine

¼ cup Parmesan cheese

1 bunch fresh Italian parsley, chopped, for garnish

Add pasta to this recipe for a truly hearty meal.

1. In a mixing bowl, combine flour, salt, pepper, and oregano. Heat the oil and butter in a large skillet over medium heat until butter melts. Add onion, garlic, rosemary, and mushrooms and sauté for 5 minutes. Add chicken and sauté an additional 5 minutes.
2. Add the marinara sauce and red wine. Cover and simmer over low heat for 45 minutes. Remove cover and place chicken on platter, simmer sauce an additional 10 minutes. Serve and spoon sauce over chicken. Sprinkle with cheese and fresh parsley.

Quick and Easy Tip
To save time, precook chicken and add during final stages of cooking. This recipe gets better with age; prepare a day ahead and reheat on stovetop.

Curried Chicken with Lentils

Serves 4

Prep time: 10 minutes
Cook time: 25 minutes
Total cost: $6.48
Calories: 250
Fat: 2g
Protein: 35g
Cholesterol: 4mg
Sodium: 240mg

1 cup lentils

3 cups water

Sea salt and red pepper flakes to taste

2 cloves garlic, chopped

1 yellow onion, chopped

Juice of 1 lemon

1 teaspoon cumin

½ cup fresh Italian parsley, chopped

1 cup yogurt

1 tablespoon curry powder

Tabasco to taste

1 pound boneless chicken breasts, skin removed, cut into 1- to 2-inch cubes

Curry is a blend of other spices including turmeric and coriander and is native to India.

1. Place lentils and water in quart boiler. Bring to a boil, reduce heat, and simmer. Just before the lentils are cooked, about 25 minutes, add the salt and pepper flakes, garlic, onion, lemon juice, cumin, and parsley.
2. Turn broiler to high. In a mixing bowl, combine yogurt, curry, and Tabasco. Toss chicken to coat. Place on aluminum foil and place under broiler for 5 minutes. Turn chicken and broil an additional 5 minutes or as needed until cooked through.
3. Mix cooked chicken into the lentils and serve with rice, if desired.

Quick and Easy Tip
Use canned lentils and you'll save about 15 minutes of cooking time. The flavor is good and you have more time for family.

Kung Pao Chicken

Serves 4

Prep time: 10 minutes
Cook time: 15 minutes
Total cost: $6.92
Calories: 260
Fat: 16g
Protein: 17g
Cholesterol: 70mg
Sodium: 338mg

3 boneless chicken breasts, skin removed

1½ tablespoons peanut oil

1 dried red chili

⅓ cup peanuts

2 tablespoons water

2 tablespoons dry sherry

1 tablespoon soy sauce

1 teaspoon sugar

1 tablespoon chili sauce

1 teaspoon fresh ginger, peeled and chopped

2 cloves garlic, minced

2 scallions, chopped

2 teaspoons rice or apple cider vinegar

1 teaspoon sesame oil

4 cups cooked white rice

This recipe calls for peanut and sesame oils, both of which are good oils to have on hand for specialty dishes like this one.

Dice the chicken into 1-inch cubes. Heat the oil in a wok or skillet and add the chili. Add the chicken and peanuts and stir-fry until the chicken is cooked. Add the remaining ingredients, except the sesame oil and rice, and bring to a boil. Cook for a few minutes. Add the sesame oil and serve over rice.

Quick and Easy Tip

Plan your weekly meals ahead of time, perhaps on Sunday afternoon. Then if you are serving several dishes during the week that need rice, make the rice ahead of time and keep in the refrigerator.

The $7 a Meal Quick & Easy Cookbook

Chicken with Tomato Salsa and Green Peppers

Serves 4

Prep time: 10 minutes
Cook time: 15 minutes
Total cost: $5.68
Calories: 420
Fat: 11g
Protein: 34g
Cholesterol: 6mg
Sodium: 790mg

3 boneless chicken breast halves, skim removed

1 tablespoon olive oil

1 15-ounce jar mild or medium salsa

¾ cup chicken broth

½ cup green bell pepper, seeded and chopped

1 cup quick-cooking rice

½ cup Cheddar cheese, shredded

Try to keep a jar of salsa in your pantry for recipes like this!

Cut the chicken into 1-inch cubes. Heat oil in a large skillet and sauté chicken until cooked, about 8 minutes. Stir in salsa, chicken broth, and green pepper. Bring to a boil. Stir in the uncooked rice. Sprinkle with cheese, cover, and remove from heat. Let stand 5 minutes until rice is cooked.

Quick and Easy Tip

Salsa is a quick and easy way to spice up lots of dishes. Its combination of tomatoes, onions, and other ingredients is a perfect complement to rice, eggs, fish, pork, and more.

Chicken, Avocado, and Wild Rice Salad

Serves 4

- Prep time: 10 minutes
- Cook time: 15 minutes
- Total cost: $5.94
- Calories: 332
- Fat: 13g
- Protein: 34g
- Cholesterol: 93mg
- Sodium: 365mg

1 4.3-ounce package mixed white and wild rice

3 cups cooked chicken, cut into bite sized pieces

4 scallions, chopped

1 cup Italian dressing

2 ripe avocados, sliced

Juice of 1 lemon

½ cup toasted pine nuts or sliced almonds

1 cup cherry tomatoes

Wild rice adds color, flavor, and texture to this dish and is a refreshing alternative to plain white rice.

1. Prepare rice according to package directions. When rice is ready, stir in the chicken and scallions; add the dressing and toss well. Pour into a serving dish and chill for up to 1 hour.
2. Toss avocados with the lemon juice. Garnish salad with avocados, nuts, and cherry tomatoes.

Quick and Easy Tip
Certain wild rice packages take up to 45 minutes to cook. Make sure you buy quick-cooking wild rice when shopping.

Easy-Baked Chicken Casserole

Serves 6

Prep time: 10 minutes
Cook time: 15 minutes
Total cost: $6.97
Calories: 270
Fat: 15g
Protein: 23g
Cholesterol: 9mg
Sodium: 780mg

2 cups cooked chicken, cubed

2 cups celery, sliced

½ cup almonds

½ teaspoon sea salt

½ yellow onion, finely chopped

Juice of 1 lemon

1 cup mayonnaise

½ cup Cheddar cheese, shredded

1½ cups crushed potato chips

Casseroles usually take tons of time to bake. With pre-cooked chicken, you save about an hour of cooking time.

Preheat oven to 425°F. In lightly greased shallow quart baking dish, combine the chicken, celery, almonds, salt, onions, lemon juice, and mayonnaise. Sprinkle with cheese and potato chips. Bake for 15 minutes or until heated through.

Quick and Easy Tip
If the chicken is chopped small enough, this recipe is also great as an appetizer! Serve with additional potato chips as an appetizer.

Baked Chicken
with Herb Stuffing

Serves 4

Prep time: 10 minutes
Cook time: 60 minutes
Total cost: $6.99
Calories: 429
Fat: 17g
Protein: 54g
Cholesterol: 29mg
Sodium: 1,596mg

4 boneless chicken breasts, skin removed

1 10-ounce can cream of chicken soup

½ can water

1½ teaspoons curry powder

Juice of 1 lemon

½ cup Cheddar cheese, shredded

½ cup mayonnaise

1 8-ounce package herb stuffing mix

This recipe takes an hour to bake, but use that time to hang out with the family—watch a football game together or, if sunny, get outside and play some ball.

Preheat oven to 350°F. Lay chicken breasts in a 9" x 12" casserole. Combine the soup and water in a small bowl. Pour the soup mixture over chicken. Mix the remaining ingredients into the stuffing mix. Spread the stuffing mix over the chicken. Bake 1 hour. If the stuffing gets too brown, cover loosely with aluminum foil.

Penne Pasta with Chicken and Sun-Dried Tomatoes

Serves 6

Prep time: 12 minutes
Cook time: 20 minutes
Total cost: $7.00
Calories: 334
Fat: 12g
Protein: 20g
Cholesterol: 31mg
Sodium: 432mg

2 tablespoons extra virgin olive oil

4 cloves garlic, chopped

2 large boneless chicken breasts, skin removed, cut into 1-inch cubes

3 cups chicken broth

½ cup oil-packed sun-dried tomatoes, chopped

2 tablespoons fresh Italian flat-leaf parsley, chopped

2 scallions, white and half of green tops, chopped

¼ cup unsalted butter, softened

Sea salt and black pepper to taste

1 pound penne pasta

Don't let the words fool you; scallions are the same thing as green onions. Use the whole thing, except for the roots, of course.

1. In a large, deep skillet, heat the oil over medium heat. Add the garlic and chicken and sauté until chicken is cooked through, about 3 to 4 minutes. Remove the chicken from the pan and set aside.
2. Pour the chicken stock into a saucepan and add the tomatoes, parsley, and scallions. Add salt and pepper to taste. Bring to a boil and reduce over high heat 5 to 10 minutes. Add the chicken to the pan and whisk in the butter, a bit at a time, to thicken the sauce. Remove from the heat until golden. Do not allow to burn.
3. Meanwhile, in a large pot, bring at least 4 quarts of water to a rolling boil. Add 1 tablespoon salt. Add the penne; stir to prevent sticking. Cook until al dente. Drain.
4. In a bowl toss the penne in the sauce, transfer to a warm platter, and serve.

Teriyaki Chicken

Serves 4

Prep time: 10 minutes
Cook time: 20 minutes
Total cost: $6.58
Calories: 292
Fat: 12g
Protein: 32g
Cholesterol: 24mg
Sodium: 1,083mg

½ cup Italian dressing

½ cup teriyaki sauce

5 boneless chicken breast
halves, skin removed

Marinate
overnight

Italian dressing is useful for all sorts of things: pasta salad, poaching chicken breasts, and even for marinating steaks. It's a great trick to add lots of flavor without all the preparation!

Combine the Italian dressing and teriyaki sauce. Marinate the chicken in this mixture overnight. Grill over hot coals for about 20 minutes, turning chicken after 10 minutes. Cook until the meat is no longer pink and the juices run clear.

Quick and Easy Tip
Marinating foods is easy and infuses flavor into your protein product. This recipe calls for marinating overnight, making for super easy cooking the next day.

Marinated Chicken Skewers

Serves 4

Prep time: 15 minutes
Cook time: 8 minutes
Total cost: $6.32
Calories: 181
Fat: 7g
Protein: 26g
Cholesterol: 72mg
Sodium: 64mg

Marinate
20 minutes

1 tablespoon lemon juice

1 tablespoon water

1 tablespoon olive oil

½ teaspoon dried tarragon, crumbled

¼ teaspoon Tabasco sauce

¼ teaspoon sea salt

1 clove garlic, chopped

4 boneless chicken breasts, skim removed, cut into 1-inch cubes

1 red bell pepper, seeded and cut into 1-inch squares

2 zucchini, cut into 1-inch thick slices

People love anything on the grill. This marinade is not sugar based so the chicken will not burn as easily when on the grill.

1. In a small bowl, combine the lemon juice, water, oil, tarragon, Tabasco sauce, salt, and garlic. Place the chicken in a lock-top plastic bag and set in a deep bowl. Pour the lemon juice mixture into the bag, secure the top closed, and let the chicken stand for 20 minutes at room temperature, turning the bag frequently.
2. Preheat the broiler. Drain the chicken, reserving the marinade. Thread the chicken, bell pepper, and zucchini alternately onto 4 10- to 12-inch long skewers. Arrange the skewers on a broiler pan. Slip under the broiler 4 to 5 inches from the heat source. Broil, turning once and brushing occasionally with the reserved marinade until the chicken is tender and cooked through, about 8 minutes. Serve immediately.

Quick and Easy Tip
A great way to save time and stress is to marinate the chicken the day before and go ahead and prepare the skewers. Then, just heat the grill and cook!

Pasta Primavera
with Chicken

Serves 4

Prep time: 15 minutes
Cook time: 10 minutes
Total cost: $6.68
Calories: 382
Fat: 12g
Protein: 12g
Cholesterol: 20mg
Sodium: 266mg

1 tablespoon olive oil

2 yellow onions, chopped

2 green bell peppers, seeded and chopped

1 clove garlic, chopped

2 zucchini squash, chopped

2 yellow summer squash, chopped

3 tomatoes, chopped

¼ cup fresh basil leaves, chopped

Sea salt and black pepper to taste

1 tablespoon plain flour

½ cup heavy cream, or ¼ cup whole milk plus ¼ cup sour cream

½ cup chicken broth

1 pound rotini

Pasta is a family hit on most occasions. Keep some on hand at all times for a quick, easy and filling meal.

1. In a large, deep skillet, heat the oil over medium heat. Add the onions, bell peppers, and garlic and sauté 3 minutes. Add the zucchini and yellow squash and sauté 1 minute. Add the tomatoes and basil and cook briefly, just until the tomatoes soften. Season with salt and pepper to taste.
2. Drain the vegetables in a colander set over a bowl to catch the juices. Let the juices cool, then add the flour to the juices. Stir well so that there are no lumps and the mixture is smooth. Add the cream and broth, stirring constantly. Stir the cream mixture into the vegetables. Bring to a simmer over low heat and cook 2 to 3 minutes. Do not boil.
3. Meanwhile, in a large pot, bring at least 4 quarts of water to a rolling boil. Add 1 tablespoon salt. Add the pasta, stir to separate, and cook until al dente. Drain. Transfer the hot pasta to a serving platter or to individual plates and spoon the vegetable mixture over the top.

Marinated Ginger Chicken

Serves 4

Prep time: 12 minutes
Cook time: 20 minutes
Total cost: $4.53
Calories: 370
Fat: 9g
Protein: 20g
Cholesterol: 14mg
Sodium: 660mg

1 2- to 3-pound whole frying chicken, cut into pieces, or 1 package whole, cut-up chicken pieces

½ cup lemon juice

½ cup canola oil

¼ cup soy sauce

1 teaspoon grated gingerroot or 1 tablespoon ground ginger

1 teaspoon onion salt

¼ teaspoon garlic powder

Marinate
4 hours

Fresh gingerroot is best for this recipe and is relatively inexpensive. Buy some fresh root and keep what you don't use in your freezer!

1. Place chicken in a shallow baking dish. In a small bowl, combine the lemon juice, oil, soy sauce, ginger, onion, and garlic powder. Pour over the chicken. Cover and refrigerate at least 4 hours or overnight, turning occasionally.
2. Grill or broil for about 20 minutes, turning after 10 minutes. Cook until the meat is no longer pink and the juices run clear, basting frequently with marinade.

Quick and Easy Tip
Marinating is an easy way to infuse flavor into foods without a long cooking time. Here, soy sauce and ginger combine for spectacular flavor. This marinade is also good on steaks!

Chicken Picatta

Serves 4

Prep time: 12 minutes
Cook time: 20 minutes
Total cost: $5.98
Calories: 202
Fat: 9g
Protein: 19g
Cholesterol: 50mg
Sodium: 721mg

4 boneless, chicken breast halves, skin removed

Sea salt and black pepper to taste

2 tablespoons butter

1 teaspoon olive oil

½ cup chicken broth

¼ cup vermouth

Juice of 1 lemon

1 tablespoon capers, drained and rinsed

Lemon slices for garnish

Picatta is a cooking style using lemon, capers, and wine and is traditional to Italian cuisine. You can also substitute veal or pork.

1. Pat chicken dry. Season with salt and pepper. Melt butter with oil in a large heavy skillet over medium-high heat. Add the chicken and cook until springy to the touch, about 4 minutes per side. Remove from the skillet; keep warm.
2. Increase heat to high. Stir the broth and vermouth into the skillet. Boil until reduced by half, scraping up any browned bits. Remove from the heat. Mix in the lemon juice and capers. Place the chicken on plates and pour the sauce over the chicken. Garnish the chicken with lemon slices.

Quick and Easy Tip
Vermouth is substituted for white wine here. Add a side of pasta for a heartier meal.

Lemon Chicken with Broccoli

Serves 4

Prep time: 10 minutes
Cook time: 20 minutes
Total cost: $6.89
Calories: 382
Fat: 11g
Protein: 28g
Cholesterol: 6mg
Sodium: 760mg

1 tablespoon olive oil

4 boneless chicken breast halves, skin removed

1 10-ounce can cream of broccoli soup

¼ cup low-fat milk or whole milk

Juice of 1 lemon

Pinch black pepper

4 thin lemon slices

Using the cream of broccoli soup as a base saves time but keeps the flavor of the dish.

Heat the oil in a skillet. Sauté the chicken breasts about 10 minutes, until browned on both sides. Pour off the fat. Combine the soup, milk, lemon juice, and pepper. Pour over the chicken. Top each chicken piece with a slice of lemon. Reduce heat to low and cover. Simmer 5 to 10 minutes until chicken is tender, stirring occasionally.

Quick and Easy Tip

Add in some fresh steamed broccoli florets, if you wish, for an even more nutritious meal without tons of extra time and money.

Stir-Fry Chicken
with Vegetables

Serves 4

Prep time: 15 minutes
Cook time: 10 minutes
Total cost: $6.44
Calories: 387
Fat: 11g
Protein: 29g
Cholesterol: 82mg
Sodium: 627mg

2 tablespoons red wine

1 tablespoon soy sauce

½ teaspoon cornstarch

1 teaspoon sugar

1 tablespoon sea salt

1 tablespoon peanut oil

2 cups blanched broccoli florets

1 cup blanched, sliced carrots

½ cup yellow onion wedges

6 ounces boneless chicken breasts, skin removed, cut into thin strips

2 cups cooked rice

Stir-fry is a healthy way to cook. If you don't have a wok, don't worry; a skillet works fine.

1. In a small bowl, make the sauce by combining the red wine, soy sauce, cornstarch, sugar, and salt. Stir to dissolve the cornstarch. Set aside. In a wok, heat the oil; add the broccoli, carrots, and onion. Cook, stirring quickly and frequently, until vegetables are tender and crisp and onions are browned. Stir in the chicken and stir-fry 2 more minutes.
2. Add the sauce to the chicken mixture and cook, stirring constantly, until the sauce is thickened, 2 to 3 minutes. Serve each portion over ½ cup cooked rice.

Quick and Easy Tip
Blanching the vegetables is a process that brings out the color of the vegetable while at the same time making them tender. Be sure not to overcook them as the vegetables will become mushy and not good for stir-fry.

Turkey Pot Pie

Serves 4

Prep time: 15 minutes
Cook time: 14 minutes
Total cost: $6.94
Calories: 253
Fat: 6g
Protein: 26g
Cholesterol: 57mg
Sodium: 943mg

1 tablespoon butter

½ yellow onion, diced

½ cup celery, chopped

1 can turkey or chicken gravy

¼ cup water

1 10-ounce package frozen mixed vegetables

1 cup turkey breasts, cut into cubes

¼ teaspoon black pepper

¼ teaspoon marjoram

1 can refrigerated biscuits

Pot pie is a wonderful dish for chilly days.

1. Preheat the oven to 400°F. In a medium ovenproof skillet, heat the butter over medium heat; sauté the onion and celery in the butter about 3 minutes. Stir in the gravy, water, vegetables, turkey, pepper, and marjoram. Bring to a boil, then remove from the heat.
2. Arrange the biscuits on top of the mixture. Bake 12 to 14 minutes, or until the biscuits are golden brown.

Quick and Easy Tip
Refrigerated biscuits make this dish the simplest ever.

Turkey, Tomatoes, and Olives with Linguine

Serves 4

Prep time: 20 minutes

Cook time: 30 minutes

Total cost: $7.00

Calories: 294

Fat: 14g

Protein: 32g

Cholesterol: 72mg

Sodium: 808mg

2 teaspoons olive oil

1 yellow onion, chopped

3 cloves garlic, chopped

¾ pound turkey breast, skin removed, cut into bite-sized pieces

1 tablespoon fresh basil, chopped

½ teaspoon dried thyme

½ teaspoon dried rosemary

12 to 16 kalamata or other olives, pitted and chopped

1½ tablespoons capers, drained

2 tomatoes, chopped

2 cups chicken broth

1 tablespoon sea salt

1 pound linguine

1 cup grated Pecorino Romano cheese or Parmesan cheese

Pecorino Romano cheese is a wonderful Italian blended cheese. If your budget is tight, go with a more traditional Parmesan instead without sacrificing flavor.

1. In a large, deep skillet, heat the oil over medium heat. Add the onion and garlic and cook until the onion is translucent. Add the turkey, basil, thyme, and rosemary and sauté until the turkey is lightly browned. Stir in the olives, capers, and tomatoes and cook briefly, until the tomatoes begin to give off liquid. Remove the turkey from the skillet. Add the chicken stock, bring to a boil, and simmer over medium heat until the broth is reduced by half. Return the turkey to the sauce and stir well.
2. Meanwhile, in a large pot, bring at least 4 quarts of water to a rolling boil. Add 1 tablespoon salt. Add the linguine, stir to separate, and cook until al dente. Drain.
3. Transfer the linguine to the skillet and toss with the sauce until the sauce is evenly distributed. Transfer to a warm serving dish, top with the cheese, and serve.

The $7 a Meal Quick & Easy Cookbook

Indian-Spiced Turkey

Serves 6

Prep time: 12 minutes

Cook time: 7 minutes

Total cost: $6.54

Calories: 229

Fat: 4g

Protein: 28g

Cholesterol: 75mg

Sodium: 130mg

2 large limes

⅓ cup plain yogurt

1 tablespoon canola oil

2 teaspoons fresh gingerroot, peeled, chopped

1 teaspoon ground cumin

1 teaspoon ground coriander

1 teaspoon sea salt

1 clove garlic, crushed

1½ pounds turkey cutlets

Fresh cilantro sprigs for garnish

Turkey cutlets are a choice cut that are perfect for the grill as they are not typically as thick as chicken and therefore take less time to cook.

1. Preheat grill. Grate the peel and extract the juice from 1 lime. Place 1 teaspoon of grated peel and 1 tablespoon juice in a large bowl. Cut the other lime into wedges and set aside. Add yogurt, oil, ginger, cumin, coriander, salt, and garlic to the lime peel and juice, and mix until blended.
2. Just before grilling, add the turkey cutlets to the bowl with the yogurt mixture, stirring to coat the cutlets. Do not let the cutlets marinate in the yogurt mixture, as their texture will become mealy.
3. Place the turkey cutlets on the grill over medium-hot coals. Cook the cutlets 5 to 7 minutes, until they just lose their pink color throughout. Serve with lime wedges. Garnish with cilantro sprigs.

Turkey Tetrazzini

Serves 6

Prep time: 10 minutes
Cook time: 45 minutes
Total cost: $6.48
Calories: 369
Fat: 6g
Protein: 17g
Cholesterol: 49mg
Sodium: 539mg

8 to 10 ounces spaghetti or linguine

1 4-ounce can mushrooms, reserve the liquid

3 cups cooked turkey

4 tablespoons butter

¼ cup plain flour

Sea salt and black pepper to taste

2 cups chicken broth

1 cup milk

½ cup sour cream

½ cup Parmesan cheese, grated

Tetrazzini is an American dish named for famed Italian-born opera star, Luisa Tetrazzini, as a chef prepared the dish for her during one of her long stays either in New York or San Francisco.

1. Break the spaghetti into pieces and cook according to package directions, but undercook slightly. Drain. In a large bowl, toss the noodles with the drained mushrooms and turkey. Preheat oven to 350°F. Melt the butter over low heat. Stir in the flour, salt, and pepper, and cook until the mixture is bubbly. Remove the pan from the heat, and stir in the broth, milk, sour cream, and reserved mushroom liquid. Stirring constantly, heat the sauce until it boils; boil 1 minute.
2. Pour the sauce over the noodle mixture and mix thoroughly. Place mixture in an 8" x 11" baking dish. Sprinkle the Parmesan cheese on top. Bake about 45 minutes, or until hot and bubbly in the center.

Quick and Easy Tip
Cream sauces don't generally freeze well, so prepare this dish and enjoy any leftovers for lunch the next day.

Turkey Meatloaf

Serves 6

Prep time: 10 minutes
Cook time: 60 minutes
Total cost: $6.32
Calories: 178
Fat: 7g
Protein: 39g
Cholesterol: 143mg
Sodium: 248mg

1 pound ground turkey

1 yellow onion, chopped

1 cup bread crumbs, plain or Italian seasoned

⅔ cup milk

¼ cup chili sauce

3 eggs

1 teaspoon dried thyme

Sea salt and black pepper to taste

¼ teaspoon nutmeg

2 strips bacon

Ground turkey is a healthy way to enjoy meatloaf. Buy in bulk and store in family-size servings.

1. Preheat oven to 350°F. Put all but bacon into food processor and process until well blended. Do not over process.
2. Pour into a 9" x 5" bread pan sprayed with nonstick cooking spray. Place this pan into a much larger pan, such as an 11" x 13" inch pan, and place in oven. Add boiling water to the larger pan. Cut bacon in half and arrange across the top of the loaf. Bake for 1 hour. Serve with mashed potatoes.

Quick and Easy Tip
The water bath here allows for even cooking temperatures during baking and will help prevent the turkey loaf from drying around the edges.

Farfalle Pasta with Turkey and Turkey Sausage

Serves 4

Prep time: 15 minutes
Cook time: 20 minutes
Total cost: $6.99
Calories: 483
Fat: 12g
Protein: 29g
Cholesterol: 66mg
Sodium: 1,862mg

1 tablespoon olive oil

1 yellow onion, chopped

2 cloves garlic, chopped

1 green bell pepper, seeded and julienned (cut into strips)

8 ounces boneless turkey breasts, skin removed, cut into ½-inch wide pieces

½ pound sweet or hot turkey sausages, cut crosswise into ½-inch thick pieces

1 16-ounce can Italian plum tomatoes, with juice, chopped

¼ cup dry red wine

½ teaspoon dried oregano

¼ teaspoon fresh basil leaves, chopped

1 teaspoon sugar

12 ounces farfalle pasta

½ cup milk

½ cup sour cream

Sea salt and black pepper

Farfalle is the Italian name for bowtie pasta and is the plural form of the word farfalla, meaning butterfly.

1. In a large, deep skillet, heat the oil over medium heat. Add the onion, garlic, and bell pepper and sauté until just softened. Add the turkey and sausage and sauté until slightly browned. Add the tomatoes with the juice, the wine, oregano, basil, and sugar. Bring to a boil, lower the heat, and simmer gently, stirring occasionally, for 10 minutes or until the tomatoes cook down and thicken slightly.
2. Meanwhile, in a large pot, bring at least 4 quarts of water to a rolling boil. Add 1 tablespoon of salt. Add the farfalle and stir to prevent sticking. Cook until al dente. Transfer to a warm serving bowl.
3. Stir in the milk, sour cream, and salt and pepper to taste to the tomato sauce and simmer for 3 minutes, or until it thickens slightly. Pour the hot sauce over the farfalle, toss well, and serve.

Turkey Lasagna

Serves 8

Prep time: 10 minutes
Cook time: 1 hour
Total cost: $6.98
Calories: 315
Fat: 11g
Protein: 36g
Cholesterol: 104mg
Sodium: 885mg

1 8-ounce box lasagna noodles

1 tablespoon olive oil

1 large zucchini, sliced

1 large squash, sliced

1 cup broccoli florets

¾ pound ground turkey

3 cups marinara sauce

1¾ cups ricotta cheese

2 eggs, slightly beaten

½ teaspoon dried basil

½ teaspoon oregano

16 ounces (2 cups) shredded mozzarella cheese

¼ cup Parmesan cheese

1 tablespoon butter for coating baking dish

Make sure you put a teaspoon or so of olive oil with the boiling noodles to help prevent them from sticking together.

1. Boil lasagna noodles until softened. While boiling, heat oil in a skillet or saucepan over medium heat. Add vegetables and sauté until they begin to brown and are tender. Remove vegetables from heat and set aside.
2. Add turkey to skillet and cook over medium heat until browned. Drain some of the fat from the pan and stir in marinara sauce.
3. In a small bowl, stir together ricotta, eggs, basil, and oregano.
4. Spread ¾ cup of turkey and marinara sauce mixture into buttered 13" x 9" x 2" baking dish.
5. Place three pieces of lasagna crosswise over sauce. Spread ⅔ cup ricotta mixture, then ¾ cup turkey sauce, then ½ cup vegetables evenly over pasta. Sprinkle with 1 cup mozzarella and Parmesan cheese. Repeat with remaining ingredients.
6. Cover with foil and bake for 30 minutes. Remove foil. Bake 10 to 15 minutes more until bubbly.

Cuban Skillet Turkey

Serves 6

Prep time: 10 minutes
Cook time: 15 minutes
Total cost: $6.78
Calories: 222
Fat: 11g
Protein: 25g
Cholesterol: 35mg
Sodium: 232mg

2 tablespoons olive oil

1½ pounds ground turkey

1 clove fresh garlic, minced

½ teaspoon all-purpose seasoning

1 cup yellow onions, chopped

1 large tomato, diced

1 tablespoon tomato paste

2 teaspoons cumin

¼ cup cilantro, chopped

¼ cup raisins

1 cup baking potatoes, cubed

1 cup water

This Cuban dish, sometimes called picadillo, is typically made with ground beef. It's often used for stuffed potatoes and tacos and is commonly served with mixed vegetables.

1. In a large skillet over medium heat, heat 1 tablespoon olive oil. Add turkey, olive oil, garlic, and all-purpose seasoning to skillet. Cook on medium high for 5 to 8 minutes, using a spatula to stir and chop turkey meat.
2. Add onions, tomatoes, tomato paste, cumin, and cilantro to skillet. Cook for 5 minutes on medium heat.
3. Add raisins, potatoes, and water. Simmer for another 8 to 10 minutes.

Quick and Easy Tip
Serve this dish with Grilled Bananas with Honey (page 318).

Baked Turkey Sausage
with Zucchini

Serves 6

Prep time: 10 minutes
Cook time: 40 minutes
Total cost: $6.92
Calories: 231
Fat: 7g
Protein: 17g
Cholesterol: 51mg
Sodium: 680mg

2 cups baking potatoes, cubed

2 cups turkey sausage, sliced

1 zucchini, sliced

1 yellow onion, chopped

½ cup chicken broth

½ teaspoon sea salt

¼ teaspoon black pepper

2 teaspoons plain flour

1 clove fresh garlic, minced

1 cup shredded mozzarella cheese

Sausages are spiced meats typically used for their powerful flavor. Substituting turkey sausage for your regular sausage is a healthy alternative that doesn't compromise flavor.

1. Coat a 9" x 13" baking dish with cooking spray or butter.
2. In a bowl, mix all ingredients except for mozzarella. Mix well and pour into sprayed dish. Top with mozzarella and cover with foil.
3. Bake at 365°F for 30 to 35 minutes.

Quick and Easy

If you keep the skin on your potatoes instead of peeling them, you'll preserve tons of nutrients. The skin is packed with phytonutrient carotenoids and flavonoids. It is also a tremendous source of fiber. In the future, save some time and don't peel those potatoes.

Turkey Sausage Stuffing
with Mushrooms

Serves 6

Prep time: 10 minutes
Cook time: 25 minutes
Total cost: $6.72
Calories: 263
Fat: 11g
Protein: 17g
Cholesterol: 51mg
Sodium: 500mg

1 clove fresh garlic, minced

½ teaspoon all-purpose seasoning

1 yellow onion, chopped

4 cups bread stuffing

½ cup carrots, chopped

½ cup celery, chopped

1 cup cremini or button mushrooms, sliced

2 cups turkey sausage, sliced

1 cup chicken broth

1 tablespoon fresh Italian parsley, chopped

1 teaspoon dried or fresh sage

1 teaspoon dried thyme

2 eggs

Sometimes it can be frustrating buying fresh herbs for such a small amount needed in a recipe. If you don't have the good fortune to have a little herb garden and you only need a very small amount, such as here, then use dried herbs.

1. Mix all ingredients together well in a large bowl.
2. Coat a 9" x 13" baking dish with nonstick spray. Pour mixture into the dish and cover with foil.
3. Bake at 350°F for 25 minutes.
4. Remove foil and bake for another 5 minutes or until top is golden brown.

Quick and Easy Tip
Enjoy this recipe as a vegetarian dish or substitute chicken or beef.

Risotto with Walnut-Crusted Turkey

Serves 8

Prep time: 10 minutes

Cook time: 25 to 30 minutes

Total cost: $6.98

Calories: 339

Fat: 13g

Protein: 24g

Cholesterol: 54mg

Sodium: 102mg

3 tablespoons olive oil

1½ pounds boneless turkey, cut into 1-inch pieces

Sea salt and black pepper to taste

1 egg, beaten

1 cup walnuts, chopped

4 cloves garlic, minced

1½ cups arborio rice

¾ cup Pinot Grigio or Sauvignon Blanc

4 cups chicken broth

½ bunch fresh Italian parsley, chopped

½ cup Parmesan or Romano cheese, grated

1 tablespoon butter, unsalted

Risotto is actually a cooking process that means reboiled. To get the creaminess of risotto, add the liquid a little at a time and stir frequently.

1. Preheat oven to 375°F. Lightly grease a baking pan with 1 table-spoon of the oil. Season the turkey with salt and pepper. Dip turkey in the egg, and lightly coat with nuts. Heat 1 tablespoon of the oil in a large saucepan. Lightly brown the turkey on each side, about 3 minutes per side. Transfer turkey to baking dish and bake for about 10 minutes, or until cooked through.
2. Add the remaining 1 tablespoon of oil to the saucepan and heat to medium. Add the garlic and rice; stir for 1 minute. Pour in the wine and stir until completely absorbed. Add the broth ½ cup at a time, stirring frequently and allowing each addition to be completely absorbed before adding the next. (You will be able to tell because the rice will begin to make that "sticking" sound.) Continue until all broth is absorbed and rice is tender. This process will take about 20 minutes.
3. Remove from heat; add turkey, parsley, cheese, and butter.

Roasted Turkey with Mascarpone

Serves 5

Prep time: 10 minutes
Cook time: 35 minutes
Total cost: $6.98
Calories: 340
Fat: 11g
Protein: 32g
Cholesterol: 49mg
Sodium: 364mg

1 tablespoon olive oil

2 pounds boneless turkey

pinch black pepper

2 yellow onions, chopped

1 stick unsalted butter

½ cup plain flour

4 cups milk

2 cups sour cream

1 cup mascarpone cheese

Mascarpone is made from soured cream but is different than our American sour cream. It is widely used in Italy in desserts such as tiramisu.

1. Preheat oven to 400°F. Grease a large roasting pan with oil. Slice the turkey into thin scaloppini-like portions, and season with pepper. Place onions and turkey in roasting pan. Cover and roast for 20 minutes. Uncover and continue roasting for another 10 to 15 minutes.
2. While turkey is roasting, make the cheese sauce by melting butter in a saucepan over medium heat. Sprinkle in flour and stir with a wooden spoon. Whisk in the milk and sour cream, stirring constantly. Simmer until the sauce thickens, about 10 minutes. Remove from heat and stir in mascarpone cheese.
3. To serve, place roasted turkey on platter and drizzle with cheese sauce. Serve remaining sauce on the side.

Quick and Easy Tip
Premake the cheese sauce and then reheat. But beware—cheese sauces are fairly delicate and cannot be left alone. Heat them over low heat and stir constantly. Do not freeze this cheese sauce.

CHAPTER 8

PORK

Apple-Stuffed Pork Chops

Serves 4

Prep time: 10 minutes
Cook time: 45 minutes
Total cost: $6.92
Calories: 312
Fat: 8g
Protein: 41g
Cholesterol: 105mg
Sodium: 86mg

½ cup olive oil

2 apples such as Granny Smith, cored, seeded, and chopped

1 yellow onion, chopped

1 tablespoon dried rosemary, chopped

¼ cup Italian parsley, chopped

½ cup cornbread crumbs

Sea salt and black pepper to taste

4 thick-cut pork rib chops

4 garlic cloves, chopped

Zest and juice of 1 lemon

½ cup chicken broth

½ cup dry white wine

1 teaspoon cornstarch mixed in 1 tablespoon water

Even at your local grocery store, the butcher can be helpful. Ask him to cut chops thick enough, about 1½ inches to 2 inches, and to cut a slit in each so as to be easily stuffed.

1. In a large saucepan, heat ¼ cup olive oil. Add apples, onion, and herbs and sauté until softened, about 5 minutes. Add the cornbread crumbs, salt, and pepper. Remove from heat and let cool. When cooled, stuff this mixture into the chops and secure with a toothpick.
2. Add ¼ cup olive oil to the saucepan and heat over medium heat. Add the stuffed chops and brown on each side. Add the remaining ingredients, except for the cornstarch-water mixture, and cover. Simmer for 40 minutes over low heat.
3. Place the chops on a warm platter and add the cornstarch-water mixture to the pork gravy in the saucepan to thicken. Add salt and pepper to taste. Serve chops and top with sauce.

Sautéed Pork Tenderloin
with Spinach and Water Chestnuts

Serves 4

Prep time: 10 minutes
Cook time: 15 minutes
Total cost: $6.94
Calories: 394
Fat: 19g
Protein: 42g
Cholesterol: 119mg
Sodium: 275mg

¼ cup plain flour

1 pinch nutmeg

¼ teaspoon ground cloves

Sea salt and black pepper to taste

2¾-pound pork tenderloins, cleaned and trimmed

¼ cup olive oil

Juice from 1 lemon

1 teaspoon Worcestershire sauce

1 large bunch fresh spinach, washed, dried, stems trimmed

½ cup sliced water chestnuts

This is a delicious, quick weeknight meal.

In a large mixing bowl, combine flour, nutmeg, cloves, salt, and pepper and coat pork. Heat olive oil in a large saucepan over medium heat. Add pork and sauté about 6 minutes per side. Add lemon juice, Worcestershire sauce, spinach, and water chestnuts. Stir to wilt leaves. If pan is dry, drizzle with a bit more olive oil or add a tablespoon or 2 of water.

Quick and Easy Tip
When sautéing meats, add a tablespoon or 2 of water, white wine, apple juice, or Italian dressing if the pan needs a little moisture to prevent from burning.

Pork Tenderloin Stuffed
with Apricots and Raisins

Serves 6

Prep time: 10 minutes
Cook time: 30 minutes
Total cost: $6.88
Calories: 257
Fat: 5g
Protein: 32g
Cholesterol: 38mg
Sodium: 96mg

3 dried apricots, chopped

¼ cup dried cranberries

2 tablespoons golden raisins

1 cup warm water

Juice of ½ lemon

2 pork tenderloins, about
    ¾ pound each

Worcestershire sauce

1 cup cornmeal

Sea salt and black pepper to
    taste

¼ cup olive oil

The tenderloin is so named because it is the most tender cut of pork.

1. Place dried fruit in a mixing bowl with the warm water and lemon juice. Let stand until most of the water is absorbed.
2. Preheat oven to 350°F. Make a tunnel through each tenderloin by using the handle of a wooden spoon, knife handle, or knitting needle. Stuff the fruit into the tunnels. Sprinkle both tenderloins (or roasts) with Worcestershire. Make a paste with cornmeal, salt, pepper, and olive oil. Spread it on the pork and roast for 30 minutes. The crust should be golden brown and the pork a healthy, cooked pink.

Quick and Easy Tip
When cooking pork, cook to a temperature of 160°F. The length of time depends upon the thickness of the pork. Do your best not to overcook as pork becomes dried and tough.

Grilled Pork Tenderloin Stuffed with Shallots and Herbs

Serves 4

Prep time: 5 minutes
Cook time: 18 minutes
Total cost: $6.84
Calories: 232
Fat: 6g
Protein: 39g
Cholesterol: 112mg
Sodium: 79mg

2 tablespoons unsalted butter

2 shallots, minced

2 tablespoons fresh rosemary, leaves chopped

1 tablespoon fresh basil, chopped

½ teaspoon ground coriander

4 pork chops, 1½ to 2 inches thick, a pocket cut from the outside edge

¼ cup olive oil

Sea salt and black pepper to taste

This is a perfect meal for a lazy afternoon feast.

1. In a large saucepan, heat the butter over medium heat. Add shallots and sauté until softened, about 4 minutes. Add herbs and sauté.
2. Stuff the chops with the shallot/herb mixture and rub with olive oil, salt, and pepper.
3. Heat an outdoor grill or use low broil of broiler and sear chops on each side, about 4 to 5 minutes per side for medium chops, depending upon thickness.

Quick and Easy Tip

Sauté the shallots and herbs and stuff the chops ahead of time. When ready to cook, take them from refrigerator to grill and be ready to serve within minutes.

Honey Mustard Pork Chops

Serves 4

Prep time: 10 minutes
Cook time: 12 minutes
Total cost: $6.24
Calories: 198
Fat: 3g
Protein: 21g
Cholesterol: 61mg
Sodium: 247mg

2 tablespoons honey

¼ cup Dijon mustard

1 tablespoon fresh rosemary, leaves chopped

1 tablespoon fresh thyme, leaves chopped

Sea salt and black pepper to taste

4 boneless pork chops, about 1 inch thick

Honey can be used as a sweetener for all kinds of dishes. Substitute for sugar in dressing recipes for a healthier dressing that has great flavor and consistency.

Preheat broiler. In a bowl, combine honey, mustard, herbs, and salt and pepper and whisk to combine well. Brush over the chops and place on aluminum foil. Then place under broiler and cook for about 5 minutes, turn once, baste with mustard mixture, and cook an additional 5 to 6 minutes or until pork reaches 160°F and is cooked through but still pinkish in color.

Quick and Easy Tip
Pork chops are a great item to buy in bulk and then freeze in family-size servings. Thaw in refrigerator overnight.

Italian-Seasoned Pork Chops

Serves 4

Prep time: 10 minutes

Cook time: 15 minutes

Total cost: $6.78

Calories: 220

Fat: 7g

Protein: 27g

Cholesterol: 44mg

Sodium: 310mg

3 tablespoons Dijon mustard

2 tablespoons Italian dressing

Sea salt and black pepper to taste

1 tablespoon olive oil

4 boneless pork chops

1 yellow onion, chopped

Dijon mustard is a must-have for your kitchen cabinet. Use it to spice up salad dressings, fish, steak, or pork.

1. In a small mixing bowl, combine mustard, dressing, and pinch of salt and pepper. Set aside.
2. In a large saucepan, heat 1 tablespoon olive oil over medium-high heat. Add chops and brown on both sides, turning once. Transfer the chops to a plate and set aside. Add the onions and cook over medium heat until soft, about 3 minutes. Push onions to the side of the skillet and return chops to skillet. Spread mustard mixture over chops, reduce heat to medium low, cover with lid, and cook until tender, about 15 minutes.

Quick and Easy Tip
Cooking with Italian dressing is a great secret I discovered after having kids! Kids love it and it adds the perfect flavor to many recipes. And, best of all, it's quick!

Herb-Crusted Pork Chops
with White Wine Sauce

Serves 4

Prep time: 10 minutes
Cook time: 40 minutes
Total cost: $6.96
Calories: 217
Fat: 5g
Protein: 24g
Cholesterol: 65mg
Sodium: 175mg

1 tablespoon fresh sage, chopped

1 teaspoon fresh rosemary, leaves chopped

2 cloves garlic, chopped

Sea salt and black pepper to taste

4 pork chops, about 1 inch thick

2 tablespoons butter

1 tablespoon olive oil

¾ cup dry white wine

Don't fear cooking with wine. The alcohol cooks out of the wine but extracts flavors from the other ingredients in the meantime.

1. Rub chops with the olive oil. Combine sage, rosemary, garlic, salt, and pepper. Press mixture firmly into both sides of the pork chops. In a large saucepan, melt butter over medium heat. Add chops and brown on both sides. Remove chops and set aside.

2. Add about ⅔ of the wine and bring to a boil. Return chops to pan, cover, and reduce heat. Simmer until chops are tender when pressed with the tip of a knife, about 25 to 30 minutes. When done, remove chops. Add remaining wine to saucepan and boil down to a syrupy glaze, about 4 minutes. Pour over chops.

Quick and Easy Tip
When cooking meats, test the level of doneness by pressing on the thickest part of the meat. More squishy means less done; firmer means more done.

The $7 a Meal Quick & Easy Cookbook

Breaded Pork Cutlets

Serves 4

Prep time: 10 minutes
Cook time: 3 minutes
Total cost: $6.08
Calories: 345
Fat: 17g
Protein: 35g
Cholesterol: 50mg
Sodium: 336mg

1 pound pork cutlets

Sea salt and black pepper to taste

½ cup plain flour

2 eggs, beaten

1¼ cups bread crumbs

2 cups canola oil

Another name for this dish is schnitzel, which translates to cutlets without bones. Schnitzel is traditional to Austria and has been made famous by Chef Wolfgang Puck, who is from Austria.

1. Using meat pounder, cover cutlets with parchment or wax paper and pound cutlets as thin as possible. Sprinkle with salt and pepper. Set up an assembly line with flour on one plate, eggs on another, and crumbs on a third. Coat each cutlet with flour, then egg, then bread crumbs.
2. Heat ¼ inch of oil in a large skillet over medium heat. Add as many cutlets as will fit without crowding. Cook until golden brown on each side, about 1½ minutes per side. Drain cutlets on paper towels and serve.

Quick and Easy Tip

Having your ingredients organized before cooking is the secret to making this recipe truly quick and easy. Heat your oil to hot, but not burning, before adding in cutlets to avoid overly oily cutlets.

Roasted Pork Meatballs
with Apples

Serves 4

Prep time: 12 minutes
Cook time: 30 minutes
Total cost: $6.98
Calories: 267
Fat: 5g
Protein: 37g
Cholesterol: 138mg
Sodium: 563mg

5 thick slices day-old or toasted Italian bread

2 tart apples, such as Granny Smith, peeled and finely chopped

1 yellow onion, chopped

2 sprigs fresh oregano, leaves chopped

1 tablespoon olive oil

1 pound ground pork

1 egg, lightly beaten

2 tablespoons chopped walnuts

Sea salt and black pepper to taste

These meatballs make great appetizers for various parties. They are a popular dish and are a tasty alternative to beef!

1. Preheat oven to 375°F. Line a baking sheet with parchment paper.
2. In a bowl, soak bread in water for 1 minute. Squeeze out liquid and set aside. In bowl, combine all ingredients and form the mixture into 2-inch balls. Place meatballs on a baking sheet. Bake for 30 minutes or until thoroughly cooked and golden brown. Drain on paper towels and serve.

Quick and Easy Tip
Look for lean ground pork to save on fat and calories without risking flavor!

Pork Ribs with Merlot Sauce

Serves 5

Prep time: 10 minutes

Cook time: 15 minutes

Total cost: $7.00

Calories: 230

Fat: 8g

Protein: 25g

Cholesterol: 65mg

Sodium: 482mg

1 tablespoon olive oil

1 yellow onion, chopped

2 pounds thick pork ribs

6 plum tomatoes, diced

1 orange, zested and juiced

2 cups beef broth

4 sprigs fresh oregano, leaves chopped

1 cup Merlot wine

½ cup honey

Sea salt and black pepper to taste

This recipe is a quick way to enjoy ribs.

1. Preheat oven to 400°F. Heat oil in a large ovenproof saucepan over medium-high heat. Add the onions and ribs. Brown together, about 5 minutes per side for the ribs. Add the tomatoes and cook for 3 minutes. Add remaining ingredients.
2. Cover the pan and place in oven for 45 minutes. Uncover and cook an additional 15 minutes. Serve.

Quick and Easy Tip

Zesting an orange means to use a grater (or zester) and scrape the peel from the orange. Only zest the top layer of the fruit, stopping at the white (or pith) part as the pith tastes bitter. Use zest in everything from dressings to desserts!

Sautéed Pork Sausage
with Red Bell Peppers

Serves 4

Prep time: 8 minutes
Cook time: 15 minutes
Total cost: $6.75
Calories: 391
Fat: 29g
Protein: 215g
Cholesterol: 65mg
Sodium: 1,052mg

1 tablespoon olive oil

1 pound pork sausage, mild or medium

1 red bell pepper, seeded and chopped

1 shallot, chopped

2 garlic cloves, chopped

2 stalks celery, chopped

1 teaspoon fresh ginger, peeled and minced

1 orange, zested and juiced

3 sprigs fresh thyme, leaves chopped

1 bay leaf

Sea salt and black pepper

Red bell peppers complement this recipe. They're great accents to grilled foods such as chicken or beef.

1. In a large saucepan, heat oil over medium-high heat. Brown the pork sausage. Add the bell peppers, shallots, garlic, celery, and ginger. Reduce heat to medium and sauté for 5 minutes.
2. Add the orange juice and zest, thyme, and bay leaf. Season with salt and pepper and simmer, uncovered, for about 20 minutes.

Quick and Easy Tip
When cooking any recipe, feel free to add your favorite ingredients. Like with this recipe, mix the red bell peppers with yellow, orange, and green ones for more color and variety. Quick note: yellow and orange bell peppers can often be a bit more expensive.

Roasted Pork with Potatoes

Serves 6

Prep time: 5 minutes
Cook time: 1 hour
Total cost: $6.98
Calories: 389
Fat: 5g
Protein: 38g
Cholesterol: 37mg
Sodium: 227mg

1 2½-pound pork roast, bone-in

2 cloves garlic, chopped

2 sprigs fresh oregano, leaves chopped

Sea salt and black pepper to taste

1 tablespoon olive oil

2 yellow onions, peeled and quartered

2 large baking potatoes, washed and cut into 2-inch chunks

This recipe takes awhile to cook, but it's easy to prepare.

Preheat oven to 375°F. Pierce the pork with a sharp knife in several places and insert garlic cloves with oregano leaves. Season with salt and pepper. Prepare roasting pan by pouring in oil. Place the pork roast in a roasting pan with a lid. Cover and roast for 40 minutes, add onions, potatoes, and oregano and stir. Roast uncovered for about 20 minutes, until the potatoes are fork-tender and the pork is cooked to an internal temperature of 160°F.

Quick and Easy Tip
For an even more nutritious, delicious meal, add carrots and celery!

Fennel-Roasted Pork Shoulder with Apples

Serves 4

Prep time: 10 minutes

Cook time: 1 to 2 hours

Total cost: $6.92

Calories: 340

Fat: 7g

Protein: 32g

Cholesterol: 128mg

Sodium: 281mg

1 2-pound boneless pork shoulder roasts

1 bulb fennel, cleaned and chopped

1 yellow onion, chopped

2 Granny Smith apples, cored and chopped (substitute pears if you prefer)

2 tablespoons olive oil

½ cup vegetable broth

Sea salt and black pepper to taste

Fennel is a vegetable that is often confused with the herb star anise because each has a mild licorice flavor. Dice or chop the fennel bulb as you would an onion and use the more bitter stalks for soups and stews.

Preheat oven to 375°F. Cut open the roast in half, sideways, creating a top and bottom and place inside up. Layer bottom half with fennel, onion, and apples. Place top half on and tie securely with butcher's twine. Coat with olive oil, salt, and pepper. Place in a roasting pan. Add broth and cover with foil. Roast (bake) for 1 hour. Uncover and roast an additional ½ hour longer until the pork is thoroughly cooked. Untie, slice, and serve.

Quick and Easy Tip

Pork shoulder is a fairly lean cut of pork that can be purchased bone in or bone out. Cooking a bone-in pork shoulder takes a little more time than boneless, however, the bone does add a little extra flavor to the meat.

Apple-Coated Baked Pork Chops

Serves 6

Prep time: 10 minutes

Cook time: 1 hour

Total cost: $6.97

Calories: 215

Fat: 4g

Protein: 20g

Cholesterol: 82mg

Sodium: 241mg

3 slices raisin bread

½ cup applesauce

6 cloves garlic

1 teaspoon olive oil

6 pork chops

Sea salt and black pepper to taste

Applesauce is the secret ingredient here. I use it as a base for many recipes including soups and other sauces.

Preheat oven to 375°F. Line a baking sheet with parchment paper. Separately, toast the bread and grate into crumbs. In food processor or blender, purée applesauce, garlic, and oil and blend until smooth. Rub the chops with the applesauce mixture, coat with bread crumbs and place the coated chops on the baking sheet, and sprinkle with salt and pepper. Bake for 30 minutes, turn and bake for an additional 30 minutes or until done.

Chili Pepper Pork with Potatoes

Serves 6

Prep time: 8 minutes

Cook time: 4½ hours

Total cost: $6.98

Calories: 293

Fat: 7g

Protein: 41g

Cholesterol: 112mg

Sodium: 84mg

1 2-pound shoulder of pork (fat trimmed)

1 yellow onion, quartered

2 whole cloves

1 cinnamon stick

1 tablespoon whole peppercorns

2 garlic cloves, chopped

1 teaspoon cumin seeds

5 whole, fresh chili peppers, your choice of pepper

3 medium new potatoes, quartered

2 tablespoons apple cider vinegar

Here, the peppers are left whole so you gain maximum flavor without having to worry about the super spicy pepper seeds.

In a large-quart boiler, place pork, onions, cloves, cinnamon, peppercorns, garlic, cumin, and chili peppers. Add enough water to cover all. Cover and cook on low for 3 hours. Stir and add the potatoes. Cook about 1½ hours longer. Remove cloves, cinnamon stick, peppercorns, and chili peppers. Add the vinegar and stir to combine. Serve hot.

Quick and Easy Tip

This is easiest when cooked in a crock pot and left to simmer all day. If you don't have a crock pot, check water every hour or so to be sure it doesn't evaporate. Add water as needed to maintain water level.

Stewed Pork with Horseradish

Serves 6

- Prep time: 10 minutes
- Cook time: 1½ to 2 hours
- Total cost: $7.00
- Calories: 213
- Fat: 6g
- Protein: 34g
- Cholesterol: 89mg
- Sodium: 322mg

Sea salt and black pepper to taste

2 tablespoons butter

2 tablespoons canola oil

1½ pounds boneless pork, cut into bite-size pieces

1 yellow onion, chopped

1 carrot, peeled and sliced

1 rib celery, sliced

2 cans beef broth

½ cup cider vinegar

¼ cup prepared horseradish

Horseradish is a root that comes from the same plant family as mustard, wasabi, and cabbage. Prepared horseradish is grated horseradish root that has been mixed with vinegar, thereby preserving the flavor and color of fresh horseradish. Prepared horseradish will keep in your refrigerator for months before it darkens, which indicates it is losing its flavor.

In a large-quart boiler, heat butter and oil over medium heat. Add pork and cook until browned, about 3 minutes. Remove pork and set aside. Add onion, carrot, and celery and cook until onions are softened, about 8 minutes. Return the pork to the boiler and add beef broth and vinegar, and bring to a boil. Reduce the heat, cover, and simmer for 1½ hours or until pork is tender. Remove from heat, stir in horseradish and serve.

Quick and Easy Tip

The vinegar used here helps break down the proteins in the pork, making the pork more tender as it cooks.

Cajun-Style Pork Chops
with Pineapple

Serves 4

Prep time: 7 minutes
Cook time: 35 minutes
Total cost: $6.99
Calories: 463
Fat: 22g
Protein: 39g
Cholesterol: 105mg
Sodium: 110mg

4 thick pork chops, boneless

Sea salt to taste

1 teaspoon cayenne pepper

1 tablespoon olive oil

1½ cups dry white wine

1 cup red bell pepper, chopped

1 yellow onion, chopped

1 clove garlic, chopped

2 tablespoons soy sauce

1 15-ounce can pineapple
   chunks, liquid reserved

Hot cooked rice

This dish keeps the pork chops nice and moist.

Sprinkle chops with salt and cayenne pepper. In a large sauce-pan, heat 1 tablespoon oil over medium to medium-high heat. Add pork chops and brown them slowly on each side. Add wine, bell pepper, onion, and garlic. Cover and simmer for 25 to 30 minutes. Remove pork chops, then add soy sauce and pineapple liquid and simmer, while stirring, until thickened. Add the pineapple chunks and bring to a boil. Serve over pork chops with cooked rice.

Quick and Easy Tip
Keep cooked rice on hand in the refrigerator for simple, fast meals in a pinch.

The $7 a Meal Quick & Easy Cookbook

Stroganoff with Pork

Serves 6

Prep time: 9 minutes
Cook time: 45 minutes
Total cost: $6.96
Calories: 326
Fat: 9g
Protein: 31g
Cholesterol: 96mg
Sodium: 513mg

Sea salt and black pepper to taste

½ cup plain flour

1½ pounds boneless pork, cut into 2-inch chunks

2 tablespoons butter

2 garlic cloves, chopped

1 yellow onion, chopped

1½ cups chicken broth

2 teaspoons Worcestershire sauce

1 cup sour cream

¼ cup Italian parsley, chopped

Stroganoff, or stroganov, is a Russian dish that includes beef and sour cream. Delicious on its own, this dish is now traditionally served over rice or noodles. Here I have substituted pork for beef.

In a large mixing bowl, combine salt, pepper, and flour. Coat pork in flour mixture. In a large saucepan, heat butter over medium heat until browning. Add garlic and onion, and cook until tender, about 3 minutes. Add pork, broth, and Worcestershire sauce. Bring to a boil, reduce heat, cover, and simmer for 30 minutes, stirring occasionally. Gradually stir in sour cream and cook an additional 5 minutes or until sour cream is well incorporated. Garnish with the parsley.

Quick and Easy Tip
To serve with noodles, use 1 pound of egg noodles cooked in water and drained.

Paprika Pork Chops

Serves 4

Prep time: 8 minutes
Cook time: 55 minutes
Total cost: $6.90
Calories: 202
Fat: 8g
Protein: 33g
Cholesterol: 89mg
Sodium: 265mg

1 cup sour cream

½ cup plain flour

1 tablespoon dried dill or 1½ tablespoons fresh dill

Sea salt and black pepper to taste

4 shoulder pork chops, 1-inch thick

4 tablespoons butter

1 yellow onion, chopped

2 cloves garlic, chopped

2 tablespoons paprika

1 cup chicken broth

Paprika, or red pepper, is native to Hungary and can be either spicy or mild. Most Hungarian paprika purchased in stores is of the mild variety.

1. In a small mixing bowl, combine sour cream, 2 tablespoons flour, and dill. Set aside. In a separate mixing bowl, combine salt, pepper, and remaining flour. Dredge pork chops in flour-salt mixture. In a large saucepan, heat the butter over medium heat until browning. Add the chops and brown for about 5 minutes on each side. Remove chops and set aside. Add onion and garlic and cook until tender, about 3 to 4 minutes. Add paprika and chicken broth, increase heat, and bring to a boil to combine all the flavors in the pan.
2. Return chops to pan, reduce heat, cover, and simmer chops for 45 minutes or until tender. Remove chops again and stir in sour cream mixture and cook over medium heat until heated, stirring constantly until thick and smooth. Pour over the chops when serving.

CHAPTER 9

BEEF

Artichokes Stuffed with Herbs and Beef

Serves 4

Prep time: 10 minutes
Cook time: 55–60 minutes
Total cost: $6.96
Calories: 378
Fat: 8g
Protein: 36g
Cholesterol: 84mg
Sodium: 649mg

4 artichokes

4 slices Italian bread

1 pound ground beef

½ yellow onion, chopped

2 cloves garlic, chopped

4 sprigs fresh oregano leaves, chopped

½ tablespoon fresh basil, leaves chopped

Sea salt and black pepper to taste

1 egg

2 tablespoons Parmesan cheese, grated

Artichokes can be prickly, so wear thick kitchen gloves if you have sensitive hands.

1. Preheat oven to 375°F. Cut the artichokes in half lengthwise, leaving stems on, and peel them with a vegetable peeler. Remove and discard the chokes (the prickly white and purple center). Bring a large boiler, ¾ filled with water, to a boil and add 1 tablespoon of salt. Add artichokes and boil them for 1 minute. Remove artichokes and transfer to a large bowl filled with ice water. Drain and set aside.
2. Separately, in a small bowl, soak bread in water for 1 minute, then squeeze out water. In a large mixing bowl, combine beef, onion, garlic, oregano, basil, pepper, salt, bread, egg, and cheese. Stuff the artichoke leaves with the beef mixture and place cut side down in a deep roasting pan.
3. Bake covered for 45 minutes. Uncover and bake for an additional 10 to 15 minutes.

Herbed Meatloaf of Beef and Pork

Serves 6

Prep time: 10 minutes
Cook time: 60 minutes
Total cost: $6.99
Calories: 335
Fat: 10g
Protein: 18g
Cholesterol: 97mg
Sodium: 328mg

3 slices toasted Italian bread

¼ cup milk

2 Roma tomatoes, seeded and diced

1 yellow onion, chopped

3 cloves garlic, chopped

1 tablespoon fresh Italian parsley, chopped

1 teaspoon fresh thyme leaves, chopped

4 green olives, chopped

4 black olives, chopped

2 slices Swiss cheese, chopped

¾ pound ground beef

¾ pound ground pork

1 egg

1 tablespoon honey

Sea salt and black pepper to taste

Meatloaf is a great way to serve a hearty, filling, nutritious meal the family will enjoy.

Preheat oven to 375°F. In a mixing bowl, soak toast in milk, then squeeze out liquid. In a large mixing bowl, combine all ingredients. Mix together well and form into desired loaf shape. Place in greased loaf pan and bake for 45 to 60 minutes or until internal temperature reaches 170°F. Slice and serve.

Quick and Easy Tip

Make a ketchup glaze by combining ketchup, brown sugar, and a bit of Worcestershire sauce. Coat the meatloaf during the last 15 minutes of baking and allow to bake uncovered.

Grilled London Broil with Merlot Marinade

Serves 4

Prep time: 5 minutes
Cook time: 15 minutes
Total cost: $7.00
Calories: 259
Fat: 13g
Protein: 37g
Cholesterol: 84mg
Sodium: 142mg

1 cup dry red wine such as Merlot

1 tablespoon olive oil

1 teaspoon ground cinnamon

1 whole clove

Sea salt and black pepper to taste

¾ pound flank steak

It's not known how London broil got its name because the dish originated in North America, not London. Flank steak is used and should be marinated or pounded to break down the otherwise tough proteins of this cut of beef. Always cut against the grain when serving.

Preheat grill. Mix together wine, oil, and seasonings. Coat the meat in the wine mixture and grill until desired doneness, 7 minutes per 1 inch of thickness.

Quick and Easy Tip

To ensure tenderness, mix together seasonings and wine and marinate overnight or up to 5 hours in the refrigerator. Remove when ready to grill.

The $7 a Meal Quick & Easy Cookbook

Top Sirloin with Black Beans and Mexican Salsa

Serves 4

Prep time: 5 minutes
Cook time: 15 minutes
Total cost: $6.96
Calories: 240
Fat: 6g
Protein: 29g
Cholesterol: 77mg
Sodium: 149mg

1 tablespoon olive oil

¾ pound top round sirloin, cut into 2-inch cubes

1 clove fresh garlic, minced

½ teaspoon all-purpose seasoning

¼ cup frozen corn

1 tablespoon cilantro, chopped

½ cup beef broth

¼ cup celery, sliced

1 yellow onion, thinly sliced

1 cup salsa

1 14-ounce can black beans, canned

¼ teaspoon black pepper

Sliced in strips, this recipe could also be served as fajitas!

1. Coat a skillet with oil. Add sirloin, garlic, and all-purpose seasoning to skillet. Sauté on medium high for 8 minutes, stirring often.
2. Mix remaining ingredients and add to skillet. Simmer for 8 to 10 minutes. Add additional beef broth if mixture gets too dry.

Quick and Easy Tip
Using dried black beans from scratch takes quite a long time. Use the canned variety instead—they're still nutritious and much faster when every second counts.

Sautéed Beef with Sugar Snap Peas and Soy Sauce

Serves 4

Prep time: 8 minutes
Cook time: 20 minutes
Total cost: $6.95
Calories: 329
Fat: 14g
Protein: 31g
Cholesterol: 44mg
Sodium: 842mg

1 tablespoon olive oil

¾ pound round sirloin steak, cut into 2 inch cubes

1 clove fresh garlic, minced

½ teaspoon all-purpose seasoning

3 tablespoons low-sodium soy sauce

1 cup chicken broth

½ cup hoisin sauce

1½ cups white or yellow onions, quartered

1 tablespoon cornstarch

1 tablespoon sesame oil

1½ tablespoons ground ginger

1½ cups sugar snap peas, fresh or frozen

2 carrots, sliced

Don't add salt to this recipe as there is plenty in the soy sauce, chicken broth, hoisin sauce, and oils.

1. Coat a skillet with olive oil. Add beef, garlic, and all-purpose seasoning to skillet. Sauté on medium high for 8 minutes, stirring often.
2. Mix remaining ingredients and add to skillet. Simmer for 8 to 10 minutes.

Spicy Beef with Onions

Serves 4

Prep time: 10 minutes
Cook time: 15 minutes
Total cost: $6.99
Calories: 146
Fat: 8g
Protein: 35g
Cholesterol: 63mg
Sodium: 302mg

1 tablespoon olive oil

¾ pound round sirloin, cut into 2-inch cubes

1 clove fresh garlic, minced

½ teaspoon all-purpose seasoning

½ teaspoon black pepper

1 teaspoon ground ginger

1 teaspoon jalapeño peppers, finely chopped

1 yellow onion, sliced

2 tomatoes, diced

1 tablespoon curry powder

1 teaspoon coriander

1 cup beef broth

1 cup sour cream

When cooking beef, the leaner cuts are top sirloin, eye of round, and bottom round, which have less than 3 grams of saturated fats per serving.

1. Coat a skillet with olive oil. Add beef, garlic, and all-purpose seasoning to skillet. Sauté on medium high for 8 minutes, stirring often.
2. Mix remaining ingredients except sour cream and add to skillet. Simmer for 8 to 10 minutes. Add sour cream and mix well. Simmer for another 5 minutes.

Quick and Easy Tip

Curry is a blend of other seasonings. There are many varieties, but the most common spices used to create it are coriander, cumin, turmeric, and fenugreek. Ginger, nutmeg, black pepper, and garlic are also commonly used.

Easy Pot Roast with Potatoes and Carrots

Serves 4

Prep time: 12 minutes
Cook time: 35 minutes
Total cost: $6.99
Calories: 239
Fat: 5g
Protein: 29g
Cholesterol: 87mg
Sodium: 237mg

¾ pound top sirloin, cut into 2-inch cubes

1 teaspoon finely chopped fresh garlic

½ teaspoon all-purpose seasoning

1 cup yucca, chopped into 2-inch cubes

1 cup sliced carrots

1 baking potato, cut into 2-inch cubes

1½ cups beef broth

1 yellow onion, quartered

1 teaspoon fresh thyme leaves, chopped

½ teaspoon fresh sage leaves, chopped

1 bay leaf

½ teaspoon black pepper

Yucca is a plant native to hot and dry climates and can be found in the southwestern United States. It is the main ingredient in tapioca pudding and can be used in place of potatoes.

1. Add all ingredients to a large saucepan and cook on medium high for 8 to 10 minutes.
2. Reduce heat and simmer for 20 to 25 minutes. Add beef broth if gravy dries out.

Quick and Easy Tip
The best way to prepare yucca is by baking, boiling, or frying, much as you would a potato.

Grilled Fillet with Feta

➤ Serves 4

Prep time: 10 minutes
Cook time: 30 minutes
Total cost: $7.00
Calories: 440
Fat: 12g
Protein: 41g
Cholesterol: 86mg
Sodium: 325mg

2 tablespoons balsamic vinegar

½ cup plus 1 tablespoon extra virgin olive oil

2 sprigs fresh thyme leaves, chopped

4 4-ounce beef tenderloin steaks

½ red onion, chopped

2 cloves garlic, chopped

4 tablespoons feta cheese, crumbled

Enjoy with Brussels Sprouts with Roasted Peanuts (page 285) for a truly unique and delicious meal.

1. Preheat grill. In a mixing bowl, whisk together vinegar, ½ cup oil, and thyme. Then place steaks in a baking pan and pour vinegar mixture over steaks. Let stand at room temperature for 10 minutes. Meanwhile, in heavy saucepan, heat 1 tablespoon olive oil over medium heat and add onion and garlic. Sauté until tender, about 6 minutes. Remove from heat and set aside.
2. Place steaks on grill; cook on medium heat for approximately 7 minutes. Turn and cook for an additional 7 minutes or until desired doneness.
3. When serving, place steaks on platter or plate and top with feta cheese, then top with onion mixture and serve.

Quick and Easy Tip

For testing the doneness of meats, put your hand palm up and touch your thumb and index finger together. Feel the pad at the base of your thumb; that's what rare steaks feel like. Touch your thumb and middle finger together; the pad will feel like a medium-rare steak. Ring finger and thumb is medium, and thumb and pinky feels like a well-done steak.

Spicy Peppered Beef

Serves 4

Prep time: 10 minutes
Cook time: 20 minutes
Total cost: $6.94
Calories: 362
Fat: 16g
Protein: 29g
Cholesterol: 71mg
Sodium: 302mg

¾ pound top sirloin

1 clove fresh garlic, minced

½ teaspoon all-purpose seasoning

1 can kernel corn, drained

1 red bell pepper, diced

½ yellow onion, diced

1 tablespoon fresh cilantro, chopped

1 tablespoon lemon juice

2 teaspoons brown sugar

½ teaspoon onion powder

1 teaspoon oregano

½ teaspoon paprika

½ teaspoon red pepper

½ teaspoon cumin

¼ teaspoon black pepper

1 cup beef broth

Quick and flavorful, this recipe is great with a side of pasta or rice.

1. Coat a skillet with nonstick spray. Add beef, garlic, and all-purpose seasoning to skillet. Sauté on medium-high heat for 8 minutes, stirring often.
2. Mix remaining ingredients and add to skillet. Simmer for 8 to 10 minutes.

Quick and Easy Tip
Mix together all ingredients, except beef, for a terrific marinade for beef, chicken, or pork.

Cube Steaks with Tomatoes and Green Chilies

Serves 4

Prep time: 10 minutes

Cook time: 30 minutes

Total cost: $6.52

Calories: 283

Fat: 10g

Protein: 26g

Cholesterol: 88mg

Sodium: 166mg

3 tablespoons plain flour

1 tablespoon chili powder

Sea salt and black pepper to taste

¾ pound beef cube steaks

2 tablespoons olive oil

1 14-ounce can diced tomatoes with green chilies

½ cup sliced mushrooms

Cube steaks are typically round steaks that have been run through a machine that pierces the steak all over to break up connective tissue so the meat is more tender. You can pound your own round steaks using the pointed side of a meat mallet.

In a mixing bowl, combine flour, chili powder, salt, and pinch of pepper. Mix well. Place steaks on parchment paper and sprinkle half of flour mixture over steaks. Pound into steaks using a meat pounder or rolling pin. Turn steaks, sprinkle with remaining flour mixture, and pound again. In a large saucepan, heat olive oil over medium-high heat. Add steaks; sauté for 4 minutes, then turn and sauté for 2 minutes. Remove steaks from saucepan. Pour tomatoes into pan; cook and stir until simmering, scraping browned bits. Add steaks back to pan along with mushrooms; simmer for 15 to 20 minutes, until tender.

Grilled Steak Skewers

Serves 4

Prep time: 10 minutes
Cook time: 20 minutes
Total cost: $6.86
Calories: 204
Fat: 8g
Protein: 26g
Cholesterol: 56mg
Sodium: 360mg

¾ pound sirloin steak

¾ cup barbeque sauce

2 tablespoons Coca-Cola

2 cloves garlic, chopped

½ teaspoon black pepper

6 cremini mushrooms, sliced

1 red bell pepper, seeded and cut into strips

The sugar acids in both the barbeque sauce and Coke blend well to add spice, flavor, and actually help cook the steak. Use as both a marinade and a basting sauce.

1. Cut steak into 1-inch cubes and combine with barbeque sauce, Coke, garlic, and black pepper. Mix well. Massage the sauce, or marinade, into the meat. Let stand for 10 minutes.
2. Meanwhile, prepare vegetables and preheat grill. Thread steak cubes, mushrooms, and bell peppers onto wooden or metal skewers. Place on grill over medium heat. Grill skewers and brush frequently with basting marinade for 7 to 10 minutes, until steak is desired doneness. Discard any remaining marinade when done.

Quick and Easy Tip

If you have time, prepare skewers the day before, pour marinade over all, and marinate overnight.

Grilled Fillet with Basil Pesto

Serves 2

Prep time: 8 minutes
Cook time: 20 minutes
Total cost: $6.89
Calories: 416
Fat: 16g
Protein: 51g
Cholesterol: 72mg
Sodium: 391mg

2 4-ounce fillet steaks, or tenderloin

1 pinch sea salt

1 pinch white pepper

½ cup basil pesto

¼ cup blue cheese

¼ cup fresh basil leaves, chopped as described in step 3

For a lighter version of this recipe, leave off the blue cheese, as pesto traditionally has Parmesan cheese already mixed in.

1. Prepare and heat grill. Place steaks on a platter and sprinkle both sides with salt and pepper.
2. Place steaks on grill and cook, over medium heat, for 5 minutes. Turn steaks, cover, and cook for 4 minutes. Top each steak with pesto and sprinkle blue cheese over the top of the pesto. Cover and grill for 4 minutes.
3. Meanwhile, roll basil leaves into a round shaped and cut into thin strips. Place steaks on a serving platter and sprinkle with basil chiffonade. Let rest for 5 minutes and serve.

Quick and Easy Tip

You can make your own basil pesto, but with so many delicious premade ones, go ahead and save yourself some time, and most likely money, by purchasing premade pesto.

Meatballs with Sesame-Ginger Vegetables

Serves 6

Prep time: 4 minutes
Cook time: 20 minutes
Total cost: $6.99
Calories: 345
Fat: 33g
Protein: 10g
Cholesterol: 74mg
Sodium: 275mg

1-pound package frozen meatballs

3 tablespoons olive oil

1 yellow onion, chopped

2 cloves garlic, chopped

1 16-ounce package frozen Asian vegetables in sesame-ginger sauce

½ cup beef broth

Asian vegetables are usually sliced differently than other frozen mixed vegetables and come with their own sauce, saving both time and money.

Thaw meatballs overnight in the refrigerator. In a large saucepan, heat oil over medium-high heat. Add onion and garlic, and cook for 5 minutes. Add meatballs, vegetables, and beef broth, cover, reduce heat, and simmer for 7 minutes. Uncover and cook an additional 3 to 5 minutes, until mixture is slightly thickened. Serve immediately.

Quick and Easy Tip
These meatballs are great on their own or served with rice.

Shepherd's Pie

Serves 4

Prep time: 10 minutes
Cook time: 1 hour
Total cost: $7.00
Calories: 381
Fat: 21g
Protein: 18g
Cholesterol: 77mg
Sodium: 127mg

2 baking potatoes, peeled, cut into 2-inch cubes

1 tablespoon canola oil

½ yellow onion, chopped

¾ pound ground beef

½ package taco seasoning

1 16-ounce package frozen broccoli, cauliflower, and carrots

¼ cup water or beef broth

¼ cup sour cream

¼ cup Parmesan cheese, grated

Shepherd's pie is traditionally a meat pie with a crust of mashed potatoes. It originated as a means of using left-over beef roast with mashed potatoes.

1. Fill large-quart boiler ½ full with water and place over high heat. Add potatoes and boil until tender, about 15 to 20 minutes. Drain and mash with fork or potato masher. Set aside.
2. Preheat oven to 400°F. In a large saucepan over medium heat, heat 1 tablespoon canola oil. Add onion and sauté for 5 minutes. Add ground beef and taco seasoning and cook for approximately 7 minutes or until beef is browned. Add frozen vegetables and ¼ cup water or broth and cook an additional 3 minutes. Add potatoes and sour cream and let cook for 5 more minutes.
3. Grease casserole dish with butter. Transfer beef mixture to casserole dish. Top with Parmesan cheese and bake for 15 minutes or until casserole is heated through.

Enchiladas with Beef and Beans

Serves 4

Prep time: 10 minutes
Cook time: 25 minutes
Total cost: $6.96
Calories: 711
Fat: 25g
Protein: 31g
Cholesterol: 85mg
Sodium: 1,408mg

1 pound flat iron steak

1 pinch sea salt

1 pinch cayenne pepper

1 tablespoon chili powder

1 teaspoon ground cumin

3 tablespoons olive oil

1 16-ounce can pinto beans, drained

1 16-ounce can enchilada sauce

6 10-inch flour tortillas

1 cup pepper jack cheese, shredded or grated

Enchiladas are one of the most popular dishes requested for Mexican buffets.

1. Preheat oven to 400°F. Cut the steak, against the grain, into thin strips. Sprinkle steak with salt, pepper, chili powder, and cumin. Heat large saucepan or skillet over medium-high heat and add oil; heat oil until hot and add steak, cook for 3 minutes, or until steak is done.
2. Add drained beans and 1 cup enchilada sauce to steak and heat through. Divide mixture among flour tortillas and top with 1 cup cheese. Roll up tortillas to enclose tortillas and filling. Place in buttered casserole dish. Drizzle with remaining enchilada sauce and sprinkle with remaining cheese. Bake for 15 to 18 minutes, or until heated through.

Quick and Easy Tip
This is a great recipe to make even several days ahead as it freezes well.

The $7 a Meal Quick & Easy Cookbook

Spaghetti with Meatloaf

Serves 6

Prep time: 8 minutes
Cook time: 15 minutes
Total cost: $6.62
Calories: 492
Fat: 19g
Protein: 31g
Cholesterol: 65mg
Sodium: 1,044mg

1 pound spaghetti pasta noodles

2 tablespoons olive oil

1 yellow onion, chopped

1 pound leftover Herbed Meatloaf of Beef and Pork (page 161), or 1 pound frozen meatballs

1 14-ounce can tomato sauce

1 28-ounce jar pasta sauce

1 cup grated Parmesan cheese

A chef I know whips up cooked pasta noodles into the meatloaf for a tasty twist on this simple recipe.

1. Fill large-quart boiler ¾ with water, heat over high heat until boiling. Add pasta, drizzle with olive oil, and pinch of salt.
2. Meanwhile, in a large saucepan, heat olive oil over medium heat. Add onions and cook for 5 minutes, until tender. Add leftover meatloaf, tomato sauce, and pasta sauce and cook for 7 to 9 minutes or until sauce is hot. Drain pasta and serve with Parmesan cheese.

Quick and Easy Tip
If you have some extra fresh Italian parsley in your refrigerator, throw a tablespoon into the pasta for added flavor.

Chili with Jalapeños

🥄 Serves 6

Prep time: 8 minutes
Cook time: 20 minutes
Total cost: $6.99
Calories: 333
Fat: 11g
Protein: 23g
Cholesterol: 47mg
Sodium: 978mg

¾ pound ground beef

1 yellow onion, chopped

2 tablespoons plain flour

2 14-ounce cans diced tomatoes, undrained

1 4-ounce can chopped jalapeños, undrained

2 8-ounce cans tomato sauce with seasonings

1 cup water

If this chili is too spicy, leave out the jalapeños.

1. In a large saucepan, cook ground beef and onion over medium heat, stirring frequently to break up the meat, about 4 to 5 minutes. When beef is browned, drain off half the liquid and grease. Sprinkle flour over beef and cook for 2 minutes, stirring once.
2. Add remaining ingredients, bring to a simmer, and simmer for 10 to 15 minutes, until flavors are blended and liquid is thickened. Serve immediately.

Quick and Easy Tip
The flour helps thicken the chili, but be careful to not add too much or you'll create another recipe entirely!

Tortellini Alfredo with Beef

Serves 4

Prep time: 5 minutes
Cook time: 18 minutes
Total cost: $6.85
Calories: 534
Fat: 34g
Protein: 25g
Cholesterol: 98mg
Sodium: 987mg

1 16-ounce package frozen beef-filled tortellini

¾ pound ground beef

1 yellow onion, chopped

½ 10-ounce jar or package four-cheese Alfredo sauce

½ 9-ounce container pesto sauce

Alfredo sauce is named for an Italian restaurateur, Alfredo, from Rome. A largely American dish now, Alfredo refers to a sauce made with melted cheese and butter.

1. Bring large-quart boiler filled ¾ with water to boil over high heat. Add pasta and cook as directed, about 5 to 8 minutes for fresh or frozen pasta.
2. While waiting to boil, in a large saucepan over medium-high heat cook beef and onion, stirring to break up beef, about 5 minutes until beef is browned. Drain off grease. Combine beef with pasta and add Alfredo sauce to saucepan. Cook over medium heat for 5 minutes, stirring occasionally until mixture is combined and sauce bubbles. Stir in pesto, cover, remove from heat, let stand for 5 minutes, and serve.

Quick and Easy Tip
For a lighter version of this recipe, leave out the beef or substitute chicken or turkey.

Marinated Flank Steak

Serves 4

Prep time: 9 minutes
Cook time: 25 minutes
Total cost: $6.96
Calories: 154
Fat: 7g
Protein: 8g
Cholesterol: 2mg
Sodium: 487mg

2 garlic cloves, minced

¼ teaspoon sea salt

1 tablespoon grill seasoning such as Tony's or other

¼ teaspoon dry mustard

¼ teaspoon cayenne pepper

2 tablespoons balsamic vinegar

1 pound flank steak

Grill seasoning contains lots of spices, usually including cumin, oregano, pepper, garlic, and sugar. Use it for hamburgers as well as grilled steaks.

1. Preheat grill. In a small bowl, mash garlic and salt together and create a paste. Add remaining ingredients, except flank steak. Prick both sides of steak with fork and rub garlic mixture into the steak. Let stand for 10 minutes.
2. Place steak on grill over medium coals and cover. Grill for 5 minutes, turn steak, cover, and grill 5 minutes longer, until medium rare or medium. Let steak stand for 5 minutes, then slice against grain to serve.

Quick and Easy Tip
Flank steak refers to the steak from the belly portion of the cow. It is best when marinated or braised and is most widely used in the Mexican dish, fajitas.

Herb-Crusted New York Strip Steak

Serves 4

Prep time: 10 minutes

Cook time: 15 minutes

Total cost: $7.00

Calories: 262

Fat: 9g

Protein: 45g

Cholesterol: 98mg

Sodium: 655mg

4 4- to 5-ounce New York strip steaks

½ teaspoon sea salt and white pepper

2 tablespoons olive oil

2 tablespoons Worcestershire sauce

2 tablespoons fresh thyme leaves, chopped

½ teaspoon dried oregano leaves

¼ cup balsamic vinegar

2 tablespoons dry mustard

Worcestershire sauce is used a lot in steak recipes. It is a blend of different spices and ingredients, including anchovies.

1. Preheat grill. Place steaks on baking sheet and pierce all over with a fork. Sprinkle both sides with salt and pepper. In a small bowl, combine remaining ingredients and mix well. Pour over steaks, turning to coat, rubbing marinade into steaks with hands. Let stand for 10 minutes.
2. Place steaks on grill over medium heat and drizzle with any remaining marinade. Cover grill and cook for 5 minutes. Turn steaks and cook for 5 minutes longer or until desired doneness. Let stand 5 minutes, then serve.

Quick and Easy Tip

An instant-read meat thermometer is always a good utensil to have on hand. When grilling steaks, 140°F is rare, 145°F is medium rare, 160°F is medium, and 170°F is well done. Be sure to let the steak stand for a few minutes before carving and serving to let the juices redistribute.

Easy Meatloaf

Serves 6

Prep time: 10 minutes
Cook time: 30 minutes
Total cost: $6.96
Calories: 359
Fat: 23g
Protein: 18g
Cholesterol: 75mg
Sodium: 719mg

1 egg

½ teaspoon Italian seasoning

1 yellow onion, chopped

¼ teaspoon garlic pepper

¾ cup soft bread crumbs

¾ cup ketchup

1 pound ground beef

¾ cup shredded jack cheese, divided

Sea salt and black pepper as desired

Meatloaves made in muffin tins are cute, fun to make, and fun to eat. Serve with some ketchup and frozen French fries to give your kids a treat.

1. Preheat oven to 350°F. In a large bowl, combine egg, Italian seasoning, onion, garlic pepper, bread crumbs, and ½ cup ketchup and mix well. Add ground beef, half the cheese, salt and pepper, and mix gently but thoroughly to combine.
2. Press meat mixture, ⅓ cup at a time, into 12 muffin cups. Top each with bit of ketchup and remaining cheese. Bake at 350°F for 15 to 18 minutes, until meat is thoroughly cooked. Remove from muffin tins, drain if necessary, place on serving platter, cover with foil, and let stand 5 minutes before serving.

Quick and Easy Tip

Meatloaf mix can be substituted for the ground beef and is found in the meat aisle of the supermarket. It usually consists of one-third beef, one-third pork, and one-third veal, but read the label to find out what the blend is in your area. The veal lightens the mixture, and the pork adds a slightly different flavor and texture.

Simple Beef Stroganoff

Serves 4

Prep time: 5 minutes
Cook time: 14 minutes
Total cost: $6.84
Calories: 352
Fat: 15g
Protein: 17g
Cholesterol: 65mg
Sodium: 283mg

2 tablespoons olive oil

1 yellow onion, chopped

1 pound ground beef

1 8-ounce package frozen cut green beans, thawed and drained

1 pound uncooked egg noodles

2 cups sour cream

Egg noodles are the traditional noodle for stroganoff. They are lighter, thinner, and cook faster than regular pasta noodles.

1. In a large-quart boiler filled ¾ with water, bring water to a boil over high heat. Meanwhile, heat olive oil in a large saucepan over medium heat. Add onion and cook for 4 minutes, until tender. Add beef and brown, about 5 minutes. Add beans and simmer for 5 minutes.
2. When water is boiling, add egg noodles and cook until tender but not mushy, about 5 minutes. Drain and set aside.
3. Stir sour cream into beef mixture, cover, and remove from heat. Place noodles on serving platter and spoon beef mixture over.

Quick and Easy Tip
Packaged frozen beef tips with gravy are a quick way to make stroganoff or any recipe. If you have beef in your freezer, use that and add an easy gravy mix to your recipe.

Swedish Meatballs

Serves 4

Prep time: 10 minute
Cook time: 2¾ hours
Total cost: $5.80
Calories: 416
Fat: 14g
Protein: 25g
Cholesterol: 135mg
Sodium: 305mg

1½ cups plain bread crumbs

1 cup milk

½ pound ground beef

½ pound ground pork, or extra beef if preferred

2 eggs

1 yellow onion, chopped

Sea salt and black pepper to taste

¼ teaspoon allspice

¼ teaspoon nutmeg

¼ teaspoon cardamom

1 10½-ounce can beef broth

2 tablespoons butter, melted

2 tablespoons plain flour

Swedish meatballs are most commonly made with both beef and pork. These meatballs are usually served with gravy, lingonberry jam, and boiled potatoes.

1. Soak bread crumbs in milk for 5 minutes in a large mixing bowl. Preheat oven to 400°F. Add beef, pork, eggs, onion, salt, allspice, nutmeg, and cardamom to bread crumbs. Mix well. Shape into 1-inch balls. Place on baking sheet lined with parchment paper and bake for 15 minutes.
2. In a large-quart boiler, place cooked meatballs, ½ can beef broth, pepper, and remaining salt. Simmer over low heat for about 2 hours, adding broth or water as needed.
3. Separately, in a small bowl, mix together melted butter and flour. Mix until a smooth paste forms. Add paste to ½ can beef broth and add to meatball mixture. Cook until thickened, about 25 minutes.

The $7 a Meal Quick & Easy Cookbook

Italian Meatballs

Serves 4

Prep time: 10 minutes
Cook time: 50 minutes
Total cost: $6.89
Calories: 438
Fat: 26g
Protein: 22g
Cholesterol: 161mg
Sodium: 394mg

1 pound ground beef

1 cup bread crumbs, soaked in ½ cup milk, excess squeezed out

1 yellow onion, chopped

¼ cup seedless raisins, chopped

¼ cup Parmesan cheese, grated

¼ cup Italian parsley, chopped

2 eggs, lightly beaten

1 teaspoon fresh thyme, stems removed, leaves chopped

Sea salt and black pepper to taste

1 tablespoon olive oil

1 clove garlic, minced

2 large tomatoes, seeded and chopped

1 teaspoon fresh oregano, stems removed, leaves chopped

½ 10-ounce package frozen peas, thawed

Italian meatballs traditionally have fresh herbs, tomatoes or tomato sauce, and, of course, garlic.

1. In a mixing bowl, combine beef, bread crumbs, raisins, cheese, parsley, eggs, thyme, salt, and pepper. Roll the mixture into 18 to 20 meatballs. Place on lightly greased baking sheet and place them under broiler, turning them once or twice until they are browned, about 5 minutes. Transfer to oven to keep warm.
2. In a saucepan, heat oil over medium heat and add onion and garlic and cook until tender, about 5 minutes. Add the tomatoes and oregano. Cover and simmer for 10 minutes. Preheat oven to 350°F. Add peas, cover, and simmer for 5 more minutes. Pour sauce over meatballs and bake, covered, for 30 minutes.

Sloppy Joes

Serves 4

Prep time: 10 minutes
Cook time: 1 hour
Total cost: $6.50
Calories: 428
Fat: 16g
Protein: 19g
Cholesterol: 77mg
Sodium: 567mg

1 pound ground beef

1 yellow onion, chopped

2 cloves garlic, minced

1 cup tomato sauce

1 cup green bell pepper, seeded and chopped

½ cup water

¼ cup brown sugar

¼ cup spicy mustard

¼ cup apple cider vinegar

1 tablespoon chili powder

4 hamburger buns

Sloppy joes are usually just that, pretty sloppy! For a neater joe, put sloppy joe mix in crescent roll dough, roll up, and bake.

In a large saucepan over medium heat, add beef, onion, and garlic. Cook until meat is browned and onion is tender. Drain off fat. In a large-quart boiler, combine remaining ingredients, except buns. Stir in meat mixture, cover and simmer over low heat for about 45 minutes, adding water if necessary to prevent from drying. Serve by spooning over hamburger buns.

Quick and Easy Tip
There are lots of uses for sloppy joe mix. Use it on tortillas with cheese or as a dip with tortilla chips.

The $7 a Meal Quick & Easy Cookbook

Curried Beef with Pine Nuts

Serves 4

Prep time: 10 minutes
Cook time: 15 minutes
Total cost: $6.68
Calories: 585
Fat: 29g
Protein: 26g
Cholesterol: 77mg
Sodium: 398mg

1 tablespoon olive oil

1 yellow onion, chopped

2 cloves garlic, chopped

1 pound ground beef

1 4-ounce package pine nuts

2 teaspoons curry powder

Sea salt and black pepper to taste

1 8-ounce can tomato sauce

1 cup water

¼ cup Italian parsley, chopped

4 cups cooked rice

Pine nuts are used in traditional pesto sauce. As an alternative, use crushed walnuts.

In a large saucepan over medium heat, add olive oil, onion, and garlic and cook until onions are tender, about 5 minutes. Add ground beef and cook until browned, about 4 minutes. Add pine nuts, curry, salt, pepper, tomato sauce, and water. Bring to a boil, then reduce heat and simmer until sauce is thickened, about 5 minutes. When ready to serve, stir in parsley. Serve over rice.

Quick and Easy Tip
Toasting nuts brings out their natural oils and flavors. Toast in a saucepan on stove top over low heat until nuts are slightly browned. Pay attention as they burn quickly.

Beef

Roast of Beef with Peppers and Onions

Serves 4

Prep time: 10 minutes
Cook time: 1 hr. 15 mins.
Total cost: $6.89
Calories: 376
Fat: 16g
Protein: 25g
Cholesterol: 56mg
Sodium: 278mg

¾ pound bottom round steak

Sea salt and black pepper

1 teaspoon ground red pepper

1 teaspoon ground white pepper

2 tablespoons plain flour

¼ cup canola oil

1 yellow onion, chopped

1 red bell pepper, seeded and chopped

1 green bell pepper, seeded and chopped

1 celery rib, chopped

1 cup beef broth

2 cups cooked rice

If you have some at home, add some sliced cremini mushrooms.

Season roast with salt and peppers. Dust with flour on all sides. In a large heavy quart boiler, heat oil over medium heat. Add the round steak and brown on all sides. Remove the meat and pour off all but 1 teaspoon of the oil. Add half the onions, bell peppers, and celery. Mix well. Add the broth. Stir well and reduce heat to low. Return roast to the pot and add remaining vegetables. Cover and cook until the meat is very tender, about 1 hour and 15 minutes. Slice the meat, serve with rice and gravy from the pot.

The $7 a Meal Quick & Easy Cookbook

CHAPTER 10

SEAFOOD

Tuna Salad on Ciabatta Bread

Serves 2 (3 slices each)

Prep time: 12 minutes
Chill time: 1 hour
Total cost: $6.98
Calories: 406
Fat: 14g
Protein: 27g
Cholesterol: 25mg
Sodium: 783mg

½ medium crisp apple, cored and chopped

Juice of ½ lemon

¼ cup water

1 hard-boiled egg, diced

½ red onion, chopped

1 can tuna in water, drained

1 tablespoon chopped walnuts

1 tablespoon extra virgin olive oil

½ tablespoon balsamic vinegar

Sea salt and black pepper to taste

½ loaf Italian bread such as ciabatta

2 to 4 green or red lettuce leaves

Ciabatta bread is a traditional Italian bread that tastes great drizzled with a little extra virgin olive oil.

1. In a mixing bowl, combine apple, lemon juice, and water. Toss well and then drain. Once drained, add the egg and onion to the apples. Toss well. Add tuna, nuts, oil, vinegar, and pinch of salt and pepper. Slice the bread in half lengthwise, then layer lettuce and mound the tuna mixture on top.
2. Wrap the loaf tightly with plastic wrap and refrigerate for 1 hour. Slice into 6 equal portions and serve.

Almond-Crusted Salmon on Tortilla Crisps

Serves 3

Prep time: 10 minutes
Cook time: 12 minutes
Total cost: $6.45
Calories: 452
Fat: 16g
Protein: 29g
Cholesterol: 50mg
Sodium: 825mg

3 flour or corn tortillas

½ serrano pepper, minced

2 tablespoons almonds, chopped

1 teaspoon chili powder

¼ cup milk

½ pound salmon fillet, rinsed and cut into 3 portions

1 tablespoon extra virgin olive oil, plus extra for drizzling

Honey

Nuts add protein, flavor, and crunch! If serving for a party, however, it's a good idea to ask if any of your guests are allergic.

1. Toast tortillas under the broiler. Mix together the serrano pepper, almonds, and chili powder. In a mixing bowl, pour in milk. Dip salmon into milk and then dredge the salmon into the almond mixture.
2. In a large saucepan over medium heat, add olive oil and heat until hot but not smoking. Add salmon and cook each side for approximately 5 minutes, until cooked. Serve on tortillas drizzle with extra virgin olive oil and honey.

Quick and Easy Tip
Buying chopped almonds is usually about the same price as whole. Save yourself a step and buy them prechopped if you can.

Grilled Fish Sandwich

Serves 4

Prep time: 12 minutes
Cook time: 10 minutes
Total cost: $5.60
Calories: 314
Fat: 9g
Protein: 18g
Cholesterol: 44g
Sodium: 565mg

4 slices bacon

1 red onion, chopped

½ pound whitefish

8 slices whole-wheat bread

1 tablespoon extra virgin olive oil

8 lettuce leaves

1 large tomato, sliced

Sandwiches are great for lunch or dinner, or try mini-sandwiches for afternoon parties in the summer.

1. In a large saucepan, cook bacon until crisp. Drain bacon on paper towels, crumble, and set aside. Drain off all but 2 tablespoons bacon drippings. Cook onion in drippings over medium heat for 3 to 4 minutes. Add fish and cook for about 3 minutes per side, depending upon thickness. Turn once.
2. Toast bread slices and brush with olive oil. Layer one bread slice with lettuce, onion, bacon, tomatoes, and fish. Top with additional bread slice.

Quick and Easy Tip
Leave onions raw, if you like, for a crisp, fresh alternative.

Fish Chowder

Serves 4

Prep time: 10 minutes

Cook time: 1 hour, 15 mins.

Total cost: $6.99

Calories: 136

Fat: 4g

Protein: 13g

Cholesterol: 137g

Sodium: 518mg

1 tablespoon olive oil

1 large baking potato, peeled and cut into 1- to 2-inch cubes

1 ear corn, kernels cut off cob

1 large tomato, chopped

½ leek, trimmed and sliced

¾ pound whitefish such as tilapia

1 teaspoon curry powder

Black pepper to taste

¼ cup white wine such as Sauvignon Blanc

16 ounces chicken broth plus 16 ounces water

½ head fresh kale, washed and chopped

½ teaspoon capers

Fish chowder can be made so many ways—try adding red and yellow bell peppers and fresh spinach.

In a large quart boiler, heat oil on medium. Add the potatoes, stir in corn, tomatoes, leeks, and fish; sauté until leeks begin to wilt, about 6 minutes. Add curry and pepper, then add wine and reduce the wine by half, about 20 minutes. Pour in the broth and water and simmer for 45 minutes. Add kale and simmer for 5 minutes, then remove from heat. Ladle into serving bowls and sprinkle with capers.

Quick and Easy Tip
Use frozen corn off the cob and save time on chopping without adding to your budget or sacrificing flavor.

Baked Tortillas with Crab and Basil

Serves 6

Prep time: 5 minutes
Cook time: 20 minutes
Total cost: $6.60
Calories: 225
Fat: 15g
Protein: 9g
Cholesterol: 42g
Sodium: 309mg

6 ounces canned crabmeat, drained

8 basil leaves, chopped

Pinch black pepper

1½ cups sour cream

2 large flour tortillas

Nonstick cooking spray

Serving anything with crab at parties is always a hit! There are many different types of crabmeat available in stores, so shop for which is most cost effective for you. My favorite is pasteurized Maryland blue crab.

Preheat oven to 375°F. Flake the crabmeat. In a mixing bowl, combine crab, basil, pepper, and sour cream. Spray pie dish or pie pan with cooking spray. Place 1 tortilla on the bottom. Spoon in crab mixture, top with second tortilla, then spray with more cooking spray. Bake for 20 minutes. Let stand 5 minutes, slice then serve.

Quick and Easy Tip
Make sure to use fresh basil with this recipe. Dried basil doesn't have the crispness of fresh and will make the dish taste a little bitter.

Broiled Oysters with Lemon

Serves 4

Prep time: 5 minutes
Cook time: 5 minutes
Total cost: $6.99
Calories: 92
Fat: 3g
Protein: 11g
Cholesterol: 56mg
Sodium: 120mg

1 pound fresh shelled oysters

1 tablespoon olive oil

Black pepper to taste

1 teaspoon grated lemon zest

¼ bunch fresh parsley, minced

Sea salt to taste

Do not eat oysters raw unless you know they come from a quality source and have been stored properly.

Preheat oven broiler. Place cleaned and opened oysters on broiler pan and drizzle each with olive oil, sprinkle with pepper and lemon zest. Place under broiler for 2 minutes or until oysters are fully cooked. The oyster meat should feel firm but not hard. Top with parsley and salt, and serve.

Quick and Easy Tip

To save time, purchase oysters from a seafood market out of the shell. Add Parmesan cheese to these before broiling for extra flavor.

Mussels in Red Wine Sauce

Serves 4

Prep time: 10 minutes
Cook time: 10 minutes
Total cost: $7.00
Calories: 122
Fat: 5g
Protein: 15g
Cholesterol: 38mg
Sodium: 563mg

1 dozen mussels, cleaned and rinsed

1 tablespoon olive oil

1 shallot, chopped

2 cloves garlic, chopped

2 large tomatoes, chopped

½ cup dry red wine

½ cup fish broth, canned

¼ teaspoon dried red pepper flakes

1 teaspoon dried oregano

This is a quick and satisfying seafood dish.

Clean the mussels. In a large quart boiler, heat oil over medium heat. Add shallots, garlic, and tomatoes. Cook for 5 minutes. Add mussels, wine, broth, pepper flakes, and oregano; simmer until mussels open. Serve.

Quick and Easy Tip
Purchase mussels in the shell at your local seafood market or in the seafood section. Be sure to debeard them (pull the fibers off) and rinse them. Discard any open shells before cooking.

Risotto with Shrimp

Serves 6

Prep time: 10 minutes
Cook time: 20 minutes
Total cost: $6.99
Calories: 212
Fat: 6g
Protein: 14g
Cholesterol: 88mg
Sodium: 486mg

2 teaspoons olive oil

½ yellow onion, chopped

2 cloves garlic, minced

1 cups arborio rice

2 tablespoons dry white wine

2½ cups vegetable or chicken broth

¾ pound cooked shrimp

¼ cup Parmesan cheese

¼ bunch fresh Italian parsley, chopped

Risotto is delicious cooked most any way. The secret is to stir continuously and wait until most liquid is absorbed before adding more. Arborio rice is a short, thick-grain rice that seems to absorb as much liquid as you give it, so keep adding until you reach the consistency you desire.

In a large saucepan, heat oil over medium heat and add onion. Cook for 3 minutes. Add the garlic and cook an additional 1 more minute. Add the rice and stir into the mixture, combining well. Pour in the wine and let reduce by half. Add the broth, ½ cup at a time, stirring each until liquid is fully incorporated before adding more. Continue the process until all liquid is used. Remove from heat. Stir in shrimp and cheese. Sprinkle with parsley and serve.

Quick and Easy Tip
Replace shrimp with a meat if you like, such as cooked sausage, or use your favorite seafood.

Shrimp in Wontons with Fresh Gingerroot

Serves 6

Prep time: 15 minutes
Cook time: 5 minutes
Total cost: $5.99
Calories: 125
Fat: 2g
Protein: 10g
Cholesterol: 62mg
Sodium: 353mg

½ pound cooked shrimp, peeled and chopped

1 bunch scallions, chopped

6 cloves garlic, chopped

1 tablespoon fresh ginger, peeled and chopped

½ cup white wine such as Sauvignon Blanc

Juice of 1 lemon

1 cup fish broth

2 tablespoons soy sauce

1 package square wonton wrappers

Wontons are great to have on hand. Try brushing them with olive oil, sprinkling with Parmesan cheese, and baking until golden for easy Parmesan crisps that are perfect by themselves or for dips.

1. In a mixing bowl, combine shrimp, half the scallions, half the garlic, and ginger. Spoon mixture into wonton wrappers, seal edges by wetting slightly with water, fold wonton in half and press to seal.
2. In a large saucepan, combine remaining garlic and ginger. Heat over medium heat and add wine, lemon juice, broth, and soy sauce. Bring to a simmer. Add the filled wontons and simmer about 2 minutes. Serve with remaining broth, garnish with remaining scallions.

Quick and Easy Tip
You can use fresh shrimp; however, peel, devein, and cook them before placing into wontons.

Polenta with Serrano Peppers and Whitefish

Serves 4

Prep time: 10 minutes
Cook time: 35 minutes
Total cost: $6.99
Calories: 265
Fat: 7g
Protein: 22g
Cholesterol: 66mg
Sodium: 812mg

2 tablespoons olive oil

½ serrano chili pepper, seeded and diced

3 cups fish broth or vegetable broth

1 cup cornmeal or masa meal

¾ pound whitefish such as cod or tilapia

Sea salt and black pepper to taste

2 tablespoons Parmigiano-Reggiano or Parmesan cheese

1 tablespoon apple cider vinegar

Many people do not realize that cornmeal is the same as polenta and is very affordable. Substitute it virtually anywhere you would use rice.

1   Preheat grill to medium heat. Heat 1½ tablespoons olive oil in a stockpot on medium. Lightly sauté the chili, then add the broth and bring to a boil.
2. Whisk in the cornmeal slowly and cook for about 20 to 30 minutes, stirring frequently, adding more broth if necessary.
3. While polenta cooks, lightly dip the fish in the remaining olive oil and place on rack to drain. Season with salt and pepper.
4. When the polenta is finished cooking, remove it from the heat and add the cheese; keep warm.
5. Grill fish for 3 to 5 minutes on each side, depending on the thickness of the fish.
6. To serve, spoon out a generous dollop of polenta on each serving plate and arrange the fish on top. Drizzle with the vinegar.

Oven-Roasted Freshwater Bass with Black Olive Chutney

Serves 6

Prep time: 10 minutes
Cook time: 20 minutes
Total cost: $6.12
Calories: 116
Fat: 4g
Protein: 13g
Cholesterol: 72mg
Sodium: 615mg

1 shallot, peeled and chopped

1 stalk celery, chopped

Sea salt and black pepper to taste

1 pound bass fillet

½ cup dry white wine

1 cup fish broth or vegetable broth

¼ cup kalamata olives, chopped

2 cloves garlic, chopped

¼ teaspoon fresh-grated lemon zest

Try to find black bass or freshwater bass. You can also use Chilean sea bass, but it is significantly more expensive.

1. Preheat oven to 400°F. In ovenproof baking dish, add shallots and celery to bottom of dish. Sprinkle with salt and pepper. Place fish on top and add the wine and broth. Cover and bake for 15 to 20 minutes.
2. While the fish cooks, prepare chutney by combining olives, garlic, and lemon zest. Remove the fish from the cooking liquid and serve with a spoonful of chutney.

Quick and Easy Tip
Chutneys are thick, usually sweet, low-fat sauces that are made of fruits with spices. They are great for cooking as they add lots of flavor and texture to your recipes.

Pan-Fried Flounder with Balsamic Reduction

Serves 2

Prep time: 5 minutes
Cook time: 15 minutes
Total cost: $6.25
Calories: 75
Fat: 2.5g
Protein: 27g
Cholesterol: 54mg
Sodium: 94mg

2 cups balsamic vinegar
¼ cup plain flour
¼ cup cornmeal

½ pound flounder fillet
1 tablespoon olive oil
Black pepper to taste

A flat whitefish, flounder is not overly fishy tasting and is good baked, broiled, grilled, or fried.

1. In a small-quart boiler, add balsamic vinegar and simmer over medium heat until liquid is reduced by two-thirds, about 15 minutes.
2. While vinegar is reducing, in a mixing bowl, combine flour and cornmeal and coat the flounder. In a large saucepan over medium heat, heat oil. Add flounder and cook about 7 minutes on each side. Serve fish by drizzling with balsamic reduction and sprinkle with pepper.

Quick and Easy Tip
If your market does not have flounder, use halibut or tilapia fillets.

Shrimp-Stuffed Halibut
with Lime and Cilantro

Serves 2

Prep time: 12 minutes
Cook time: 8 minutes
Total cost: $7.00
Calories: 184
Fat: 4g
Protein: 35g
Cholesterol: 122mg
Sodium: 145mg

½ pound halibut fillet

¼ pound shrimp, peeled and deveined, chopped

1 lime, zested and juiced

1 tablespoon fresh cilantro, stems removed, leaves chopped

2 cloves garlic, chopped

1 tablespoon extra virgin olive oil

Black pepper to taste

Halibut is a perfect fish for grilling. Because halibut has a flaky texture when cooked, try to turn it only once when cooking, especially on the grill.

1. Soak 12 wooden skewers in water for about 1 hour. Preheat grill.
2. Butterfly the halibut fillet lengthwise to make a ½- to ¾-inch thick fillet. Lay the fillet out, then layer the shrimp, half the lime zest, half the cilantro, and garlic. Gently roll up the stuffed filet, then cut into 6 pinwheels. Insert 2 skewers into each pinwheel, forming an X to hold the pinwheels together. Brush with half of the oil, and grill for 4 minutes on each side.
3. To serve, sprinkle each with pepper and the remaining zest and cilantro. Drizzle with remaining olive oil.

Quick and Easy Tip
Use a grill basket to grill the halibut as it makes the fish easy to turn.

The $7 a Meal Quick & Easy Cookbook

Pan-Fried Trout

Serves 4

Prep time: 10 minutes
Cook time: 15 minutes
Total cost: $7.00
Calories: 165
Fat: 5g
Protein: 23g
Cholesterol: 66mg
Sodium: 79mg

½ cup plain flour

¼ cup cornmeal

½ teaspoon garlic powder

Sea salt and black pepper to taste

2 egg whites

1 tablespoon cold water

4 small prepared trout

2 tablespoons olive oil

¼ bunch fresh Italian parsley

Trout is usually cooked whole. Be careful when eating to discard any bones.

1. In a small bowl, combine flour, cornmeal, garlic powder, and pepper. In a separate bowl, mix together egg whites and water. Coat trout with cornmeal mixture, then dip in egg mixture, then dip again in cornmeal mixture. Shake off excess.
2. Heat oil to medium temperature in a large skillet. Cook trout about 5 minutes on each side until golden brown and cooked through. Remove trout from pan and drain on rack covered with paper towels. Sprinkle with parsley and salt before serving.

Quick and Easy Tip
Trout is a wonderful fish when smoked. If you have a stovetop smoker, smoke trout for 20 to 25 minutes using cherry wood chips.

Peppercorn-Crusted Tuna

Serves 2

Prep time: 4 minutes
Cook time: 5 minutes
Total cost: $6.99
Calories: 150
Fat: 2g
Protein: 26g
Cholesterol: 51mg
Sodium: 110mg

½ cup balsamic vinegar

2 tablespoons freshly cracked peppercorns

½ pound tuna steaks, sliced into 2 equal portions

Pinch sea salt

2 tablespoons unsalted, chilled butter

Lemon wedges

Tuna is a delicious fish and can be cooked so many ways. When buying, make sure to purchase top-grade tuna, sushi grade if possible.

1. Heat the vinegar in a small saucepan and bring to a boil. Lower heat and cook until vinegar is reduced to about 3 tablespoons. Set aside. Press the cracked peppercorns firmly into one side of each tuna steak. Sprinkle the tuna lightly with salt. Heat 1 tablespoon of the butter in a large nonstick skillet over medium-high heat and cook the fish, peppered side down, until seared, about 3 minutes. Turn fish and cook for 1 to 2 minutes, until the fish is seared on the outside yet still very pink in the center. Transfer the fish to a plate and cover loosely with foil to keep warm.
2. Add the remaining butter and reduced vinegar to the saucepan. Whisk constantly and cook over high heat until thick, about 1 to 2 minutes. To serve, place tuna steak, peppered side up, on serving plate and drizzle with balsamic sauce. Garnish with lemon wedges.

Salmon Smothered with Onions, Mushrooms, and Zucchini

Serves 2

Prep time: 10 minutes
Cook time: 10 minutes
Total cost: $6.14
Calories: 239
Fat: 15g
Protein: 29g
Cholesterol: 80mg
Sodium: 259mg

1 cup chicken broth

1 tomato, chopped

½ green bell pepper, seeded and chopped

½ yellow onion, chopped

1 cup sliced cremini mushrooms

1 zucchini, sliced

1 clove garlic, chopped

2 teaspoons Italian seasoning

Sea salt and black pepper to taste

½ pound skinless salmon fillets

2 tablespoons grated Parmesan cheese

Salmon is packed full of omega-3 fatty acids, which help give your skin a healthy glow, and it tastes delicious and is very filling.

1. Combine the broth, tomatoes, peppers, onions, mushrooms, zucchini, garlic, seasoning, salt, and pepper in a large saucepan, and heat over medium-high heat. Cover and bring to a boil.
2. Using wooden spoon, move vegetables aside and add the salmon fillets. Reduce heat to medium, cover, and gently simmer until the fish is opaque and firm throughout, about 8 to 10 minutes. Transfer salmon to serving plates, spoon vegetables over salmon and sprinkle with Parmesan cheese.

Quick and Easy Tip
Buy whole salmon fillets and cut into individual serving sizes and freeze.

Broiled Whitefish with Lemon Dijon

Serves 4

Prep time: 7 minutes
Cook time: 7 minutes
Total cost: $6.74
Calories: 143
Fat: 8g
Protein: 18g
Cholesterol: 51mg
Sodium: 247mg

1 stick (½ cup) unsalted butter

2 tablespoons shallots, chopped

Juice of ½ lemon

1 teaspoon paprika

2 tablespoons Dijon mustard

Pinch sea salt and black pepper

¾ pound cod fillets

1 tablespoon fresh Italian parsley, chopped

Cod is a light, flaky whitefish that tends to take on the flavors of the ingredients around it. Salmon and halibut are also great fish to pair with this sauce.

1. Preheat broiler. Heat butter in a small saucepan over medium-low heat. Add shallots and cook until soft, about 2 minutes. Add lemon juice, paprika, mustard, salt, and pepper. Remove from heat and whisk until creamy and well blended. Transfer the butter sauce to a small bowl.
2. Dip the fillets in butter sauce, coating both sides. Place the fillets in a single layer in shallow broiler pan. Spoon any remaining butter sauce over tops of fillets.
3. Broil the fish until browned and cooked through, about 4 to 5 minutes. Baste with pan juices several times during the cooking process. To serve, transfer fillets to a platter and pour pan juices over the fish. Top with parsley.

Quick and Easy Tip
If the fresh fish selection does not look as fresh as it should, substitute frozen.

Sautéed Shrimp with Curry

Serves 4

Prep time: 8 minutes
Cook time: 5 minutes
Total cost: $6.99
Calories: 130
Fat: 4g
Protein: 23g
Cholesterol: 172mg
Sodium: 182mg

1 pound shrimp, peeled and deveined

1½ tablespoons curry powder

Pinch chili powder

1 tablespoon olive oil

¼ cup scallions, chopped

½ cup chili sauce

Sea salt and black pepper to taste

Shrimp are perfect to use for a quick meal because they cook in 2 minutes or less! Keep some in your freezer for last-minute meals.

In a mixing bowl, combine shrimp, curry, and chili powder, and toss to coat. Heat oil in a large skillet over medium heat. Add shrimp and cook, stirring often, until shrimp turns pink, about 2 minutes. Add scallions and chili sauce and stir. Cook until heated through, about 3 minutes. Season to taste with salt and pepper.

Quick and Easy Tip
Serve this over pasta or rice as a tasty alternative.

Proscuitto-Wrapped Shrimp with Honey and Lemon

Serves 4

Prep time: 10 minutes

Cook time: 5 minutes

Total cost: $6.94

Calories: 173

Fat: 6g

Protein: 22g

Cholesterol: 142mg

Sodium: 445mg

2 ounces prosciutto, thinly sliced, cut into ½-inch-wide x 3-inch-long strips

¾ pound shrimp, peeled and deveined

2 tablespoons olive oil

Black pepper to taste

¼ cup chicken broth

1 tablespoon lemon juice

1 tablespoon honey

Proscuitto-wrapped shrimp is popular at parties. Before wrapping, spread a little Dijon mustard on the prosciutto for another layer of flavor.

1. Wrap prosciutto around shrimp and press lightly to seal. In a large saucepan, heat oil over medium-high heat. Add shrimp and cook, turning once, until shrimp turn pink, about 3 minutes. Season with pepper. Transfer shrimp to plate and cover loosely.
2. Add the broth, lemon juice, and honey to the pan and bring to a simmer. Add the shrimp and any accumulated juices to the pan and stir to coat the shrimp evenly, being careful not to damage the prosciutto wrapping. Heat through, about 1 to 2 minutes. Season to taste.

Quick and Easy Tip
Honey is a natural sweetener. Use in place of sugar for sauces and even some desserts.

Whitefish with Caper Cream Sauce

Serves 4

Prep time: 10 minutes
Cook time: 12 minutes
Total cost: $7.00
Calories: 335
Fat: 25g
Protein: 29g
Cholesterol: 51mg
Sodium: 80mg

¾ pound whitefish fillets

Sea salt and black pepper to taste

3 tablespoons plain flour

4 tablespoons unsalted butter

1 tablespoon shallots, chopped

½ cup dry white wine

2 tablespoons capers, rinsed and drained

2 teaspoons grain mustard

½ cup heavy cream, room temperature

If you'd rather not use heavy cream (it tastes good but is typically expensive and high in fat and calories), use ½ cup low-fat sour cream and ½ cup milk.

Season each fillet with salt and pepper. Sprinkle both sides with flour. In a large saucepan, heat 3 tablespoons of butter over medium heat. Add the fish, and cook until cooked through, about 2 minutes per side. Remove fillets and set aside. Add shallots to the pan and additional butter. Cook for about 1 minute, until soft but not browned. Add wine, capers, and mustard and simmer for about 3 minutes, until sauce starts to thicken. Slowly add cream, stirring constantly until incorporated. Cook about 6 minutes until the sauce begins to thicken. Adjust seasoning as desired. Serve by placing fish on platter and pouring sauce over.

Quick and Easy Tip
When cooking with any kind of cream sauce, stir frequently to avoid burning.

Tilapia Fillets with Spinach

Serves 4

Prep time: 8 minutes
Cook time: 20 minutes
Total cost: $6.46
Calories: 261
Fat: 6g
Protein: 26g
Cholesterol: 56mg
Sodium: 222mg

10 ounces frozen spinach, thawed and drained

3 shallots, minced

⅓ cup chicken broth

Pinch nutmeg

2 tablespoons butter

1 pound tilapia fillets

½ cup buttermilk

2 eggs, beaten

Dash hot pepper sauce such as Tabasco

2 tablespoons Romano cheese, grated

Sea salt and black pepper to taste

Tilapia is a whitefish with a slightly pinkish color. Native to Africa, tilapia can now be found around the world. This fish is low in fat and is perfect for grilling.

1. In a large saucepan over medium heat, combine spinach, shallots, broth, and nutmeg and cook, covered, for about 4 minutes, stirring occasionally.
2. Separately, in an ovenproof skillet, heat butter over medium-high heat. Tilt pan so butter is spread evenly across pan. Transfer spinach mixture to ovenproof skillet and spread evenly throughout skillet. Top spinach mixture with tilapia fillets.
3. In a small bowl, combine buttermilk, eggs, and pepper sauce and mix until blended. Pour mixture over tilapia and top with grated cheese. Season with salt and pepper, being sure not to oversalt as the cheese has a high sodium content.
4. Preheat broiler to medium high. Transfer skillet to oven and broil until the sauce is evenly browned and fish is cooked through, about 12 minutes. Turn skillet once or twice to prevent overly browning some areas. Remove from heat and let rest for 4 or 5 minutes. Cut into 4 equal portions and serve.

The $7 a Meal Quick & Easy Cookbook

Lime-Jalapeño Grouper

Serves 4

Prep time: 8 minutes
Cook time: 10 to 12 mins.
Total cost: $7.00
Calories: 225
Fat: 84g
Protein: 36g
Cholesterol: 34mg
Sodium: 75mg

½ stick (¼ cup) unsalted butter, room temperature

2 tablespoons jalapeños, seeded and chopped

Juice of 1 lime

Sea salt and black pepper to taste

¾ pound grouper fillets

¼ cup plain flour

3 tablespoons olive oil

Grouper is a whitefish known to the Gulf and Atlantic coasts. It is very mild in flavor and is great for grilling, broiling, or poaching.

1. In a small bowl, combine butter, jalapeños, lime juice, and salt (for a smoother butter, combine in food processor). Set aside. Season fillets with salt and pepper. Place flour in a small bowl and coat the fish in the flour.
2. In a large saucepan over medium-high heat, add the oil and fish and cook until browned, about 3 to 5 minutes. Carefully turn the fish and cook for an additional 3 to 4 minutes or until fish is golden on both sides and texture is flaky. When serving, dollop fish with jalapeño butter.

Quick and Easy Tip

When seeding jalapeños, be sure to wear gloves as the fire is in the seeds. If you do accidentally seed them without gloves, soak your hands in milk to calm the burn.

Baked Salmon with Shallots and Horseradish Dijon

![spoon icon] **Serves 2**

Prep time: 7 minutes
Cook time: 12 minutes
Total cost: $6.96
Calories: 245
Fat: 15g
Protein: 35g
Cholesterol: 80mg
Sodium: 228mg

½ pound salmon fillets, skin on

2 tablespoons olive oil

Pinch sea salt and black pepper

4 tablespoons butter, room temperature

2 tablespoons prepared horseradish

1 tablespoon Dijon grainy mustard

½ large shallot, peeled and minced

1 tablespoon fresh chives, chopped

Some chefs consider the skin side of fish to be "presentation side," but you can plate it skinless or skin side down if you prefer.

1. Preheat oven to 375°F. Line a baking sheet with parchment paper and place salmon skin side down. Drizzle with olive oil and season with salt and pepper. Bake salmon for about 12 minutes.
2. Separately, combine butter, horseradish, mustard, and shallot in a small bowl and blend well. Season with salt and pepper. Serve baked salmon with a dollop of butter mixture. Top with chopped chives.

Quick and Easy Tip

There are lots of ways to spice up butter, and this recipe is great for meats, poultry, and fish. If you find you really like this one, make a double batch of the butter mixture and use with other foods.

Pan-Grilled Salmon with Wasabi

Serves 2

Prep time: 9 minutes
Cook time: 12 minutes
Total cost: $7.00
Calories: 270
Fat: 17g
Protein: 34g
Cholesterol: 117mg
Sodium: 34mg

½ pound salmon fillets

Pinch sea salt

2 tablespoons butter

¼ cup heavy cream, room temperature

Juice of 1 lemon

1 tablespoon wasabi paste

Black pepper to taste

1 tablespoon fresh chives, chopped

Wasabi paste is available in the Asian or ethnic section of your grocery store.

1. Season salmon with salt. In a large saucepan over medium heat, heat butter until melted. Add salmon, skin side down. Cook about 4 minutes or until skin begins to brown. Flip salmon and cook an additional 4 minutes. Transfer salmon to plate and cover loosely with foil.
2. Add the cream and lemon juice to the pan and stir to blend. Bring to a simmer and cook for 2 minutes. Remove from heat and let cool for 2 minutes. Add the wasabi paste and stir to blend well. Adjust seasoning as desired. Transfer salmon to serving platter and top with wasabi mixture, pinch of pepper, and chives.

Quick and Easy Tip
Bring cream to room temperature; however, don't let it sit out too long. If you get distracted and find you are cooking later, put the cream back in the refrigerator.

Broiled Halibut with Basil Pesto and Tomatoes

Serves 4

Prep time: 4 minutes
Cook time: 14 minutes
Total cost: $6.99
Calories: 405
Fat: 6g
Protein: 50g
Cholesterol: 1mg
Sodium: 1,041mg

¾ pound halibut fillets

1 tablespoon olive oil

Sea salt and black pepper to taste

2 cups chopped, seeded tomatoes

¾ cup pesto sauce

¼ cup Parmesan cheese, grated

Halibut is among the largest fish in the sea and is dominant in the Pacific Northwest. It is a whitefish and is delicious, not overly fishy tasting, and flakes nicely when cooked properly.

1. Preheat broiler. Place fillets on broiler pan lined with aluminum foil and brush with half the olive oil; sprinkle with salt and pepper. In a small bowl, combine tomatoes, remaining olive oil, pesto, and Parmesan cheese; season with salt and pepper.
2. Broil halibut fillets for 10 to 12 minutes or until fish is firm when touched. Top with tomato mixture and broil an additional 1 to 2 minutes being careful not to burn.

Quick and Easy Tip
Allow about 10 minutes cooking time per 1 inch of thickness for any type of fish.

The $7 a Meal Quick & Easy Cookbook

Shrimp and Sausage Jambalaya

Serves 4

Prep time: 6 minutes
Cook time: 30 minutes
Total cost: $6.48
Calories: 366
Fat: 19g
Protein: 26g
Cholesterol: 40mg
Sodium: 952mg

1 8-ounce package yellow rice mix

2 tablespoons olive oil

1 yellow onion, chopped

1 14-ounce can diced tomatoes with green chilies, undrained

½ pound frozen cooked shrimp, thawed

1 Italian or Polish sausage, cooked and sliced into ½-inch slices

Jambalaya is traditional to New Orleans and is a combination of Spanish and French culture. Jambalaya is the New World answer to Old World paella.

Prepare rice mix as directed on package. Meanwhile, in a large saucepan heat olive oil over medium heat. Add onion; cook and stir for 4 to 5 minutes, until tender. Add tomatoes, shrimp, and sliced sausage; bring to a simmer, and cook for 3 to 4 minutes. When rice is cooked, add to saucepan; cook and stir for 8 minutes, until blended. Serve immediately.

Quick and Easy Tip
Add any combination of vegetables to this dish to create your own version. In the South, we add okra and green beans.

Basil Pesto Ravioli with Shrimp

Serves 4

Prep time: 8 minutes
Cook time: 15 minutes
Total cost: $7.00
Calories: 498
Fat: 6g
Protein: 45g
Cholesterol: 43mg
Sodium: 410mg

1 tablespoon olive oil

1 red bell pepper, seeded and chopped

½ pound frozen shrimp, peeled and deveined

1 9-ounce package refrigerated or frozen cheese ravioli

1½ cups water

¾ cup pesto sauce

½ cup grated Parmesan cheese

Pesto sauce is traditionally Italian. It's usually made fresh with crushed basil, pine nuts, olive oil, and Parmesan. It is easy to make your own, but be aware of the cost difference. Sometimes with pesto sauce, it's cheaper to buy the premade, which is available both in jars and refrigerated plastic containers.

1. In a large saucepan over medium heat, heat olive oil. Add bell pepper and sauté for 4 minutes until slightly tender. Add shrimp and cook for about 4 minutes, until shrimp turn pinkish. Remove all from skillet and set aside.
2. Add ravioli and water to skillet and bring to a boil over high heat. Reduce heat to medium, cover, and simmer for 5 minutes, until ravioli are hot, stirring occasionally. Drain off excess water, then return pasta, shrimp, and peppers to skillet. Mix gently so as not to break ravioli. Stir in pesto sauce and cook until heated, about 1 to 2 minutes. Top with Parmesan and serve.

Scallops in White Wine and Peppers

Serves 4

Prep time: 5 minutes
Cook time: 10 minutes
Total cost: $7.00
Calories: 398
Fat: 9g
Protein: 40g
Cholesterol: 75mg
Sodium: 212mg

2 tablespoons olive oil

4 cloves garlic, chopped

1 serrano pepper, seeded and minced

1 cup dry white wine such as Sauvignon Blanc

¾ pound sea scallops

Pinch sea salt

Pinch cayenne pepper

2 tablespoons butter

There are three major kinds of scallops. Sea scallops are the largest, with a yield of anywhere between 20 to 30 per pound. Allow 1 to 3 per person, depending upon size. Bay scallops are smaller, sweet in flavor, yield about 50 per pound, and are great for appetizers. Calico scallops are the smallest of the scallop family and are not widely used in cooking, as they are darker in color and more tough in texture.

1. In a large saucepan, heat olive oil over medium heat. Add garlic and serrano pepper; cook for 2 to 3 minutes, stirring occasionally. Add wine, reduce heat to low, and simmer for 2 minutes. Add scallops, salt, and cayenne pepper, cover, and simmer for 3 minutes or until scallops turn opaque in color and are slightly firm. Be careful not to overcook as the scallops will become tough.
2. When scallops are cooked, stir in butter until melted and serve.

Pasta with Mussels, Garlic, and Red Bell Pepper

Serves 4

Prep time: 8 minutes
Cook time: 18 minutes
Total cost: $6.96
Calories: 273
Fat: 9g
Protein: 27g
Cholesterol: 47mg
Sodium: 820mg

½ pound spaghetti noodles

3 cloves garlic, chopped

2 tablespoons olive oil

½ yellow onion, chopped

1 red bell pepper, seeded and chopped

½ teaspoon dried oregano leaves

1 cup dry white wine

1 cup vegetable or chicken broth

Sea salt and black pepper to taste

1 pound cleaned mussels

Be sure to check for fresh, live mussels before cooking by tapping lightly on any open shells. If the shells close, the mussel is still alive and is suitable for consumption. If the shell does not close, the mussel has died and should be instantly discarded as it will become toxic. Mussels are an excellent source of selenium, vitamin B12, and zinc.

1. Bring a large pot of water with a small drizzle of olive oil to a boil; cook spaghetti pasta until tender, drain (do not rinse), and set aside.
2. In a large stockpot, heat olive oil over medium-high heat. Add onion and garlic and cook until fragrant, about 1 minute. Add bell pepper and cook for about 3 to 4 minutes, until tender. Add oregano, white wine, and broth. Bring to a boil. Add salt and pepper, then add mussels. Cover pot and reduce heat to medium low. Cook for about 7 minutes or until all mussels are opened (some mussels may not open; discard them). Remove mussels from pot and place in a mixing bowl. Then add cooked spaghetti to pot with liquid, toss, and transfer to serving platter. Place mussels on top of spaghetti and serve.

CHAPTER 11

VEGETARIAN

Parmesan-Stuffed Mushrooms

Serves 6

Prep time: 7 minutes
Cook time: 12 minutes
Total cost: $5.05
Calories: 125
Fat: 11g
Protein: 6g
Cholesterol: 5mg
Sodium: 145mg

1 pound cremini mushrooms, stems removed and reserved

3 tablespoons butter, unsalted

1 yellow onion, chopped

¾ cup bread crumbs

Sea salt and black pepper to taste

1 teaspoon dried thyme leaves

¼ cup Parmesan cheese, grated

2 tablespoons fresh Italian parsley, chopped

Get a jump-start on this recipe by making the filling mixture the day before. Wait, however, to broil the mushrooms until just before serving.

1. Preheat broiler. Chop mushroom stems. In a large saucepan over medium heat, melt butter. Add onion and cook for 2 minutes. Add mushroom stems and cook 2 to 3 minutes more. Stir in bread crumbs, salt, pepper, and thyme. Cook an additional 1 minute. Remove from heat and stir in cheese.
2. Using a small spoon, fill each mushroom cap with mushroom mixture. Place filled mushrooms on a baking sheet and put under preheated broiler for 6 minutes, or until tops are browned and caps have softened slightly and become juicy. Sprinkle tops with parsley.

The $7 a Meal Quick & Easy Cookbook

Fresh Fennel Bulb with
Lemon and Asiago Cheese

Serves 4

Prep time: 7 minutes
Cook time: none
Total cost: $6.68
Calories: 65
Fat: 3g
Protein: 3g
Cholesterol: 1mg
Sodium: 345mg

2 bulbs fresh fennel, cleaned

½ fresh lemon

1 4-ounce wedge Parmigiano-Reggiano or asiago cheese

1 tablespoon high-quality extra virgin olive oil

Pinch sea salt

Simple and Italian, just the way they like it!

Trim fennel stems and wispy fronds from fennel tops. Break the bulbs apart, layer by layer, using your hands to make long, bite-size pieces. Discard the core. Arrange the pieces onto a serving platter. Squeeze lemon over fennel. Using a vegetable peeler, shave curls of cheese over fennel, allowing them to fall where they may. Make about 10 curls. Drizzle olive oil over all and sprinkle with salt.

Quick and Easy Tip
Precut fennel and keep in the refrigerator. Fennel is a vegetable that has a licorice taste. The citric acid in the lemon and tart flavor help balance the bitterness of fresh fennel.

Roasted Fresh Beets
with Feta

Serves 4

Prep time: 10 minutes
Cook time: 45 to 55 mins.
Total cost: $5.62
Calories: 181
Fat: 4g
Protein: 3g
Cholesterol: 12mg
Sodium: 125mg

2 pounds fresh beets, washed and cut into 2-inch cubes

1 tablespoon olive oil

Sea salt and black pepper to taste

1 cup feta cheese

1 bunch fresh Italian flat-leaf parsley, chopped

Most people hear "roasted beets" and think, yuk! Boy are they wrong! This is one of my most popular dishes in my cooking classes.

1. Heat oven to 375°F. Toss beets with olive oil, salt, and pepper. Spread onto parchment-lined baking sheet in single layer. Roast in middle rack of oven for 45 minutes or until tender. Check about halfway through cooking and toss if needed.
2. Remove from oven, toss with feta and parsley, and serve.

Quick and Easy Tip
Add a little lemon zest to perk up the flavor, if you like.

Vegetarian Custard of
Carrots, Tarragon, and Parmesan

Serves 4

Prep time: 10 minutes
Cook time: 56 minutes
Total cost: $6.79
Calories: 425
Fat: 35g
Protein: 18g
Cholesterol: 130mg
Sodium: 457mg

1 tablespoon unsalted butter

2 cups carrots, peeled and sliced

2 shallots, chopped

2 tablespoons Port wine

Pinch sea salt and black pepper

Pinch nutmeg

1 cup whipping cream

3 large eggs

¼ cup Parmesan cheese, grated

2 tablespoons fresh tarragon, chopped

These custards bake in a bain-marie, which is a French term for water bath, to ensure them cooking evenly. Don't be afraid to try this; it's actually very easy. Just be careful not to scald yourself with the hot water when placing in or taking out of the oven.

1. Preheat oven to 375°F. Butter 4 6-ounce ramekins or custard cups. In a medium saucepan over medium heat, melt 1 tablespoon butter; add the carrots and cook until soft, about 3 to 4 minutes. Reduce heat and add shallots, Port wine, salt, pepper, and nutmeg. Let simmer for 2 minutes while you separately heat the cream in a small boiler until hot but not boiling. Quickly whisk the eggs into the vegetable mixture, then gradually whisk in the cream. Gently stir in the Parmesan.
2. Divide the entire mixture into the prepared ramekins. Place them in a shallow baking dish. Add enough hot tap water to come two-thirds up the sides of the ramekins. Cover entire dish with foil and place in center of oven. Bake for 30 minutes, until almost set. Open oven door and bake an additional 10 minutes. Remove from oven and allow to rest for 10 minutes before serving. Unmold by loosening with a knife and turning over (or serve in ramekins) and top with tarragon.

Sautéed Parsnips and Pears with Mango Chutney

Serves 4

Prep time: 12 minutes
Cook time: 21 minutes
Total cost: $6.35
Calories: 245
Fat: 2g
Protein: 5g
Cholesterol: 2mg
Sodium: 205mg

1½ pounds parsnips, cut into 1-inch pieces

2 tablespoons olive oil

1 red onion, thinly sliced

2 Bosc pears, cored and thinly sliced

1 teaspoon curry powder

½ teaspoon ground coriander

Sea salt and black pepper to taste

¼ cup plain yogurt

¼ cup mango chutney

2 tablespoons fresh cilantro, chopped

Coriander is the seed that fresh cilantro is grown from. Native to Southwest Asia and North Africa, coriander is used in many cooking cultures including Middle Eastern, Mediterranean, and Indian.

Partially boil the parsnips, about 5 minutes. In a large saucepan over medium heat, add oil. Add onion, pears, curry, and coriander and cook for about 10 minutes, stirring regularly. Add the parsnips and season with sea salt and pepper, and cook an additional 5 minutes, until parsnips brown lightly. Remove from heat and then stir in yogurt, chutney, and cilantro. Serve.

Quick and Easy Tip
Parsnips are root vegetables related to carrots. They typically grow in cold climates, not warm, as frost enhances their flavor.

Sweet Potatoes with
Candied Gingerroot

Serves 4

Prep time: 10 minutes
Cook time: 25 minutes
Total cost: $5.36
Calories: 249
Fat: 3g
Protein: 5g
Cholesterol: 1mg
Sodium: 422mg

4 large sweet potatoes, peeled and cut into 2 to 3-inch cubes

¼ cup milk

2 tablespoons butter

1 tablespoon mashed candied ginger, or 1 tablespoon brown sugar plus ½ teaspoon ground ginger

Sweet potatoes, found in North and South America, are commonly confused with yams, which are native to Africa and Asia. A tasty alternative to baking potatoes, sweet potatoes are loaded with beta carotene and vitamin C.

Place potatoes in a large-quart boiler filled ¾ with water. Bring to a boil and cook potatoes until tender, about 20 minutes. Drain and return to pan. In a small saucepan, heat the milk with the butter. Add milk mixture to potatoes, along with candied ginger. Mash by hand using potato masher or with an electric mixer.

Quick and Easy Tip
Fresh ginger is the underground stem of the ginger plant. This root can be candied and eaten as a snack or combined with other foods as a spice. Fresh gingerroot can be kept in the refrigerator for up to three weeks or in the freezer for up to five months.

Traditional Potato Cakes

Serves 4

Prep time: 12 minutes

Cook time: 12 minutes

Total cost: $4.56

Calories: 274

Fat: 8g

Protein: 4g

Cholesterol: 20mg

Sodium: 310mg

2 eggs

3 large baking potatoes, peeled and grated

1 medium yellow onion, grated using box grater or food processor

Sea salt and black pepper to taste

1 tablespoon plain flour, plus a little extra if needed

Canola oil for frying

Potato pancakes are great to make as an appetizer for parties. Serve with sour cream and, if budget allows, a little lumpfish caviar.

1. Beat egg in a large bowl. Add potato, onion, salt, and pepper and combine. Add flour and toss together being careful not to overwork the mixture.
2. In a large saucepan over medium-high heat, pour in oil about ¼-inch deep. Heat oil to hot but not burning. From potato batter, make 8 pancakes. Gently squeeze out any excess water and place pancakes in batches into hot oil. Cook slowly, without moving them for the first 5 minutes. Loosen with spatula and turn after about 8 minutes. When the top appears to be about one-third cooked, flip pancake and finish cooking, about 4 more minutes. Drain on paper towels and serve.

Quick and Easy Tip

The key here is not to handle the pancakes too much. Otherwise the flour gets absorbed and you end up adding more and more flour for a "cakey" pancake.

Grilled Portabello Mushrooms

Serves 4

Prep time: 15 minutes
Cook time: 6 minutes
Total cost: $6.20
Calories: 120
Fat: 1g
Protein: 7g
Cholesterol: 2mg
Sodium: 199mg

4 large portabello mushrooms, stems removed
½ cup extra virgin olive oil
1 cup red wine vinegar
2 tablespoons soy sauce

1 tablespoon sugar
½ cup variety fresh herbs, chopped, such as parsley, thyme, rosemary, chives

Portabello mushrooms are like a vegetarian burger! Try using them as "bread" for a portabello mushroom sandwich layering cheese, mixed greens, and tomato slices.

1. Brush any dirt from the mushrooms, but do not wash them. Whisk together olive oil, vinegar, soy sauce, sugar, and herbs. In shallow dish, pour the marinade over the mushrooms; marinate 10 minutes, turning after 5 minutes.
2. Preheat grill. Grill 2 to 3 minutes on each side. Serve whole or sliced with leftover marinade.

Quick and Easy Tip
Add a tablespoon or slice of Gruyère or Swiss cheese and cook until melted for an extra culinary treat.

Wild Mushroom Risotto

Serves 6

Prep time: 10 minutes
Cook time: 30 minutes
Total cost: $6.95
Calories: 330
Fat: 11g
Protein: 14g
Cholesterol: 7mg
Sodium: 741mg

½ cup asparagus tips

2 tablespoons butter, unsalted

2 ounces dried morel mushrooms, soaked in water, liquid reserved, chopped

Sea salt and black pepper to taste

2 tablespoons olive oil

1 medium yellow onion, chopped

2 cloves garlic, chopped

½ cup cremini (or button) mushrooms, chopped

1½ cups arborio rice

½ cup dry white wine such as Sauvignon Blanc

5 cups chicken or vegetable broth

¼ cup Parmesan cheese

Zest of ½ lemon

¼ cup fresh chives, chopped

The flavors in this risotto infuse into the mushrooms, making a perfect combination.

1. Cook asparagus pieces in boiling salted water until vibrant, about 1 minute. Drain and set aside. In a large saucepan over medium heat, heat 1 tablespoon butter and add morel mushrooms with liquid. Season with salt and pepper and let cook for 5 minutes. Set aside.
2. In a large-quart boiler, heat 1 tablespoon olive oil over medium heat and add onion, garlic, and cremini mushrooms and cook for about 3 minutes. Then add rice and stir with wooden spoon to coat with other ingredients, about 1 minute. Pour in wine and stir constantly until all wine is absorbed.
3. Add 1 cup of broth, and stir constantly until absorbed. Repeat with remaining broth, adding ½ cup to 1 cup at a time until rice is mostly tender (about 20 minutes). Remove from heat and stir in cheese and remaining butter and mix well. Add mushrooms, asparagus, lemon zest, and season to taste. Serve with chives and any extra Parmesan cheese.

Olive-Stuffed Artichokes

Serves 4

Prep time: 12 minutes
Cook time: 35 minutes
Total cost: $6.32
Calories: 153
Fat: 9g
Protein: 3g
Cholesterol: 1mg
Sodium: 201mg

4 large artichokes, trimmed and split lengthwise

4 quarts water

½ fresh lemon, zested and juiced

1 cup cooked white rice

7 green olives, chopped

7 kalamata olives, chopped

Sea salt and black pepper to taste

2 tablespoons fresh Italian flat leaf parsley, chopped

3 tablespoons butter, melted

1 egg

1 clove garlic, minced

I always use Italian flat-leaf parsley, as it has a better flavor and texture than curly parsley. Besides, among chefs, curly parsley is a bit out of fashion.

1. Boil the artichokes in 4 quarts of water with lemon juice and lemon zest for 20 minutes. Drain and place on a parchment-lined baking sheet, cut side up.
2. Preheat oven to 350°F. Mix the rest of the ingredients together in a large bowl. Spoon filling over the artichokes, pressing between the leaves. Bake for 15 minutes or until hot.

Quick and Easy Tip
Artichokes can be a little tricky. Wear gloves to tear off the outer leaves and trim the stem. Either steam them, boil them, or bake them to make them tender.

Veggie Burger-Stuffed Red Bell Peppers

Serves 4

Prep time: 5 minutes
Cook time: 33 minutes
Total cost: $6.96
Calories: 277
Fat: 5g
Protein: 5g
Cholesterol: 12mg
Sodium: 324mg

4 large garlic cloves, minced

1 large onion, minced

¼ cup olive oil

2 veggie burgers, frozen

Sea salt and black pepper to taste

4 large red bell peppers

When shopping for bell peppers, stick with buying red or green as the yellow and orange bell peppers are slightly more rare and are usually more expensive. You do not sacrifice flavor by buying red or green ones.

1. Sauté the garlic and onion for 3 minutes in a large saucepan with 1 tablespoon olive oil over medium heat. Add veggie burgers, breaking up with a wooden spoon, and cook until heated through and broken down, about 4 minutes. Add salt and pepper as desired. Preheat oven to 350°F.
2. Cut the peppers in half lengthwise and scoop out seeds and cores. Fill with the burger mixture, drizzle with remaining olive oil, and place on parchment-lined baking sheets and bake for 25 minutes.

Quick and Easy Tip
If you don't have veggie burgers, substitute firm tofu or extra vegetables with rice or other grain.

Oven-Baked Eggplant with Ricotta and Parmesan

Serves 4

Prep time: 15 minutes
Cook time: 40 minutes
Total cost: $6.35
Calories: 196
Fat: 6g
Protein: 6g
Cholesterol: 4mg
Sodium: 124mg

2 medium eggplants, cut into 16 round slices and salted

1 cup corn flour

Black pepper to taste

¼ cup olive oil, or as needed

2 cups tomato sauce

1 pound (16 ounces) ricotta cheese

1 cup grated Parmesan cheese

2 eggs

1 tablespoon dried oregano

1 cup mozzarella cheese

Eggplant is native to India but is used in cooking worldwide. Raw eggplant can taste bitter so salting and rinsing, a process called "degorging," helps extract the bitterness and make the eggplant more tender.

1. Stack salted eggplant slices on a plate and place another place on top. Place a weight on top plate to press out the brown liquid. Separately, in a medium mixing bowl, mix flour and pepper. Dredge the eggplant slices in the flour mixture. Heat olive oil in a large saucepan over medium-high heat. When hot but not burning, add eggplant and fry until browned, about 5 minutes.
2. Preheat oven to 325°F. Prepare a 2-quart casserole dish with nonstick spray and spread a thin layer of tomato sauce. In a large bowl, mix ricotta cheese, ½ cup of Parmesan cheese, eggs, and oregano. Place a tablespoon of the egg-cheese mixture on each slice of eggplant and roll, placing seam side down in a baking dish.
3. Spread with sauce, sprinkle with remaining Parmesan, top with mozzarella, and bake for 35 minutes.

Asparagus Frittata with Cheese

● **Serves 8**

Prep time: 7 minutes
Cook time: 15 minutes
Total cost: $6.75
Calories: 225
Fat: 21g
Protein: 21g
Cholesterol: 312mg
Sodium: 340mg

1 10-ounce box frozen chopped asparagus

6 eggs

½ cup Cheddar cheese, grated

¼ cup Monterey jack cheese, shredded

Fine zest of one lemon

Sea salt and black pepper to taste

2 tablespoons butter, unsalted

Asparagus contains no fat or cholesterol and is low in calories and sodium. It's also a good source of folic acid, potassium, and fiber.

1. In a large ovenproof saucepan over medium heat, add asparagus and cook for 2 to 3 minutes or until heated through. Drain, chop, and set aside in a separate bowl.
2. Preheat broiler. In another bowl, beat eggs and then mix in cheeses, lemon zest, salt, and pepper. Mix well. In the large saucepan, heat butter over medium heat. Add egg mixture, then distribute asparagus throughout egg mixture and reduce heat, cooking slowly for about 10 minutes. To finish cooking, place saucepan under broiler for about 30 seconds and brown very slightly on top.

Quick and Easy Tip

If you do not have an ovenproof saucepan or skillet, don't worry. When cooking the frittata, use a spatula to run around the sides of the frittata to lift. Tilt the pan and let some of the runny egg mixture in the center of the frittata run to the sides. This is similar to cooking an omelet.

Baked Potatoes Stuffed
with Spinach and Cheese

Serves 4

Prep time: 10 minutes
Cook time: 1 hour
Total cost: $5.50
Calories: 249
Fat: 3g
Protein: 5g
Cholesterol: 1mg
Sodium: 422mg

4 baking potatoes

1 10-ounce package frozen chopped spinach, thawed, with excess water squeezed out

1 cup sour cream

Pinch nutmeg

1 cup white American cheese, grated

Sea salt and black pepper to taste

½ cup sharp Cheddar cheese, shredded

Stuffed potatoes are easy, filling, and taste great! Add crispy bacon crumbles and chopped chives for a truly delicious potato.

Preheat the oven to 350°F. Bake the potatoes for 40 minutes. Then cool the potatoes and split them in half lengthwise. Spoon out the insides of the potatoes, leaving skin intact. Place potato filling in a mixing bowl. Add the spinach to the potato filling. Stir in sour cream and nutmeg. Add the American cheese and season with salt and pepper. Restuff the potato skins and arrange cheddar cheese on top. Bake for another 20 minutes, and serve hot.

Quick and Easy Tip
When scooping out the potato, scoop out as much as possible but leave a slight potato edge along the skin. This helps keep the potato skin from breaking.

Omelet of Red Peppers and Gorgonzola

Serves 2

Prep time: 7 minutes

Cook time: 10 minutes

Total cost: $2.70

Calories: 325

Fat: 28g

Protein: 15g

Cholesterol: 471mg

Sodium: 480mg

2 teaspoons unsalted butter

4 eggs, well beaten

2 ounces gorgonzola cheese, crumbled

½ red bell pepper, seeded and chopped

Sea salt and black pepper to taste

Enjoy breakfast for dinner for a welcome change of pace. You'll be surprised; your family will probably love it!

Heat a 10-inch nonstick pan over medium-high heat. Melt the butter and swirl to coat pan. Add eggs and swirl pan to distribute evenly. Place cheese and bell pepper on one side of omelet. Season with salt and pepper as desired. Cook until just set, when the consistency is like custard. Carefully but quickly flip plain side of omelet over side with cheese and peppers. Cut in half and serve.

Quick and Easy Tip

For extra flavor, sauté half a yellow onion, chopped, with the red peppers for about 2 minutes in a tablespoon of olive oil. Or substitute other ingredients such as mushrooms, green beans, tomatoes, or fresh herbs.

The $7 a Meal Quick & Easy Cookbook

Asian Crepes with Snow Peas and Water Chestnuts

Serves 4

Prep time: 7 minutes
Cook time: 15 minutes
Total cost: $4.83
Calories: 223
Fat: 8g
Protein: 12g
Cholesterol: 125mg
Sodium: 263mg

4 eggs

2¼ cups milk

2 cups plain flour

Pinch sea salt

¼ cup (half a stick) melted butter, plus 2 to 3 tablespoons for cooking

¼ cup peanut oil

1 pound snow pea pods, ends trimmed slightly

½ fresh lemon, zested and juiced

1 8-ounce can sliced water chestnuts, drained

½ cup roasted, unsalted peanuts

2 tablespoons soy sauce

1 tablespoon fresh gingerroot, minced

Tabasco or other red pepper sauce as desired

Water chestnuts are actually an aquatic vegetable that grows in marshes and are native to China.

1. In a medium mixing bowl, whisk together eggs, milk, flour, butter, and salt. Mix to combine well, but don't overly mix. In nonstick skillet, add ½ to 1 tablespoon of the butter and heat over medium heat. Swirl pan to coat. Pour in ¼ cup of batter and swirl to cover pan. Cook for 1 to 1½ minutes, lifting edges with spatula. Crepe should easily slide out of pan. As crepes are cooked, transfer to plate to hold, stacking them is okay.
2. In a large saucepan or nonstick skillet, heat oil over medium-high heat. Add snow pea pods, lemon zest and juice, and stir to coat. Add water chestnuts and peanuts, and stir occasionally, cooking for 5 minutes. Add remaining ingredients, mix well and serve with crepes.
3. To wrap crepes, place crepe flat on plate, add ⅓ cup filling, fold crepe in half, then fold again.

Vegetarian Chili

Serves 6

Prep time: 3 minutes
Cook time: 20 minutes
Total cost: $5.88
Calories: 324
Fat: 11g
Protein: 24g
Cholesterol: 0mg
Sodium: 437mg

2 15-ounce cans spicy chili beans, undrained

1 14-ounce can diced tomatoes with green chilies, undrained

1 12-ounce jar tomato salsa

1 tablespoon chili powder

1 green bell pepper, chopped

1 cup water

As a chef you grow to love tasty, easy recipes like this one. Perfect for a Super Bowl party!

In heavy saucepan, combine all ingredients. Bring to a boil, then reduce heat and simmer for 15 to 20 minutes, stirring occasionally, until peppers are crisp-tender and mixture is heated and blended. Serve immediately, topped with sour cream, grated cheese, and chopped green onions, if desired.

Quick and Easy Tip
Use this chili on taco salad or baked potatoes!

Burritos with Black Beans, Broccoli, and Cauliflower

Serves 4

Prep time: 5 minutes
Cook time: 14 minutes
Total cost: $4.60
Calories: 175
Fat: 8g
Protein: 14g
Cholesterol: 1mg
Sodium: 421mg

2 tablespoons olive oil

1 yellow onion, chopped

½ teaspoon crushed red pepper flakes or hot sauce

2 cups frozen broccoli and cauliflower combo, thawed

1 15-ounce can black beans, drained

4 10-inch flour tortillas

1½ cups shredded pepper jack cheese

This is a healthy way to enjoy Mexican food. If you have some sour cream in your refrigerator, add a dollop.

1. In a large saucepan over medium heat, heat olive oil and add onion. Cook about 4 minutes, until tender. Sprinkle with red pepper flakes and stir together. Drain vegetables and add to onion mixture. Cook for about 4 minutes. Stir in black beans, cover, and let simmer for 4 minutes.
2. Meanwhile, warm tortillas by layering in microwave-safe paper towels and microwaving on high for 1 to 2 minutes. Spread tortillas on cutting board or other work surface and divide vegetable mixture among tortillas. Sprinkle with cheese, fold in sides, and roll up.

Quick and Easy Tip
Other great ingredients for this recipe are chopped green beans, corn, and red bell peppers. Add extra spice by adding chili powder or cayenne pepper.

Linguine with Brie and Tomatoes

Serves 4

Prep time: 5 minutes
Cook time: 15 minutes
Total cost: $6.20
Calories: 241
Fat: 10g
Protein: 5g
Cholesterol: 36mg
Sodium: 180mg

5 large tomatoes

¼ cup olive oil

1 12-ounce box linguine pasta

Pinch sea salt

¼ bunch fresh basil, chopped

1 6-ounce wedge Brie cheese

Soft cheeses include Brie, Camembert, and Reblochon. When you need to slice these cheeses, place them in the freezer for about 15 minutes. The cheese will harden and it will be easier to handle.

Cut tomatoes in half and squeeze out seeds. Coarsely chop tomatoes and combine in a large bowl with olive oil. Bring large pot of water to a boil and cook linguine pasta as directed on package. Meanwhile, add salt and basil to tomatoes and toss gently. Cut Brie into small cubes and add to tomatoes. Drain pasta and immediately add tomato mixture. Toss, using tongs, until mixed.

Quick and Easy Tip
Hothouse tomatoes are good for this recipe as are tomatoes from the vine, which tend to be the most flavorful.

The $7 a Meal Quick & Easy Cookbook

Salad of Jicama and Mango with Black Beans

Serves 4

- Prep time: 15 minutes
- Cook time: none
- Total cost: $6.89
- Calories: 102
- Fat: 1g
- Protein: 1g
- Cholesterol: 0mg
- Sodium: 3mg

1 cup peeled and diced jicama

⅓ cup mango, diced

½ cup canned black beans, drained and rinsed

½ cup diced red onion

⅓ cup mandarin oranges, drained

2 tablespoons fresh lime juice

2 tablespoons fresh orange juice

2 tablespoons fresh cilantro, chopped

Pinch sea salt and black pepper

Jicama is a Mexican vine, and the edible part is the root. It is high in fiber and up to 90 percent water.

1. Combine the jicama, mango, black beans, red onion, and mandarin oranges in a medium bowl and toss to mix.
2. Separately, mix together the lime juice, orange juice, cilantro, salt, and pepper in a bowl. Pour over jicama mixture and toss well. Let stand at room temperature for 10 minutes to allow flavors to blend.

Quick and Easy Tip
This is the perfect salad for a brunch. Make the day before and keep in the refrigerator until ready to serve.

Teriyaki Vegetables

Serves 4

Prep time: 5 minutes
Cook time: 18 minutes
Total cost: $5.32
Calories: 228
Fat: 1g
Protein: 9g
Cholesterol: 0mg
Sodium: 379mg

1 cup broccoli florets

1 cup sugar snap peas

½ cup sliced water chestnuts, drained

½ cup baby corn, drained

1 cup cauliflower, in chunks

1 cup shiitake mushrooms, sliced

⅓ cup low-sodium teriyaki sauce

If you prefer to use frozen vegetables instead of fresh, you may have to increase your cooking time about 5 minutes to allow for thawing.

1. Coat a skillet with nonstick spray. Add all ingredients, except teriyaki sauce, to skillet.
2. Cook vegetables for 15 minutes on medium high or until broccoli is tender. Pour teriyaki on veggies and simmer for 3 minutes.

Quick and Easy Tip
Did you know that shiitake mushrooms traditionally sprout off of logs? They're the most common type of mushroom used in Asian dishes, and they add a deep flavor and chewy texture. If you prefer an even more intense flavor from your mushrooms, buy your shiitake mushrooms dried instead of fresh.

The $7 a Meal Quick & Easy Cookbook

Baked Sweet Potato Fries

Serves 6

Prep time: 5 minutes
Cook time: 30 minutes
Total cost: $4.50
Calories: 136
Fat: 3g
Protein: 2g
Cholesterol: 0mg
Sodium: 14mg

2 pounds peeled sweet potatoes

2 teaspoons ground cinnamon

1 tablespoon olive oil

This recipe offers a nutritional step up from regular baked fries because the sweet potatoes are packed full of beta carotene. And they are a tasty alternative.

1. Preheat oven to 450°F. Cut potatoes into matchsticks, about ½-inch thick. Toss potatoes, cinnamon, and olive oil in a bowl.
2. Coat a large baking sheet with nonstick spray. Bake for 25 to 30 minutes or until potatoes are fairly crispy.

Quick and Easy Tip
These make a great snack food for kids!

Squash Casserole with Saltine Crust

Serves 6

Prep time: 5 minutes
Cook time: 45 minutes
Total cost: $6.42
Calories: 122
Fat: 3g
Protein: 11g
Cholesterol: 72mg
Sodium: 156mg

10 medium yellow squash, sliced

1 yellow onion, chopped

Salt and black pepper to taste

6 ounces shredded Cheddar cheese

2 eggs

10 saltine crackers, crushed

If you love this recipe but are looking for a change, try substituting zucchini for the yellow squash. These vegetables are traditionally interchangeable because of similar flavors and textures.

1. Coat a 9" x 13" baking dish with nonstick spray. Place squash and onion in dish. Sprinkle with salt and pepper and bake at 350°F for 15 minutes.
2. Drain water from veggies and stir in cheese. Beat eggs and mix into veggies. Stir in crackers until thick. Return dish to oven and bake at 325°F for 30 minutes.

PIZZA AND PASTA

Meatball Pizza

Serves 2

Prep time: 5 minutes
Cook time: 15 minutes
Total cost: $6.89
Calories: 678
Fat: 33g
Protein: 21g
Cholesterol: 41mg
Sodium: 1,670mg

2 6-inch prepared pizza crusts, such as Boboli

1 cup pizza sauce

½ teaspoon dried oregano leaves

½ teaspoon dry mustard

4 ounces frozen meatballs, thawed and cut in half

½ cup frozen onion and bell pepper stir-fry combo

1 cup shredded mozzarella

Boboli pizza crusts are delicious, convenient, and inexpensive. They're also great for kids' pizza parties!

Preheat oven to 400°F. Place pizza crust on work surface. In a small bowl, combine pizza sauce with oregano and dry mustard. Mix well. Spread over pizza crust. Cut meatballs in half and arrange, cut side down, on pizza sauce. Sprinkle onion and bell pepper on pizza and top with cheese. Place pizza directly on rack in center of oven. Bake for 15 minutes or until crust is golden brown and cheese has melted and begins to brown.

Quick and Easy Tip
Buying precooked frozen meatballs is the way to go for any meatball recipe unless you have lots of helping hands to roll them out. You can always add your own special touch to the sauce!

Three-Cheese Pizza

Serves 2

Prep time: 7 minutes
Cook time: 15 minutes
Total cost: $6.98
Calories: 410
Fat: 18g
Protein: 6g
Cholesterol: 94mg
Sodium: 824mg

1 cup pizza marinara sauce

2 6-inch prepared pizza crusts such as Boboli

1 cup shredded provolone cheese

1 cup shredded mozzarella cheese

1 cup pepper jack cheese

6 cloves fresh garlic, minced

1 tablespoon olive oil

The Italians in Napoli claim to be the originators of pizza. I don't know if they were the first ones to create pizza, but theirs sure taste delicious.

Preheat oven to 425°F. Ladle the sauce over the crust, spreading it out evenly over the surface. Top with the cheeses, and sprinkle with garlic. Drizzle with olive oil. Place directly in oven on center rack. Bake for 15 minutes, until cheese is melted and crust is cooked through.

Quick and Easy Tip
If you prefer to use fresh pizza dough, lots of stores now have pre-made, fresh, unbaked pizza dough, and it is not very expensive.

Pizza with Herbs and Black Olives

Serves 2

Prep time: 5 minutes
Cook time: 15 minutes
Total cost: $6.89
Calories: 320
Fat: 10g
Protein: 13g
Cholesterol: 25mg
Sodium: 670mg

2 6- to 8-inch prepared pizza crusts such as Boboli

½ cup tomato sauce

1 cup shredded mozzarella cheese

¼ cup grated Romano cheese

4 sprigs fresh basil, chopped

4 sprigs fresh oregano leaves, chopped

¼ cup chopped black olives

Black pepper to taste

1 tablespoon olive oil

Boboli pizza crusts come in small and large sizes. Use the small ones for pizza parties so everyone can make their own individual pizzas! It's easy, fun, and easy on cleanup, which is the best part of all.

Preheat oven to 425°F. Place crust on work surface. Ladle sauce over the crust, spreading out evenly over entire surface. Top with cheese, herbs, olives, and pepper. Drizzle with oil and place in center of oven directly on rack. Bake about 15 minutes or until crust is cooked through.

Quick and Easy Tip
If you are planning a pizza party, purchase your ingredients a day or two ahead of time and prep the day before.

The $7 a Meal Quick & Easy Cookbook

BBQ Chicken Pizza

Serves 2

Prep time: 5 minutes
Cook time: 15 minutes
Total cost: $6.99
Calories: 458
Fat: 11g
Protein: 24g
Cholesterol: 85mg
Sodium: 600mg

2 6- to 8-inch Boboli pizza
  crusts

1 tablespoon olive oil

1 cup cooked boneless,
  skinless chicken breasts,
  chopped into 1-inch chunks

1 cup barbeque sauce

1 cup mozzarella cheese

Preheat oven to 425°F. Place pizza dough on work surface. Brush crust with olive oil. In a mixing bowl, toss chicken with barbeque sauce to coat. Spread chicken on pizza crust and top with cheese. Bake directly on rack in center of oven for 15 minutes or until crust is crispy and golden.

Hawaiian-Style Pizza with Pineapple

Serves 2

Prep time: 5 minutes
Cook time: 15 minutes
Total cost: $6.97
Calories: 375
Fat: 19g
Protein: 32g
Cholesterol: 126mg
Sodium: 563mg

2 6- to 8-inch Boboli pizza
  crusts

1 tablespoon olive oil

1½ cups thick deli ham, chopped

1½ cups canned, chopped
  pineapple, drained

1½ cups mozzarella cheese

This is a great recipe to add basil or thyme. Be sure to use fresh herbs for this recipe, however, as the dried herbs would taste a little bitter.

Preheat oven to 425°F. Place pizza crust on work surface. Brush with olive oil. Top with ham, pineapple, and cheese. Bake directly on rack in oven for about 15 minutes or until crust is golden and crispy.

Pizza with Roasted Red Peppers

Serves 2

Prep time: 5 minutes
Cook time: 15 minutes
Total cost: $6.68
Calories: 310
Fat: 10g
Protein: 8g
Cholesterol: 59mg
Sodium: 641mg

2 6- to 8-inch Boboli pizza crusts

2 tablespoons olive oil

1 jar roasted red bell peppers, drained and chopped

1 bunch fresh basil, chopped

Sea salt and black pepper to taste

1½ cups shredded mozzarella

Add chopped or sliced fresh or canned mushrooms to this pizza for extra flavor and color. If you use canned mushrooms, make sure they are well drained.

Preheat oven to 425°F. Place pizza crust on work surface. Brush with 1 tablespoon olive oil. In a mixing bowl, toss peppers with basil and season with salt and pepper as desired. Spread onto pizza. Top with cheese and drizzle with remaining olive oil. Place in oven directly on center rack. Bake for 15 minutes or until pizza is crisp and golden.

Spinach Mushroom Pizza

Serves 2

Prep time: 5 minutes
Cook time: 15 minutes
Total cost: $6.98
Calories: 321
Fat: 9g
Protein: 6g
Cholesterol: 72mg
Sodium: 689mg

2 6- to 8-inch Boboli pizza
    crusts

2 tablespoons olive oil

1 cup frozen spinach, thawed
    and well drained

1 cup canned sliced
    mushrooms, well drained

1 cup shredded mozzarella

Add black olives, tomatoes, feta cheese, or even goat cheese for extra delicious flavor without a lot of work!

Preheat oven to 425°F. Place pizza crust on work surface. Brush with 1 tablespoon olive oil. Top pizza with spinach, mushrooms, and cheese. Drizzle with remaining olive oil. Place directly on rack in center of oven. Bake for 15 minutes or until done.

Pizza Margherita

Serves 2

Prep time: 5 minutes
Cook time: 15 minutes
Total cost: $6.69
Calories: 306
Fat: 18g
Protein: 6g
Cholesterol: 64mg
Sodium: 499mg

2 6- to 8-inch Boboli pizza crusts

1 tablespoon olive oil

½ cup shredded mozzarella

1 bunch basil, chopped

3 Roma tomatoes, sliced

Sea salt and black pepper to taste

Feel free to add cooked sausage for tons of flavor and protein!

Preheat oven to 425°F. Place pizza crust on work surface. Brush with olive oil. Top with cheese, basil, and tomatoes. Season with salt and pepper as desired. Bake in center rack of oven directly on rack for 15 minutes or until crust is cooked through.

BBQ Chicken Pizza on Pita

Serves 2

Prep time: 3 minutes

Cook time: 6 to 8 mins.

Total cost: $4.00

Calories: 187

Fat: 11g

Protein: 14g

Cholesterol: 75mg

Sodium: 301mg

1 cup cooked chicken breast, boneless, skinless, chopped

2 tablespoons sweet barbecue sauce

1 large whole-wheat pita

¼ cup shredded mozzarella cheese

Sea salt and pepper to taste

Making pizzas using pita bread is a great way to cut down on costs, calories, and fat without sacrificing flavor.

Preheat oven to 350°F. In a bowl, mix together chicken and barbeque sauce. Top pita with chicken mixture, mozzarella, salt, and pepper. Place on parchment-lined baking sheet and cook in oven for 6 to 8 minutes or until cheese has melted.

Quick and Easy Tip
Use whole-wheat or regular pita, depending upon your taste.

English Muffin Pizza

Serves 1

Prep time: 2 minutes

Cook time: 20 to 30 secs.

Total cost: $1.27

Calories: 138

Fat: 2g

Protein: 12g

Cholesterol: 9mg

Sodium: 450mg

1 whole-wheat or regular
English muffin, split

2 tablespoons marinara sauce

2 tablespoons shredded
mozzarella cheese

This is the perfect breakfast or lunch for someone looking for lots of flavor on little effort. It's so simple, little kids can make it.

Toast English muffin halves in toaster. Top each muffin half with 1 tablespoon marina topped with 1 tablespoon mozzarella. Cook in microwave for 20 to 30 seconds or until cheese has melted.

Quick and Easy Tip
If you are not a huge English muffin fan, substitute a plain bagel.

Pita Pizza with Buffalo Chicken Wings

Serves 2

Prep time: 5 minutes

Cook time: 6 to 8 mins.

Total cost: $3.02

Calories: 170

Fat: 2g

Protein: 17g

Cholesterol: 59mg

Sodium: 471mg

1 large whole-wheat pita

2 tablespoons Crystal Wing Sauce

1 cup cooked, boneless chicken wings (available in the freezer section)

1 ounce shredded mozzarella cheese

The combination of crispy chicken, wing sauce, and cheese makes for a wildly flavorful and textured pizza. Make it for football parties!

Preheat oven to 350°F. Top pita with sauce, chicken, and mozzarella in that order. Place on parchment-lined baking sheet and place in oven. Bake for 6 to 8 minutes or until cheese has melted.

Quick and Easy Tip
Substitute your favorite wing sauce, if you like. And in true Buffalo wing fashion, serve with celery and blue cheese dressing.

The $7 a Meal Quick & Easy Cookbook

Pita Pizza with Eggplant and Gorgonzola

Serves 2

Prep time: 5 minutes
Cook time: 6 to 8 mins.
Total cost: $5.78
Calories: 138
Fat: 4g
Protein: 8g
Cholesterol: 28mg
Sodium: 429mg

1 large whole-wheat pita

2 tablespoons marinara sauce

¼ cup eggplant, peeled and diced

1 tablespoon sun-dried tomatoes, chopped

2 tablespoons shredded mozzarella cheese

1 tablespoon Gorgonzola cheese

The combination of eggplant and tomatoes is a lycopene dream. Lycopene is great for both your heart and your vision.

Preheat oven to 350°F. Top pita with marinara, eggplant, tomatoes, mozzarella, and Gorgonzola. Place on parchment-lined baking sheet and bake for 6 to 8 minutes or until cheese has melted.

Quick and Easy Tip
Pita bread is also good sliced into triangles and baked until crispy. Mix all these ingredients together, except for pita, and serve as an eggplant salsa with pita crisps.

Pita Pizza with Spinach and Feta

Serves 2

Prep time: 5 minutes
Cook time: 6 to 8 mins.
Total cost: $4.24
Calories: 118
Fat: 2g
Protein: 8g
Cholesterol: 26mg
Sodium: 313mg

1 large whole-wheat or plain pita

3 tablespoons shredded mozzarella cheese

1 tablespoon feta cheese

½ cup fresh spinach, chopped

2 tablespoons Roma tomatoes, chopped

½ teaspoon fresh garlic, minced

Just like it did for Popeye, spinach will make you strong. It's full of iron, vitamin A, and fiber, which is helpful in blood cell production and brain cell development.

Preheat oven to 350°F. Top pita with mozzarella, feta, spinach, tomatoes, and garlic. Place on parchment-lined baking sheet and cook for 6 to 8 minutes or until cheese has melted.

Quick and Easy
The often-used feta and spinach combination is popular in Greek cuisine. Add mushrooms, peppers, and your favorite cheese as an alternative to this tasty, healthy dish.

Ricotta Cheese Pita Pizza

Serves 2

Prep time: 5 minutes
Cook time: 6 to 8 mins.
Total cost: $4.16
Calories: 110
Fat: 1g
Protein: 8g
Cholesterol: 35mg
Sodium: 257mg

1 large whole-wheat or plain pita

2 tablespoons shredded mozzarella cheese

2 tablespoons ricotta cheese

2 tablespoons Roma tomatoes, sliced

½ teaspoon fresh garlic, minced

Ricotta cheese is an Italian sheep milk or cow milk cheese and is generally lower in fat than other cheeses. Ricotta means "recooked" as it is produced from the whey (the liquid that separates from the cheese) when in production.

Preheat oven to 350°F. Top pita with mozzarella, ricotta, tomatoes, and garlic. Place pita on parchment-lined baking sheet. Place in oven and bake for 6 to 8 minutes or until cheese has melted.

Quick and Easy
Add fresh basil to this for a truly Italian meal.

Pita Pizza with Thanksgiving Turkey and Sweet Potatoes

Serves 2

Prep time: 5 minutes

Cook time: 5 to 6 mins.

Total cost: $2.10

Calories: 205

Fat: 3g

Protein: 12g

Cholesterol: 24mg

Sodium: 223mg

1 whole-wheat or plain pita

¼ cup leftover sweet potatoes or leftover sweet potato casserole

2 ounces leftover oven-roasted turkey breast, cut in small chunks

1 tablespoon leftover turkey gravy

Sea salt and black pepper as needed

Tired of turkey sandwiches? This is a delicious alternative to holiday leftovers.

Preheat oven to 350°F. Top pita with sweet potatoes, turkey, and top with gravy. Season with salt and pepper, if desired. Transfer to a parchment-lined baking sheet and bake until heated through, about 5 minutes.

Quick and Easy Tip
This proves that pizzas can be made with just about everything. Create your own at home using whatever leftovers are in your refrigerator!

Pita Pizza with Grilled Vegetables

Serves 6

Prep time: 8 minutes
Cook time: 13 minutes
Total cost: $6.78
Calories: 117
Fat: 1g
Protein: 8g
Cholesterol: 15mg
Sodium: 347mg

1 tablespoon olive oil

1 yellow onion, diced

1 red bell pepper, seeded and diced

½ cup broccoli florets, chopped

2 tomatoes, seeded and diced

Sea salt and black pepper as needed

6 large whole-wheat pitas

6 tablespoons marinara sauce

½ cup shredded mozzarella cheese

1 tablespoon fresh basil, chopped

Grilled vegetables are great on anything. If you don't have any leftover grilled vegetables on hand, buy fresh or use some frozen vegetables from your freezer.

1. In a large sauté pan over medium heat, add olive oil and heat until warmed, about 15 seconds. Add onion, bell pepper, broccoli, and tomatoes, and season with salt and pepper as desired. Cook until tender, about 5 minutes.
2. Place pita on parchment-lined baking sheet. Top pita with marinara, mozzarella, basil, and vegetables. Place in oven and bake for 6 to 8 minutes or until cheese has melted.

Quick and Easy Tip
This is the perfect recipe for any leftover grilled vegetables from a summer cookout or another recipe you made earlier in the week.

Rotini Pasta with Red Bell Peppers, Peas, and Green Onions

Serves 8

Prep time: 15 minutes
Chill: 2 hours
Total cost: $6.35
Calories: 199
Fat: 6g
Protein: 6g
Cholesterol: 22mg
Sodium: 349mg

1 cup plain nonfat yogurt

½ cup low-fat mayonnaise

½ cup grated Parmesan cheese

1 tablespoon fresh basil, or dill leaves, chopped

2 cloves garlic, chopped

Sea salt and black pepper to taste

2 red bell peppers, seeded and chopped

1 cup blanched peas

½ cup chopped green onions

1 pound rotini pasta, cooked and drained

Pasta salad is great for parties. It is inexpensive, filling, and goes a long way when it comes to serving.

In a large bowl, blend yogurt, mayonnaise, Parmesan cheese, basil or dill, garlic, salt, and pepper. Add the bell peppers, peas, and green onions, and mix well. Add pasta and toss to coat. Cover and refrigerate for 2 hours.

Quick and Easy Tip

Keep cooked pasta on hand in the refrigerator for super quick and easy meals. After pasta is cooked and drained, drizzle with 1 teaspoon of olive oil and toss to coat, then refrigerate. The oil helps keep pasta from sticking together.

The $7 a Meal Quick & Easy Cookbook

Tortellini Pasta with Salmon

Serves 8

Prep time: 10 minutes

Chill: 2 to 4 hours

Total cost: $6.97

Calories: 283

Fat: 6g

Protein: 20g

Cholesterol: 53mg

Sodium: 410mg

1 8-ounce package frozen or fresh cheese tortellini

1 zucchini, sliced

1 red bell pepper, cut into narrow strips (julienned)

1 6.5-ounce cans salmon, drained and flaked

½ cup plain yogurt

¼ cup Parmesan cheese, grated

¼ cup fresh Italian parsley, chopped

1 teaspoon dried oregano, crumbled

When it comes to fresh or frozen, pasta is one of those food products that freezes well. Use whichever is the most cost effective for your budget.

1. Cook tortellini as directed on package. Drain well. In a medium bowl, toss together pasta, zucchini, and bell pepper. Add salmon and mix to combine.
2. In a small bowl, stir together yogurt, cheese, parsley, and oregano. Mix well. Add to pasta mixture and toss gently to coat. Cover and refrigerate for several hours before serving so dairy ingredients thicken.

Quick and Easy Tip
Using canned salmon is a cost-effective and time-saving way to enjoy this healthy fish.

Pasta with Mushrooms and Crispy Bacon

Serves 8

Prep time: 8 minutes
Cook time: 23 minutes
Total cost: $5.23
Calories: 125
Fat: 8g
Protein: 6g
Cholesterol: 8mg
Sodium: 366mg

2 tablespoons olive oil, plus a drizzle for pasta

2 slices bacon, chopped

½ yellow onion, chopped

2 cups fresh cremini or button mushrooms, sliced

1½ cups frozen peas

1 teaspoon unsalted butter

2 cups chicken broth

Sea salt and black pepper to taste, plus 1 tablespoon salt for pasta water

1 pound pasta shells or penne pasta

½ cup Parmesan cheese, grated

If your budget allows, substitute the bacon for more traditional Italian prosciutto. Dice the prosciutto as you would the bacon; however, the cooking time for the prosciutto will be less because prosciutto is traditionally sliced thinner than bacon.

1. In a large skillet or saucepan, heat oil over medium heat. Add bacon and onion and cook until bacon is crisp and onion is tender. Add mushrooms and cook until the moisture has almost all evaporated, about 5 minutes. Add peas, butter, and broth. Simmer until liquid is reduced by half, about 10 minutes. Season with salt and pepper to taste.
2. Meanwhile, in a large pot, bring at least 4 quarts of water to a rolling boil. Add 1 tablespoon salt and a drizzle of olive oil. Add the pasta, stir to separate, and cook until not quite al dente, about 8 minutes or so. Drain. Transfer pasta to skillet and combine with the hot sauce. Cook briefly to heat through. Transfer all to large bowl and toss with the Parmesan.

Penne Pasta with Garlic and Tomatoes

Serves 8

Prep time: 8 minutes
Cook time: 18 minutes
Total cost: $6.32
Calories: 382
Fat: 25g
Protein: 12g
Cholesterol: 20mg
Sodium: 266mg

2 tablespoons olive oil, plus a drizzle for cooking pasta

6 cloves garlic, chopped

3 cups chicken broth

6 Roma tomatoes, chopped

¼ bunch fresh Italian parsley, chopped

8 scallions, white part and half the green tops, chopped

Sea salt and black pepper to taste, plus 1 tablespoon salt for pasta water

¼ cup unsalted butter, softened

1 pound penne pasta

As a delicious alternative, add cooked, chopped chicken breasts.

1. In a large saucepan over medium heat, heat olive oil and add garlic, sauté until golden. Add chicken broth, tomatoes, parsley, and scallions. Add salt and pepper as desired. Bring to a boil and reduce over medium-high heat, about 5 to 8 minutes. Whisk in butter, a little at a time, to thicken sauce. Remove from heat and keep warm.
2. Meanwhile, in a large pot filled ¾ with water, bring water to a boil. Add 1 tablespoon of salt and a drizzle of oil. Add pasta and stir to prevent sticking. Cook until al dente, about 8 to 10 minutes. Drain. Transfer pasta to serving bowl and toss with sauce.

Frittata of Fettuccini, Tomatoes, and Basil

Serves 8

Prep time: 8 minutes
Cook time: 15 minutes
Total cost: $6.80
Calories: 187
Fat: 5g
Protein: 5g
Cholesterol: 73mg
Sodium: 650mg

1 tomato, diced

½ pound package egg
  fettuccini noodles

3 tablespoons prepared pesto

3 eggs, lightly beaten

¼ cup milk

1 tablespoon fresh basil,
  leaves chopped

½ cup Parmesan cheese, grated

This unique twist on a traditional frittata is delicious and filling. Substitute your favorite ingredients or, even better, whatever you have leftover in your refrigerator.

1. Bring large pot of water to boiling, add the tomatoes and noodles. Cook until al dente, about 8 to 10 minutes. Drain well. Return to the pot. Add the pesto and toss until pasta is well coated.
2. In a small bowl, beat together the eggs and milk until blended. Pour over the noodle mixture. Cook over medium heat, gently turning with a spatula until the eggs are thickened and cooked. Serve with fresh basil and cheese.

Quick and Easy Tip
Once the pasta is cooked, you can also cook this in a large skillet by adding the eggs and tossing the mixture once to distribute the eggs. Then place skillet in a 400°F oven for 5 to 8 minutes, until eggs are cooked. Remove from oven and slice like a pie, and top with basil and cheese.

CHAPTER 13

VEGETABLES AND SIDE DISHES

Grilled Garlic Bread

Serves 6

Prep time: 5 minutes
Cook time: 10 minutes
Total cost: $6.00
Calories: 172
Fat: 6g
Protein: 3g
Cholesterol: 22mg
Sodium: 400mg

½ cup extra virgin olive oil

4 cloves garlic, crushed and minced

Pinch onion salt

3 tablespoons butter, melted

1 teaspoon fresh Italian parsley, chopped

1 loaf French bread

Garlic bread is the best and customary accompaniment to most Italian dishes. Just be sure to serve fresh parsley with it for those who have intense garlic breath.

Preheat grill or grill pan. Combine all ingredients, except bread, in a mixing bowl, stirring well. Using a pastry brush, brush butter mixture on both sides of bread slices. Wrap entire loaf in aluminum foil and put on the grill or grill pan. Turn after 5 minutes and heat for another 5 minutes.

Quick and Easy Tip
The secret to great garlic bread is mixing all the ingredients together with melted or super softened butter. That way, all the flavors meld together and coat the bread evenly.

Asian Slaw

Serves 6

Prep time: 15 minutes
Chill: 1 hour
Total cost: $5.70
Calories: 103
Fat: 7g
Protein: 1g
Cholesterol: 22mg
Sodium: 170mg

1 head Chinese cabbage, shredded

½ 8.25-ounce can crushed pineapple, drained

1 8-ounce can sliced water chestnuts

1 large bunch fresh Italian parsley, chopped

¼ cup green onions, chopped

¼ cup mayonnaise

1 tablespoon prepared mustard

1 teaspoon fresh gingerroot, minced

Chinese cabbage is also called snow cabbage. It is lighter in texture than American cabbage and has a sweeter flavor.

Combine cabbage, pineapple, water chestnuts, parsley, and onion. Cover and chill. For the dressing, combine mayonnaise, mustard, and gingerroot. Cover and chill separately. When ready to serve, pour dressing over cabbage and toss to coat.

Quick and Easy Tip
Chinese cabbage is great for salads and for stir-frying with other vegetables. Treat as you would American cabbage or other leafy vegetable.

Guacamole

Serves 6

Prep time: 8 minutes
Cook time: none
Total cost: $6.36
Calories: 153
Fat: 13g
Protein: 2g
Cholesterol: 14mg
Sodium: 358mg

2 ripe avocados, peeled and lightly mashed

1 medium, small, ripe or canned tomato, diced

1 small onion, chopped

½ teaspoon finely chopped jalapeños

2 tablespoons lemon or lime juice

1 teaspoon fresh cilantro, chopped

Sea salt and black pepper to taste

¼ cup salsa

Fresh avocados are delicious and good for you! This simple recipe is perfect for parties or for your own family Mexican fiesta.

In a medium mixing bowl, combine all ingredients. Mix well, keeping the guacamole lumpy.

Quick and Easy Tip
The acid in the lemon juice is what keeps the guacamole from turning brown. If you have both lemons and limes, use 1 table-spoon of each!

Long-Grain Rice with Fresh Thyme

Serves 6

Prep time: 5 minutes
Cook time: 25 minutes
Total cost: $6.84
Calories: 192
Fat: 2g
Protein: 4g
Cholesterol: 1mg
Sodium: 13mg

1 tablespoon olive oil

1 yellow onion, chopped

2 ribs celery, chopped

1 clove garlic, minced

1 tablespoon fresh thyme, stems removed, leaves chopped

1 bay leaf

2½ cups water

1 cup uncooked long-grain rice

My nickname for thyme is tedious thyme because it takes a lot of time to remove the leaves! This recipe requires only a small amount of fresh thyme, thankfully. For those that require more thyme, have your family help you remove the leaves.

In a large saucepan over medium heat, heat oil until warm. Add onion, celery, garlic, and thyme. Sauté for 5 minutes until tender. Add bay leaf and water. Bring to a boil and add the rice. Cover and simmer for 20 minutes or until all the water is absorbed and the rice is tender. Remove the bay leaf and serve.

Quick and Easy Tip

Thyme is one of my favorite herbs and I use it in almost everything I make. I combine it with fresh rosemary on most occasions. Both thyme and rosemary will last up to 3 weeks in your refrigerator. Just keep them wrapped loosely with a damp paper towel.

Steamed Asparagus and Carrots with Lemon

Serves 6

Prep time: 2 minutes
Cook time: 20 minutes
Total cost: $6.78
Calories: 74
Fat: 0g
Protein: 4g
Cholesterol: 0mg
Sodium: 194mg

½ pound baby carrots, rinsed

1 8-ounce package frozen asparagus spears

2 tablespoons lemon juice

1 teaspoon lemon pepper

Pinch sea salt (optional)

Steaming is a great way to cook vegetables as it brings out their color and maintains their nutrients. Plus, it's easy on clean up, which is perhaps the best thing of all!

1. Place carrots in a steamer basket above boiling water. Cover and steam about 15 minutes or till crisp tender. Rinse the carrots in cold water; drain.
2. Meanwhile, cook the frozen asparagus spears according to package directions. Rinse the asparagus in cold water; drain. Place both carrots and asparagus in serving bowl and drizzle with lemon juice and pepper; add salt if desired. Cover and chill until ready to serve.

Quick and Easy Tip
The perfect make-ahead recipe for any dinner occasion. Add a teaspoon of fresh thyme if you have some on hand.

Three-Bean Salad

Serves 8

Prep time: 5 minutes
Cook time: 10 minutes
Total cost: $4.56
Calories: 118
Fat: 7g
Protein: 2g
Cholesterol: 0mg
Sodium: 95mg

1 16-ounce can green beans, drained

1 16-ounce can yellow beans, drained

1 16-ounce can kidney beans, drained

1 yellow onion, chopped

½ cup olive oil

½ cup apple cider vinegar

½ cup sugar

Sea salt and black pepper to taste

Three-bean salad is a popular catering item for lunch buffets. It's easy, quick, tastes great, and appeals to a large number of people. If you are having out-of-town guests, serve this!

1. In a medium boiler, bring 2 cups of water to boiling and add green beans and wax beans and cook for 8 minutes. Drain and transfer to mixing bowl or serving bowl. Add the kidney beans and onions and toss to mix.
2. In a small mixing bowl, combine oil, vinegar, sugar, salt, and pepper. Whisk together well. Pour vinegar mixture over beans and toss. Refrigerate until ready to serve.

Quick and Easy Tip
The fresh beans are the perfect complement to the canned beans. Make this recipe and serve with potato salad and grilled chicken for a spring picnic.

Oven-Roasted Potatoes

Serves 4

Prep time: 2 minutes
Cook time: 20 minutes
Total cost: $4.56
Calories: 205
Fat: 5g
Protein: 3g
Cholesterol: 15mg
Sodium: 28mg

4 large potatoes (about 2 pounds), quartered and then cut in half again, skin on

2 tablespoons butter, melted

Seasoned salt such as McCormicks Steak Seasoning or other salt seasoning

There are lots of ways to prepare potatoes. Even though I am known as The Bikini Chef for my figure-flattering flavors, one dish I love is pan-fried potatoes. Prepare parboiled potatoes (see Quick and Easy Tip), but then pan-fry in ¼ inch of hot (but not smoking) canola oil for about 5 minutes.

Preheat oven to 400°F. Place potatoes on parchment-lined baking sheet and coat with butter and salt seasoning. Toss well to coat. Place in oven and bake for 20 minutes or until fork tender and nicely browned.

Quick and Easy Tip
To ensure tender potatoes when baked, parboil for 10 minutes in a large-quart boiler filled ¾ with water. Drain potatoes, then toss potatoes as directed above and bake for 10 minutes.

The $7 a Meal Quick & Easy Cookbook

Polenta with Parmesan Cheese

Serves 6

Prep time: 10 minutes
Cook time: 10 minutes
Total cost: $6.72
Calories: 156
Fat: 2g
Protein: 4g
Cholesterol: 5mg
Sodium: 222mg

¼ cup olive oil

Sea salt and black pepper to taste

2 cups finely ground cornmeal

½ stick (4 tablespoons) unsalted butter, room temperature

½ cup Parmesan cheese, grated

Here's a recipe from Beccofino Ristorante & Wine Bar, a restaurant I worked at in Florence, Italy. We made polenta as described here and added whole garlic cloves and fresh basil. The polenta was then spread into a baking sheet and baked in the oven for about 15 minutes, making the polenta more like a dense cake. The polenta was sliced into 2- or 3-inch squares and topped with sun-dried tomato pesto.

Bring 8½ cups water to a boil in a large heavy boiler. Add olive oil, salt, and pepper. Slowly add cornmeal (polenta) and stir continuously. After all cornmeal has been added, cook and stir over low heat until polenta pulls away from sides of boiler. This should only take a few minutes as the water is absorbed quickly. Polenta should be thick, smooth, and creamy. Stir in butter and cheese.

Quick and Easy Tip
Other cheeses can be used depending upon your preference. Some tasty alternatives are Cheddar, provolone, or any smoked cheese. Also, for a creamier polenta, add ½ cup milk to the water.

Rice with Salsa and Black Beans

Serves 6

Prep time: 12 minutes
Cook time: 20 minutes
Total cost: $5.60
Calories: 204
Fat: 5g
Protein: 12g
Cholesterol: 3mg
Sodium: 466mg

1 tablespoon olive oil

½ yellow onion, diced

2 cloves garlic, minced

1 strip bacon, chopped

2 16-ounce cans black beans, undrained

½ cup picante salsa

Sea salt and black pepper to taste

4 cups cooked long-grain white rice

Rice is a good base as a side dish as you can enjoy it as is with olive oil or butter, or add fresh herbs, asparagus, green beans, red bell peppers, mushrooms, or your favorite ingredients.

In a large saucepan over medium heat, heat oil and add onions. Sauté (cook) until tender, about 5 minutes. Add garlic and bacon and cook until bacon is cooked but not crisp, about 3 minutes. Stir in the beans and salsa. Mix well and simmer about 10 minutes. Cover, stirring occasionally. Add salt and pepper to taste. Serve over rice in a bowl.

Quick and Easy Tip
Add some fresh cilantro for extra flavor and color.

Italian Risi e Bisi with Parmesan

Serves 6

Prep time: 5 minutes
Cook time: 25 minutes
Total cost: $5.75
Calories: 192
Fat: 2g
Protein: 4g
Cholesterol: 2mg
Sodium: 341mg

2 tablespoons olive oil

1 onion, finely chopped

1½ cups long-grain white rice

2 10-ounce cans chicken broth

½ cup water

1 cup frozen peas

½ cup Parmesan cheese, grated

Risi e bisi, or rice and peas, is a popular Italian dish. Stick to the simplicity of this dish rather than adding ingredients and trying to change it.

1. In heavy saucepan, heat olive oil over medium heat. Add onion; cook and stir until onion is tender, about 5 minutes. Add rice; stir to combine and cook about 2 minutes. Add chicken broth and water and bring to a boil. Cover pan, reduce heat, and simmer for an additional 15 minutes, until rice is almost tender.
2. Add peas, cover, and cook over medium-low heat until peas are hot and rice is tender, about 3 to 4 minutes. Stir in cheese and serve.

Sautéed Green Beans and Red Bell Peppers

Serves 6

Prep time: 6 minutes
Cook time: 9 to 10 mins.
Total cost: $4.18
Calories: 59
Fat: 4g
Protein: 4g
Cholesterol: 1mg
Sodium: 18mg

2 tablespoons olive oil

1 onion, finely chopped

3 cups frozen green beans

1 red bell pepper, seeded and cut into strips

Juice of ½ lemon

Sea salt and black pepper to taste

1 teaspoon fresh thyme leaves, stems removed, leaves chopped

Nutritionists teach that a colorful plate is a healthy plate, and this recipe helps prove that theory. Enjoy good nutrition and color with this easy-to-follow recipe.

In heavy saucepan, heat oil over medium heat. Add onion and cook until onion is tender, about 5 minutes, stirring occasionally. Add green beans and sauté for about 1 minute. Add bell pepper, lemon juice, salt, pepper, and thyme leaves. Stir occasionally while cooking about 3 minutes, or until peppers are tender and beans are heated through.

Quick and Easy Tip
Use fresh or frozen vegetables to make this simple yet flavorful dish.

Acorn Squash with Tarragon

Serves 4

Prep time: 5 minutes
Cook time: 20 minutes
Total cost: $4.08
Calories: 102
Fat: 1g
Protein: 2g
Cholesterol: 24mg
Sodium: 35mg

1 acorn squash

2 tablespoons water

2 tablespoons butter, unsalted

2 tablespoons brown sugar

1 tablespoon honey

½ teaspoon dried tarragon leaves

Sea salt and white pepper to taste

A very hard squash, acorn squash requires quite a bit of baking time to soften. Bake ahead and reheat for serving the next day.

1. Cut squash in half lengthwise, then cut in half again crosswise. Remove seeds and fibers from center. Place the squash halves, cut side down, on work surface and cut crosswise into 1-inch pieces. Place skin side down, in microwave safe dish. Sprinkle with 2 tablespoons water. Cover with plastic wrap, vent one corner, and microwave on high for 12 to 15 minutes, until flesh is tender when tested with fork. Uncover and drain. Set aside to reheat.
2. Separately, in a small boiler, combine remaining ingredients and heat over medium heat, stirring until smooth. Keep warm over low heat. To serve, place acorn squash on a plate and pour sauce over.

Quick and Easy Tip
Acorn squash is a winter squash that has a hard rind that is only edible after cooking.

Couscous with Herbs

Serves 6

Prep time: 3 minutes
Cook time: 15 minutes
Total cost: $5.75
Calories: 244
Fat: 6g
Protein: 8g
Cholesterol: 1mg
Sodium: 376mg

2 tablespoons olive oil

1 yellow onion, finely chopped

2 cups chicken broth

½ teaspoon dried oregano leaves

½ teaspoon dried marjoram leaves

1 cup couscous

If you end up with soggy couscous, don't worry; you can salvage it. Spread it out on parchment-lined baking sheets and dry it out in a 375°F oven for 10 minutes. Couscous is all about the balance of grain versus moisture. If you have too much moisture, just dry it out.

In a large saucepan, heat oil over medium heat. Add onion and cook until tender, about 5 minutes. Add chicken broth and herbs and bring to a boil. Stir in couscous, cover pan, and remove from heat. Let stand for 5 to 10 minutes, until liquid is absorbed. Fluff couscous with fork and serve.

Quick and Easy Tip
Couscous is actually not a grain. It is ground semolina pasta that is usually precooked. Because the ground pasta is precooked, it absorbs hot liquid extra fast making for super-fast cooking when combined with other ingredients.

Sautéed Green Beans
with Garlic

Serves 6

Prep time: 5 minutes
Cook time: 13 minutes
Total cost: $4.68
Calories: 92
Fat: 8g
Protein: 4g
Cholesterol: 8mg
Sodium: 21mg

4 cups water

1 pound green beans, ends trimmed, beans washed and dried

1 tablespoon olive oil

1 tablespoon butter

6 cloves garlic, chopped

1 shallot, chopped

Sea salt and pepper to taste

Garlic is good for your immune system but not for your breath. If you find yourself consuming lots of fresh garlic, make sure you have equal amounts of fresh parsley around to freshen your breath.

1. In a large saucepan over medium-high heat, add water and bring to a boil. Add green beans and lower heat to simmer. Simmer for 7 minutes, until beans are tender but still crisp.
2. Meanwhile, in a separate saucepan, combine oil, butter, garlic, and shallots. Heat over medium-high heat and cook until fragrant, about 2 minutes. Drain beans well and add to garlic mixture. Season with salt and pepper. Cook an additional 4 minutes. Serve.

Quick and Easy Tip
Use these same instructions for cooking asparagus and broccoli.

Sautéed Sugar Snap Peas

Serves 6

Prep time: 5 minutes
Cook time: 8 minutes
Total cost: $4.24
Calories: 56
Fat: 4g
Protein: 2g
Cholesterol: 0mg
Sodium: 8mg

3 cups sugar snap peas

2 tablespoons olive oil

½ teaspoon dried marjoram
  leaves

½ teaspoon garlic salt

½ teaspoon black pepper

Sugar snap peas are very sweet peas that are completely edible, pod included. Look for bright green peas with no dark or light spots, and select the pods that are plump and crisp. Pay attention not to cook them too long; 2 minutes in boiling water is plenty of time!

Preheat oven to 425°F. Place peas (in pods) on parchment-lined baking sheet. Sprinkle with remaining ingredients. Mix together with your hands until peas are well coated. Place in oven and roast for 6 minutes, until peas begin to brown a little and are tender but crisp.

Quick and Easy Tip
Use these delicious, naturally sweet peas in any stir-fry recipe, Asian or non-Asian.

Broccoli with Sesame Seeds

Serves 5

Prep time: 2 minutes
Cook time: 15 minutes
Total cost: $3.98
Calories: 30
Fat: 5g
Protein: 2g
Cholesterol: 3mg
Sodium: 8mg

4 cups water

1 head broccoli, stems chopped, florets only

2 tablespoons olive oil

1 tablespoon butter

1 yellow onion, chopped

3 cloves garlic, chopped

2 tablespoons toasted sesame seeds

Bring out the color by boiling the broccoli in water for about 1 minute. Not only does this bring out the color, it makes the broccoli tender but not mushy. Easy!

1. In a large saucepan over medium-high heat, add water and bring to a boil. Once boiling, reduce heat to simmer, add broccoli, and simmer for 6 minutes.
2. Meanwhile, place olive oil and butter in a separate saucepan over medium heat. Add onion and garlic. Cook and stir for 5 minutes. Drain broccoli and add to onion and garlic mixture. Sprinkle with sesame seeds, toss to coat, and serve.

Quick and Easy Tip

In place of sesame seeds, use pine nuts, cashews, or almonds for an added crunch and extra protein.

Oven-Roasted Beets

Serves 5

Prep time: 5 minutes
Cook time: 25 minutes
Total cost: $5.20
Calories: 137
Fat: 8g
Protein: 3g
Cholesterol: 8mg
Sodium: 108mg

1 pound baby beets

2 tablespoons olive oil

Sea salt and pepper to taste

3 tablespoons butter

1 tablespoon fresh oregano leaves

Beets are a root vegetable not commonly thought of for everyday meals. When most people think of beets, they think of canned beets in vinegar. However, beets can be truly flavorful if grilled, baked, and tossed with fresh herbs, olive oil, or cheese.

Preheat oven to 400°F. Cut off beet tops and root, if attached. Scrub beets and then cut in half. Place beets in a large roasting pan, drizzle with olive oil, and sprinkle with salt and pepper. Toss to coat. Place in oven and roast for 25 minutes or until beets are tender when pierced with a fork. Place in serving bowl and toss with butter and oregano.

Quick and Easy Tip
You can find baby beets in most grocery stores and at farmer's markets. Look for candy cane beets, which are red and white striped, golden, or white beets.

The $7 a Meal Quick & Easy Cookbook

Red Potatoes with Herbs

Serves 6

Prep time: 6 minutes
Cook time: 20 minutes
Total cost: $4.76
Calories: 197
Fat: 3g
Protein: 4g
Cholesterol: 2mg
Sodium: 351mg

1 pound baby red potatoes

¼ cup butter

3 cloves garlic, minced

2 tablespoons fresh thyme
leaves, chopped

2 tablespoons fresh Italian
parsley, chopped

Sea salt and pepper to taste

Baby potatoes cook fast because they are so small.
Removing a strip of skin from the middle of the potato
helps prevent them from splitting as they cook.

1. Peel a strip of skin from the middle of each potato. Place
   potatoes in a large pot, cover with water, and bring to a boil
   over high heat. Cook until tender when pierced with a fork,
   about 15 minutes.
2. Meanwhile, combine butter and garlic in a small saucepan.
   Cook over medium heat for 2 to 3 minutes, until garlic is
   fragrant. Remove from heat.
3. When potatoes are done, drain thoroughly, then return
   potatoes to pot. Place pot over medium heat and pour butter
   mixture over potatoes. Sprinkle with remaining ingredients,
   toss gently, then serve.

Quick and Easy Tip
To prepare fresh herbs that have tiny leaves, such as oregano,
rosemary, marjoram, and thyme, simply pull the leaves backward
off the stem. Chop the leaves to open up the natural oils and
flavors of the herb.

Vegetables and Side Dishes

Cauliflower with Red and Orange Bell Peppers

Serves 6

Prep time: 7 minutes

Cook time: 17 minutes

Total cost: $6.86

Calories: 91

Fat: 2g

Protein: 2g

Cholesterol: 5mg

Sodium: 88mg

3 tablespoons olive oil

1 red onion, chopped

½ teaspoon turmeric

3 cups cauliflower florets

2 green chili peppers, seeded and chopped

1 each red and orange bell pepper, seeded and sliced into ¼-inch strips

Sea salt and black pepper to taste

Turmeric provides intense color and subtle flavor to this dish and is traditional to Indian cuisine.

Heat oil in nonstick skillet over medium-high heat. Add red onion and cook until soft, about 3 minutes. Add turmeric, stir and cook for 1 minute. Add the cauliflower and reduce heat to medium, cook, stirring occasionally, for about 8 minutes. Add the chilies and bell peppers, cook about 5 minutes, until peppers are tender. Season with salt and pepper to taste. Serve hot.

Quick and Easy Tip

Chili peppers add great flavor to recipes and are very affordable. Just be sure to seed them while wearing gloves so the seeds don't burn your hands.

Creamed Spinach with Nutmeg

Serves 4

Prep time: 5 minutes
Cook time: 8 minutes
Total cost: $4.20
Calories: 166
Fat: 10g
Protein: 16g
Cholesterol: 35mg
Sodium: 80mg

2 tablespoons butter, unsalted

1 pound baby spinach leaves

1 tablespoon water

Sea salt and black pepper to taste

2 tablespoons plain flour

½ cup evaporated milk

Pinch ground nutmeg

Creamed spinach is great when paired with a juicy steak.

1. Melt butter in a medium nonstick skillet over medium-high heat. Tip skillet to coat bottom with butter. Reduce heat to medium and add spinach leaves. Add water and stir. Cook until leaves start to wilt, about 3 minutes. Season with salt and pepper.
2. Sprinkle flour over spinach and stir to evenly distribute. Add evaporated milk and nutmeg, and stir. Cook, uncovered, until sauce starts to thicken, about 5 minutes. Serve hot.

Quick and Easy Tip

As an alternative to evaporated milk, substitute sour cream. It adds flavor and creaminess, and you can use it in other recipes more easily than evaporated milk.

Green Beans with Blue Cheese and Walnuts

Serves 4

Prep time: 4 minutes
Cook time: 6 minutes
Total cost: $7.00
Calories: 103
Fat: 2g
Protein: 4g
Cholesterol: 6mg
Sodium: 129mg

1 pound green beans, ends trimmed, cut into 2-inch pieces

4 slices bacon

4 ounces blue cheese, crumbled

¼ cup walnut pieces, toasted

Try adding a squeeze of lemon to enhance the already delicious flavors.

1. Bring medium-sized saucepan of salted water to a boil. Add the beans and cook until crisp and tender, about 4 minutes. Drain and set aside.
2. Cook bacon until crisp, drain on paper towels. To assemble, place beans on serving platter and sprinkle with a few bacon pieces and cheese, then add walnuts on top.

Quick and Easy Tip
For extra flavor, after draining the beans, chop the bacon and then sauté the beans with the bacon. Yum!

Brussels Sprouts with Roasted Peanuts

Serves 4

Prep time: 5 minutes
Cook time: 15 minutes
Total cost: $5.42
Calories: 75
Fat: 1g
Protein: 5g
Cholesterol: 4mg
Sodium: 89mg

2 cups quartered Brussels sprouts, ends trimmed

¼ cup coarsely chopped unsalted dry roasted peanuts

1 tablespoon olive oil

Sea salt and black pepper to taste

Lots of people cringe when they hear you are serving Brussels sprouts; however, there are many ways to make people fall in love with them. Use this recipe as a base and then try alternative ingredients such as balsamic vinegar and honey.

1. Add 1 inch salted water to a medium-sized saucepan fitted with a vegetable steamer. Bring to a boil and add the Brussels sprouts. Cover and cook over medium heat until crisp and tender, about 7 minutes. Set aside.
2. Add peanuts to a large nonstick skillet. Toast the nuts over medium heat, tossing frequently, about 3 minutes. Add the sprouts, oil, salt, and pepper. Sauté until heated through, about 5 minutes. Taste and adjust the seasoning as desired and serve.

Quick and Easy Tip
Brussels sprouts are best when tender but not mushy. No matter how you cook them—baked, sautéed, steamed, or boiled,—make sure you don't overcook them.

CHAPTER 14

BREADS AND SANDWICHES

Pumpkin Bread

Serves 10

Prep time: 5 minutes
Cook time: 1 hour
Total cost: $4.50
Calories: 170
Fat: 6g
Protein: 3g
Cholesterol: 36mg
Sodium: 338mg

1 cup plain flour

¼ cup whole-wheat flour

¾ cup sugar

½ teaspoon ground cinnamon

1 3-ounce package instant butterscotch pudding mix

½ teaspoon baking soda

½ teaspoon baking powder

½ cup butter, melted

2 eggs

1 cup canned pumpkin pie filling

Quick breads use baking soda and powder for leavening. For best results, measure all ingredients carefully and mix wet and dry ingredients until just combined. Over-mixing makes the bread tough.

1. Preheat oven to 400°F. Spray a 9" x 5" loaf pan with non-stick cooking spray. In a large bowl, combine flour, whole-wheat flour, sugar, cinnamon, pudding mix, baking soda, and baking powder, and stir to blend. Add melted butter, eggs, and pumpkin pie filling and stir just until blended. Pour into prepared pan.
2. Place bread in oven and bake for 1 hour, or until an inserted toothpick comes out clean. Remove from oven and let cook on rack for about 10 minutes. Using a table knife, loosen bread by going around sides of pan. Turn loaf pan upside down, transferring bread to plate. Slice and serve.

Quick and Easy Tip
It's important to use pumpkin pie filling and not canned pumpkin purée because the pie filling has spices that add flavor to the bread.

Mexican Cornbread

Serves 9

Prep time: 5 minutes
Cook time: 23 minutes
Total cost: $2.79
Calories: 223
Fat: 7g
Protein: 5g
Cholesterol: 6mg
Sodium: 749mg

1 cup buttermilk

¼ cup frozen corn kernels, thawed

¼ cup vegetable or canola oil

1 egg

1¼ cups pancake mix

¾ cup yellow cornmeal

½ teaspoon paprika

Adding the corn kernels makes for a Mexican-style cornbread. You can also add roasted red bell peppers and cheese.

1. Preheat oven to 400°F. Grease a 9-inch square baking pan and set aside. In a medium bowl, combine buttermilk, corn kernels, oil, and egg, and beat with a wire whisk. Stir into dry ingredients just until combined. Pour into prepared pan.
2. Bake for 17 to 23 minutes or until edges are golden brown and top springs back when touched with finger. Serve warm with butter.

Quick and Easy Tip

Leftover cornbread can be crumbled and used as bread crumbs for other dishes such as baked chicken.

The $7 a Meal Quick & Easy Cookbook

Orange-Blueberry Muffins

Serves 10

Prep time: 3 minutes
Cook time: 15 minutes
Total cost: $6.60
Calories: 84
Fat: 7g
Protein: 4g
Cholesterol: 2mg
Sodium: 179mg

1 9-ounce package blueberry quick bread mix

5 tablespoons orange juice

¾ cup milk

¼ cup oil

1 egg

½ cup powdered sugar

Mini muffins are a perfect quick breakfast or snack for kids.

1. Preheat oven to 375°F. Line 44 mini muffin cups with paper liners and set aside. In a large bowl, combine quick bread mix, 4 tablespoons orange juice, milk, oil, and egg and stir just until dry ingredients disappear. Fill prepared muffin cups two-thirds full of batter. Bake for 10 to 15 minutes or until muffins spring back when gently touched with finger. Cool for 3 minutes, then remove to wire rack.

2. In a small bowl combine powdered sugar and 1 tablespoon orange juice; drizzle this mixture over the warm muffins and serve.

Quick and Easy Tip
Make muffins ahead of time and store in airtight containers, then reheat for best taste and texture. To reheat, place muffins on microwave-safe dish, cover with paper towels, and heat for 10 seconds per muffin, until warm.

Cinnamon Oat Scones

Serves 6

Prep time: 6 minutes
Cook time: 15 minutes
Total cost: $4.56
Calories: 300
Fat: 12g
Protein: 4g
Cholesterol: 38mg
Sodium: 265mg

2 cups plain flour

⅔ cup oatmeal

⅓ cup brown sugar

1½ teaspoons baking powder

½ teaspoon cinnamon

6 tablespoons butter

2 eggs

6 tablespoons heavy cream

1 tablespoon sugar

Try adding chopped nuts, raisins, or dried cranberries. Serve the scones hot with butter, honey, or jam.

1. Preheat oven to 400°F. Line a baking sheet with parchment paper and set aside. In a large bowl combine flour, oatmeal, brown sugar, baking powder, and half the cinnamon. Cut in butter until particles are fine.
2. In a small bowl, combine eggs and 5 tablespoons cream and beat until smooth. Add to oatmeal mixture and mix until a dough forms. Shape into a ball and press into a 9-inch circle on a baking sheet. Cut dough into 6 wedges and separate slightly. Brush with remaining 1 tablespoon cream and sprinkle with 1 tablespoon sugar mixed with remaining cinnamon. Bake for 12 to 15 minutes until edges are golden brown. Serve hot with butter.

Quick and Easy Tip
As with most types of bread dough, be sure not to overwork or overmix the dough as the final result will be bread bricks!

The $7 a Meal Quick & Easy Cookbook

Breadsticks with Parmesan Cheese

Serves 8

Prep time: 8 minutes
Cook time: 16 minutes
Total cost: $5.04
Calories: 172
Fat: 8g
Protein: 2g
Cholesterol: 22mg
Sodium: 390mg

3 tablespoons butter

2 cloves garlic, minced

½ cup Parmesan cheese, grated

¼ cup Romano cheese, grated

½ teaspoon dried Italian seasoning

1 11-ounce can refrigerated breadstick dough

Breadsticks are great with soup, salad, or just by themselves. Keep them stored in an airtight container for freshness.

1. Preheat oven to 375°F. Line baking sheets with parchment paper and set aside. In a microwave-safe dish, place butter and garlic. Cook on full power for 1 minute, until garlic is fragrant. Pour butter mixture onto a shallow plate and let stand for 5 minutes.
2. Meanwhile, on another shallow plate, combine cheeses and Italian seasoning mix. Open dough and separate into 8 breadsticks; cut each in half crosswise to make 16 breadsticks. Dip each breadstick into butter mixture, then roll in cheese mixture to coat. Place on baking sheets, about 2 inches apart. Bake breadsticks for 12 to 16 minutes or until they are puffed and light golden brown.

Quick and Easy Tip
Parmesan and Romano cheeses are often used together. Parmesan cheese is made from cow's milk and is milder and less salty than Romano cheese, which is made from sheep's milk or goat's milk.

Two-Cheese Garlic Bread

Serves 6

Prep time: 5 minutes
Cook time: 21 minutes
Total cost: $6.56
Calories: 165
Fat: 4g
Protein: 5g
Cholesterol: 14mg
Sodium: 292mg

1 loaf French bread

4 cloves garlic, minced

½ tablespoon cayenne pepper

2 tablespoons fresh Italian flat-leaf parsley, leaves chopped

½ cup butter

1 teaspoon lemon pepper

¼ cup Parmesan cheese

¼ cup Cheddar cheese

This crispy bread is perfect with spaghetti and meatballs or a salad. Use leftovers to make bread crumbs or croutons.

1. Slice bread into ¼-inch thick slices. In a heavy skillet, heat olive oil over medium heat and sauté garlic until soft and fragrant, about 2 to 3 minutes. Pour oil and garlic into medium bowl and let stand for 10 minutes. Add butter, lemon pepper, cayenne, parsley, and cheeses and mix well.
2. Preheat broiler. Spread butter mixture onto both sides of bread. Place on a baking sheet and broil about 6 inches from heat source for 3 to 5 minutes, until light brown. Turn and broil for 3 minutes on second side, until light brown and crisp. Pay attention because broiling bread can result in burned bread if not watched carefully.

Basic Flatbread

Serves 10

Prep time: 10 minutes
Cook time: 8 minutes
Total cost: $2.20
Calories: 100
Fat: 0.8g
Protein: 3g
Cholesterol: 18mg
Sodium: 326mg

4 cups plain flour

½ teaspoon sea salt

1⅓ cups cold water

1 teaspoon olive oil

Chill

1 hour

For a little sweetness, add 1 tablespoon of honey to the dough.

1. Sift together flour and salt. Mix flour with water in a mixer using a large dough hook for 3 minutes or until ingredients are incorporated and the dough is formed. Let dough rest for 1 hour in the refrigerator.
2. Once chilled, form dough into small balls, approximately 20 balls. On floured surface, use a floured rolling pin to roll out each ball into a circles about ½-inch thick. Lightly grease skillet with oil and heat to medium heat. Add flatbread and cook about 4 minutes per side, using tongs to flip, or until lightly browned on each side.

Quick and Easy Tip
Once the flatbread is cooked, drizzle with olive oil and sprinkle with sea salt and freshly chopped rosemary leaves.

Flatbread with Onion

Serves 10

Prep time: 10 minutes
Cook time: 8 minutes
Total cost: $2.70
Calories: 100
Fat: 1g
Protein: 3g
Cholesterol: 19mg
Sodium: 329mg

3½ cups plain flour

½ teaspoon sea salt

1 cup cold water, adding up to ¼ cup extra if needed

1 large yellow onion, chopped

1 teaspoon olive oil

Chill
1 hour

This recipes uses chopped fresh onion. You can also sauté the onion for about 5 minutes and then add to the mixture for a slightly different flavor.

1. Sift together flour and salt. Mix flour and water in mixer using a large dough hook for 3 minutes or until all ingredients are incorporated and the dough is formed. Add onion and incorporate into dough. Let dough rest for 1 hour in the refrigerator. Form dough into approximately 20 small balls. On a floured surface, use a floured rolling pin to roll out dough into circles about ½-inch thick.
2. Lightly grease skillet with oil and heat to medium heat. Add flatbread and cook about 4 minutes per side, using tongs to flip, or until lightly browned on each side.

Quick and Easy Tip
Developing a feel for how much to knead your dough comes with time and experience. If you overwork it, you overdevelop the gluten in the dough, making it tough. This causes the bread to have a chewy, unpleasant texture. A few quick motions should be all the kneading your dough needs.

Whole-Wheat Flatbread with Herbs

Serves 10

- Prep time: 8 minutes
- Cook time: 8 minutes
- Total cost: $3.12
- Calories: 112
- Fat: 1g
- Protein: 4g
- Cholesterol: 18mg
- Sodium: 330mg

Chill
1 hour

3 cups whole-wheat flour

1 cup plain flour

½ teaspoon sea salt

1 cup cold water, plus up to an extra ¼ cup if needed

2 tablespoons fresh thyme, stems removed, leaves chopped

2 tablespoons fresh rosemary, stems removed, leaves chopped

1 teaspoon olive oil

When adding water to dough, add a little at a time to incorporate into mixture. If dough still feels too dry, add a little more water.

1. Sift together flour and salt. Mix flour and water in mixer using a large dough hook for 3 minutes or until all ingredients are incorporated and the dough is formed. Add herbs and incorporate into dough. Let dough rest for 1 hour in the refrigerator. Form dough into approximately 20 small balls. On a floured surface, use a floured rolling pin to roll out dough into circles about ½-inch thick.
2. Lightly grease skillet with oil and heat to medium heat. Add flatbread and cook about 4 minutes per side, using tongs to flip, or until lightly browned on each side.

Quick and Easy Tip
Use only fresh herbs in this recipe as dried herbs do not have the crisp, fresh flavor that fresh herbs do.

Garlic Herb Focaccia

Serves 10

Prep time: 5 minutes

Cook time: 1 hour

Total cost: $5.90

Calories: 236

Fat: 3g

Protein: 7g

Cholesterol: 11mg

Sodium: 197mg

2 teaspoons olive oil

1¼-ounce package dry active yeast

½ cup warm water, not hot and not cold

6 cups plain flour

¼ teaspoon sea salt

2 cups water

½ bunch fresh basil, leaves finely chopped

3 cloves garlic, minced

Resting time
2 hours

If you are making bread dough from scratch (not using a bread mix), go easy on yourself the first time. Getting the feel for the right amount of moisture can be a little tricky at first.

1. Lightly grease a 13" x 9" baking pan with 1 teaspoon olive oil. In a small bowl, stir together the yeast and warm water. Let stand for 5 minutes, until foamy. Sift together the flour and salt. Add yeast mixture into flour mixture by hand or using mixer. If doing by hand, gently incorporate yeast mixture into flour mixture. If using mixer, use dough hook, and combine mixture on slow speed for about 3 minutes or until dough forms together. Remove from bowl, cover with a clean but damp kitchen towel. Let rest on a floured surface for about 1 hour.
2. Combine basil and garlic in a small bowl. Place dough in prepared pan, forming as desired. Using your fingers, gently press garlic-basil mixture into dough. Cover with kitchen towel and let rest again in warm place for about 1 hour.
3. Preheat oven to 425°F. Bake bread for 1 hour, until lightly golden brown.

Simple Chicken Wraps

Serves 4

Prep time: 8 minutes
Cook time:
Total cost: $5.52
Calories: 272
Fat: 19g
Protein: 11g
Cholesterol: 2mg
Sodium: 181mg

Resting time
1 hour

3 ounces cream cheese, room temperature

1 tablespoon mayonnaise

1 tablespoon fresh lemon juice

Pinch sea salt and black pepper

2 8-inch flour tortillas, room temperature

2 cups cooked chicken, cubed

½ red onion, diced

1 cup baby spinach leaves

Wraps are perfect for afternoon appetizer parties. Wrap the finished wrap tightly in plastic and refrigerate for about 1 hour. Remove from plastic and slice into 1-inch slices.

1. Mix together cream cheese, mayonnaise, lemon juice, salt, and pepper in a small bowl. Mix well until smooth.
2. Place tortillas on clean work surface. Spread half the cream cheese mixture on the upper third of each tortilla, about ½ inch from edge. Place half of the chicken on the lower third of each tortilla. Top each with onions and spinach. Roll up each wrap starting from the bottom and fold the tortilla over the filling and roll upward. Compress lightly to form a firm roll. Press at the top to seal the wrap closed with cream cheese mixture. Cut sandwich in half and wrap in plastic film. Refrigerate until ready to serve.

Roast Beef Wrap with Red Bell Peppers and Blue Cheese

Serves 4

Prep time: 10 minutes

Cook time: none

Total cost: $4.36

Calories: 176

Fat: 10g

Protein: 4g

Cholesterol: 10mg

Sodium: 361mg

3 ounces cream cheese, room temperature

1 tablespoon mayonnaise

2 ounces blue cheese crumbles

Sea salt and black pepper to taste

2 8-inch flour tortillas, room temperature

⅓ pound deli roast beef, cut into ½-inch strips

¼ cup diced roasted red bell peppers

1 cup romaine lettuce, chopped

Flour or whole-wheat tortillas are the best for making wraps. Use them at room temperature for ease in folding.

1. In a small mixing bowl, combine cream cheese, mayonnaise, blue cheese, salt, and pepper. Blend until smooth. Place tortilla on clean work surface. Spread half of cream cheese mixture on upper third of each tortilla, about ½ inch from edge. Place half the roast beef on the lower third of each tortilla. Top each with peppers and lettuce.
2. Roll up each wrap starting from the bottom and fold tortilla over the filling, compressing slightly to form a firm roll. Press at the top to seal the wrap closed with the cream cheese mixture. Cut the sandwich in half and wrap in plastic film. Refrigerate until ready to serve.

Quick and Easy Tip

If you don't care for blue cheese, substitute your favorite cheese.

The $7 a Meal Quick & Easy Cookbook

Honey-Roasted Turkey Wraps with Mixed Greens

Serves 4

Prep time: 7 minutes
Cook time: none
Total cost: $4.38
Calories: 389
Fat: 9g
Protein: 8g
Cholesterol: 24mg
Sodium: 324mg

3 ounces cream cheese, room temperature

1 tablespoon mayonnaise

2 tablespoons cranberry sauce

Sea salt and black pepper to taste

2 8-inch flour tortillas

⅓ pound deli sliced honey-roasted turkey breast

¼ pound Cheddar cheese, shredded (about ½ cup)

1 cup mixed greens

Consider using smoked meats in place of regular meats. Smoked meats add an extra layer of flavor without adding fat or calories.

1. Mix together cream cheese, mayonnaise, cranberry sauce, salt, and pepper in a small bowl. Place tortillas on clean work surface. Spread half the cream cheese mixture on upper third of each tortilla, about ½ inch from the edge. Place half the turkey on the lower third of each tortilla. Top each with Cheddar cheese and greens.
2. Roll up each wrap starting from the bottom and fold the tortilla over the filling, compressing slightly to form a firm roll. Press at the top to seal wrap closed with the cream cheese mixture. Cut the sandwich in half and wrap in plastic film. Refrigerate until ready to serve.

Grilled Vegetable Sandwiches

Serves 6

Prep time: 5 minutes
Cook time: 5 minutes
Total cost: $6.99
Calories: 263
Fat: 9g
Protein: 4g
Cholesterol: 10mg
Sodium: 361mg

¼ cup olive oil

½ eggplant, cubed

1 red bell pepper, seeded and diced

1 sweet red onion, diced

Sea salt and black pepper to taste

6 club sandwich rolls

2 ounces goat cheese, room temperature

Goat cheese is a very flavorful cheese that tastes even better when warmed!

1. Heat 1 tablespoon olive oil on grill pan over medium heat. Add all vegetables to grill; season with salt and pepper. Grill until cooked but al dente, about 5 minutes.
2. Brush rolls with remaining oil. Spread goat cheese onto rolls. Layer grilled vegetables onto roll. Serve a whole sandwich to 6 persons or cut in half and serve 12 persons.

Quick and Easy Tip

This is great recipe for using leftover grilled vegetables. Use any combination of vegetables you have. Reheat the vegetables by grilling as instructed above but for only 3 minutes.

Sandwich of Pita with Cucumbers and Feta Cheese

Serves 6

Prep time: 6 minutes
Cook time: none
Total cost: $5.88
Calories: 181
Fat: 8g
Protein: 5g
Cholesterol: 11mg
Sodium: 321mg

6 pita bread

2 cucumbers, peeled and diced

1 large red onion, chopped

¼ bunch fresh oregano, leaves chopped

3 ounces feta cheese, crumbled

1 tablespoon olive oil

Fresh ground black pepper

Feta is a very salty cheese so you most likely do not need to add any salt to this recipe to enjoy.

Slice each pita in half and then open to create a pita pocket. Stuff pocket with cucumber, onion, oregano, and feta. Drizzle with oil and sprinkle with black pepper.

Quick and Easy Tip

A great recipe for a weekend lunch. Mix all ingredients ahead of time, let marinate, and then stuff pita pockets just before serving. Add sliced black olives for a truly Greek dish.

BBQ Beef Sandwich

Serves 6

Prep time: 5 minutes

Cook time: 12 minutes

Total cost: $6.79

Calories: 318

Fat: 19g

Protein: 16g

Cholesterol: 53mg

Sodium: 361mg

1 tablespoon olive oil

½ yellow onion, chopped

6 tablespoons steak sauce

1 8-ounce can tomato sauce

1 pound thinly sliced cooked deli roast beef, largely chopped

6 sandwich buns, toasted

Perfect for using up leftover roast beef, this recipe can also be used with chicken.

In heavy skillet, heat oil over medium heat. Add onion and cook, stirring frequently for 5 minutes. Add steak sauce and tomato sauce and bring to a simmer. Stir in roast beef and simmer an additional 5 minutes, stirring frequently until sauce thickens slightly and roast beef is heated through.

The $7 a Meal Quick & Easy Cookbook

Corned Beef on Rye with Swiss Cheese

Serves 4

Prep time: 3 minutes
Cook time: none
Total cost: $6.80
Calories: 381
Fat: 22g
Protein: 17g
Cholesterol: 53mg
Sodium: 428mg

¼ cup mustard

¼ cup mayonnaise

8 slices deli pumpernickel rye swirl bread

¾ pound corned beef

2 cups deli coleslaw

4 slices deli Swiss cheese

These are perfect sandwiches for St. Patrick's Day parties. Serve with a pickle and side of potato salad.

In a small mixing bowl, combine mustard and mayo. Spread mustard mixture onto bread slices and make sandwiches with the corned beef, coleslaw, and Swiss cheese. Cut in half and serve.

Quick and Easy Tip
When you're using any kind of prepared salads in sandwich recipes, you may need to drain the salad by placing it in a colander and letting it stand for a few minutes, or use a slotted spoon to scoop the salad out of the container. If you're making sandwiches ahead of time, leave the salad out and add it just before serving.

Crispy Grilled Sandwich of Ham, Turkey, and Cheese

Serves 4

Prep time: 5 minutes
Cook time: 8 minutes
Total cost: $4.32
Calories: 535
Fat: 24g
Protein: 18g
Cholesterol: 34mg
Sodium: 460mg

¼ pound thinly sliced deli ham

¼ pound thinly sliced deli turkey

¼ pound thinly sliced deli Colby cheese

8 slices whole-grain bread

1 cup fish batter mix

¼ cup oil as needed

Grilled sandwiches taste great with a dipping sauce. For a spicy dip, combine ½ cup mayonnaise with 2 table-spoons honey Dijon mustard and a teaspoon of chili sauce. Blend well and enjoy.

1. Make sandwiches using ham, turkey, and cheese on bread. In shallow bowl, prepare batter mix as directed on package.
2. Pour oil into heavy saucepan and heat over medium heat until drop of water sizzles and evaporates. Dip sandwiches in batter mixture and place immediately in oil. Cook over medium heat, turning once, until bread is golden brown and cheese has melted, about 4 minutes per side. Cut sandwiches in half and serve.

Quick and Easy Tip

You can find fish batter mix near the seafood section in the grocery store. The batter adds a light crispiness to these sandwiches.

The $7 a Meal Quick & Easy Cookbook

CHAPTER 15

DESSERTS

Strawberry Angel Food Cake

Serves 8

Prep time: 5 minutes

Freeze time: 15 minutes

Total cost: $7.00

Calories: 364

Fat: 6g

Protein: 6g

Cholesterol: 8mg

Sodium: 432mg

1 whole angel food cake

2 cups strawberry frozen
yogurt, thawed slightly

1 pint strawberries, stemmed
and sliced

Angel food cake is great for making all kinds of desserts. Used here with strawberry yogurt, this cake is also great with chocolate syrup and whipped cream.

Cut the cake in half horizontally. Spread the strawberry yogurt on bottom half of cake. Place half of strawberry slices on top of yogurt. Replace top half of the cake. Place more strawberry slices on top of cake. Freeze 15 minutes before serving.

Quick and Easy Tip
If you prefer, substitute your favorite frozen fruit yogurt and combine the corresponding fresh fruit, say raspberry, for example.

The $7 a Meal Quick & Easy Cookbook

Oven-Baked Pears with Whipped Cream

Serves 6

Prep time: 10 minutes
Cook time: 30 minutes
Total cost: $6.90
Calories: 268
Fat: 8g
Protein: 4g
Cholesterol: 95mg
Sodium: 123mg

Juice of 1 lemon

6 pears, peeled and cored

2 to 4 tablespoons sugar

Ready whipped cream as desired

Pears also taste terrific when grilled. If grilling, grill on each side about 2 minutes. Grilling the pears saves time, adds flavor and color to the pears, and doesn't heat your house as much as the oven does.

Preheat oven to 375°F. In a 2-quart baking dish, combine lemon juice with enough water to cover the bottom. Add the pears, cover, and bake for 15 to 20 minutes, or until tender. Remove from oven. Uncover and sprinkle each pear with 1 to 2 teaspoons sugar. Bake, uncovered, for 10 minutes. Serve warm or chilled with whipped cream.

Quick and Easy Tip

For a truly Italian dish, substitute the whipped cream with mascarpone, an Italian cream cheese, if your budget allows. Mascarpone is a little more expensive than whipped cream and provides a less sweet flavor to the pears.

Chocolate Candy Bar Cookies

Serves 12

Prep time: 10 minutes
Cook time: 15 minutes
Total cost: $4.36
Calories: 399
Fat: 22g
Protein: 7g
Cholesterol: 37mg
Sodium: 210mg

1¼ cups plain flour

¾ teaspoon baking powder

¼ teaspoon sea salt

½ cup unsalted butter, softened

½ cup sugar

1 egg

1 teaspoon vanilla extract

1 cup chopped chocolate-covered candy bars (about 6 ounces, ½-inch thick pieces)

Heath bars work great for this recipe, and Baby Ruth bars also work well. Just be sure you don't eat all the candy bars before you need them for the recipe.

Preheat oven to 325°F. In a bowl, sift together flour, baking powder, and salt. In a large bowl, using an electric mixer set on medium speed, beat together the butter and sugar until fluffy and smooth, about 30 seconds. Mix in the egg and vanilla and beat for 1 minute, stopping mixer halfway through to scrape down the sides with rubber spatula. Reduce the speed to low and add the flour mixture, mixing just until incorporated. Gently mix in the candy bar pieces. Drop the batter by large tablespoons onto ungreased baking sheets. Bake for 15 minutes, or until lightly browned. Remove while warm to prevent sticking. Cool on wire racks.

The $7 a Meal Quick & Easy Cookbook

Simplest Ever Chocolate Mousse

Serves 6

Prep time: 10 minutes
Chill: 2 hours
Total cost: $4.02
Calories: 307
Fat: 12g
Protein: 3g
Cholesterol: 54mg
Sodium: 135mg

1 6-ounce package chocolate
pudding mix

¾ cup milk

1 teaspoon instant coffee
powder

1 8-ounce package cream
cheese, cubed

Lots of people are intimidated just by the thought of making chocolate mousse. But this recipe is so simple you can make it with your kids!

In a medium saucepan, combine pudding mix, milk, and instant coffee and stir well. Place over medium heat and cook, stirring constantly, until the mixture comes to a boil. Add the cream cheese and beat until blended. Pour into a 1-quart mold. Chill before serving.

Quick and Easy Tip
Nothing goes better with chocolate than fresh berries. Add some fresh raspberries when serving for a beautiful dish that tastes delicious!

Cream Cheese Pound Cake

Serves 10

Prep time: 15 minutes
Cook time: 1½ hours
Total cost: $7.00
Calories: 502
Fat: 38g
Protein: 8g
Cholesterol: 173mg
Sodium: 368mg

1½ cups butter

3 cups sugar

1 8-ounce package cream cheese

6 eggs

1 teaspoon vanilla

3 cups cake flour

1 tablespoon powdered sugar, for serving

Pound cakes taste delicious, slice easily, and hold up well for parties.

1. Preheat oven to 300°F. Grease a Bundt pan with softened butter, dusted with flour. Tap out the excess flour from the pan.
2. With mixer, cream together butter, sugar, and cream cheese until light and fluffy. Add eggs one at a time, beating well after each one. Then add the vanilla. Mix well. Add flour slowly until combined. Pour into bundt pan and bake for 1½ hours. When serving, dust with powdered sugar.

Quick and Easy Tip
Pound cake can be used in strawberry shortcakes as a substitute for angel food cake.

The $7 a Meal Quick & Easy Cookbook

Oven-Baked Peaches with Brown Sugar Crust

Serves 4

Prep time: 10 minutes
Cook time: 45 minutes
Total cost: $4.56
Calories: 202
Fat: 7g
Protein: 12g
Cholesterol: 124mg
Sodium: 263mg

1 20-ounce can sliced peaches, drained

Zest of ½ lemon

¼ cup dry pie crust mix

¾ cup packed brown sugar

2 tablespoons butter, cut into pieces

Whipped cream

Lemon zest is the rind of the lemon that has been grated off. When grating, use the small side of a large grater or invest in a zester, and be sure to stop when you see the white pith of the lemon. The pith has a bitter taste that will transfer to your food.

Preheat oven to 325°F. Place peaches in a medium-sized baking dish. Add lemon zest. Crumble pie crust mix into a bowl. Add the brown sugar and mix well. Dust peaches with pie-crust mixture and dot liberally with the butter. Bake for 45 minutes or until top is crusty. Serve warm with whipped cream or ice cream.

Quick and Easy Tip
Using canned peaches certainly saves time, but if you have some helpers, use fresh peaches that you have peeled and removed the pits.

Oatmeal-Crusted Baked Apples

Serves 6

Prep time: 5 minutes
Cook time: 20 minutes
Total cost: $4.14
Calories: 298
Fat: 6g
Protein: 3g
Cholesterol: 31mg
Sodium: 91mg

1 21-ounce can apple pie filling
¾ cup brown sugar
1 teaspoon cinnamon
¼ teaspoon nutmeg
½ cup plain flour
½ cup oatmeal
¼ cup butter, melted

The secret that makes this recipe good is the crumbly sugary crust on top.

1. Preheat oven to 400°F. Place pie filling into 1½-quart casserole dish. In a medium bowl, combine sugar, cinnamon, nutmeg, flour, and oatmeal and mix well. Add melted butter and mix until crumbs form. Sprinkle crumbs over pie filling.
2. Bake for 15 to 20 minutes or until pie filling bubbles and crumb mixture is browned.

Quick and Easy Tip
Apple pie filling, or any canned pie filling, can also be added to cake mixes for a more dense, flavorful cake. Add the same crumbly crust to the top of the cake before baking. Yum!

Easy No-Bake Chocolate Custard

Serves 6

Prep time: 5 minutes
Freeze time: 4 hours
Total cost: $4.52
Calories: 127
Fat: 7g
Protein: 1g
Cholesterol: 6mg
Sodium: 2mg

1 cup chocolate syrup

1 15-ounce can sweetened
condensed milk

1 16-ounce container frozen
whipped topping, thawed

½ teaspoon vanilla

¼ cup sliced almonds, toasted

Whenever a recipe calls for vanilla, use real vanilla extract as opposed to imitation vanilla, even if you are shopping on a budget. Imitation vanilla has very little flavor, and you end up using five times as much to try to get the same amount of flavor.

In a large bowl, combine syrup and sweetened condensed milk and beat until smooth. Fold in whipped topping and vanilla. Sprinkle with almonds and serve immediately as a custard or place in casserole dish, top with almonds, and freeze until hardened.

Quick and Easy Tip
Pour this mixture into a prepared pie crust (ready-made crust, available in the freezer section) and freeze until solid. Top with chocolate shavings.

Parfait of Raspberries and Pecans

● Serves 6

Prep time: 8 minutes
Cook time: none
Total cost: $6.99
Calories: 311
Fat: 18g
Protein: 4g
Cholesterol: 69mg
Sodium: 152mg

1½ cups whipping cream

½ cup powdered sugar

½ teaspoon vanilla

2 pints raspberries

½ cup chopped pecans, toasted

½ cup grated semisweet chocolate

You can use Cool Whip for some recipes, but making your own whipped cream is so much more fun and you can add your own flavors to it. As a guide, 1 cup unwhipped cream equates to about 2 cups whipped!

1. Place cream in a large mixing bowl. Begin whipping over high speed with electric mixer. While whipping, add sugar and vanilla. Beat until stiff peaks form. In a separate small bowl, add raspberries and crush them slightly so some are puréed and some are still whole.
2. Layer raspberries with whipped cream mixture, pecans, and grated chocolate in 6 parfait, martini, or wine glasses. Serve immediately or cover and refrigerate.

Quick and Easy Tip
For truly fluffy whipped cream, begin whipping cream by itself. Then as cream begins to thicken a little, add the other ingredients. Be careful and don't wait too long, however, or cream will be whipped!

The $7 a Meal Quick & Easy Cookbook

Peanut Butter Cup Pie
with Chocolate Ice Cream

Serves 8

Prep time: 10 minutes
Freeze time: 4 hours
Total cost: $7.00
Calories: 495
Fat: 29g
Protein: 13g
Cholesterol: 144mg
Sodium: 383mg

30 fudge-covered graham crackers

¼ cup butter, melted

2½ pints chocolate ice cream

¾ cup peanut butter

4 ounces peanut butter cups, chopped

This is a great dessert for parties as it usually appeals to a lot of people.

1. Crush graham crackers and combine with butter. Press crumbs into a 9-inch pie pan and set aside.
2. In a blender or food processor, combine ice cream and peanut butter. Blend or process until combined. Fold in chopped peanut butter cups until mixed well. Pour into pie crust and freeze until firm.

Quick and Easy Tip
For best results when serving, remove from freezer and let stand for about 10 minutes. Slice and then serve.

Chocolate Parfait with Oatmeal Cookies and Crumbled Toffee

Serves 4

Prep time: 10 minutes
Cook time: none
Total cost: $4.89
Calories: 269
Fat: 8g
Protein: 3g
Cholesterol: 26mg
Sodium: 88mg

1 3-ounce package instant chocolate pudding mix

1 cup chocolate milk

1 cup whipping cream

5 oatmeal cookies, broken into pieces

¼ cup toffee candy bits

Substitute any type of cookie you wish for this dessert or change the flavor of pudding mix.

1. In a medium bowl, combine pudding mix and chocolate milk. Mix well. With wire whisk, whisk until smooth and thickened. In a small bowl, beat cream until stiff peaks form. Fold into pudding mixture.
2. Layer pudding mixture, cookies, and candy bits into parfait, martini, or wine glasses. Serve immediately or refrigerate.

Amaretto Bread Pudding

Serves 10

Prep time: 15 minutes
Cook time: 50 minutes
Total cost: $7.00
Calories: 594
Fat: 26g
Protein: 12g
Cholesterol: 190mg
Sodium: 361mg

¼ cup unsalted butter

1 large loaf day-old or toasted Italian bread

6 eggs

1½ cups whole milk

1½ cups heavy cream

¼ cup amaretto liqueur

¼ cup honey

¼ cup granulated sugar

Bread pudding is a simple dessert that can be made with raisins, berries, nuts, or any combination of the above. Just add bread pieces, milk, sugar, and eggs and you have the makings of bread pudding.

1. Preheat oven to 375°F. Lightly grease a rectangular 13" x 9" baking dish with 1 teaspoon of butter. Melt remaining butter. Tear bread into large 2-inch pieces. Combine with melted butter in a bowl. Beat eggs in a separate bowl. Whisk in milk, cream, liqueur, honey, and sugar. Place bread mixture in prepared pan. Pour egg mixture over top and stir to combine.
2. Bake for 30 minutes, uncovered. Stir, and return to oven. Bake for about 15 to 20 minutes longer until set. Serve warm with whipped cream or ice cream.

Quick and Easy Tip

This is the perfect recipe for any leftover bread! Don't let any foods go to waste. There is always a recipe for any food you have; you just have to be creative! Remember, recipes are guidelines, not hard, fast rules.

Grilled Bananas with Honey

🥄 Serves 6

Prep time: 5 minutes

Cook time: 6 minutes

Total cost: $4.25

Calories: 132

Fat: 1g

Protein: 1g

Cholesterol: 0mg

Sodium: 3mg

6 bananas, peeled

Cooking spray

2 tablespoons honey

¼ cup almonds, whole or
    chopped

¼ cup light brown sugar

2 teaspoons fresh cilantro,
    leaves chopped

There are hundreds of types of bananas. The most familiar banana is the Cavendish banana; however, some markets may carry red bananas, which are sweeter, or the Manzano banana, which has an apple flavor.

1. Preheat grill. Spray bananas with cooking spray and place on grill. Turn them while grilling to get crossed grill marks on the bananas. Grill them for 3 minutes on each side.
2. When serving, slice bananas on bias, fan on plate, drizzle with honey, and sprinkle with almonds, brown sugar, and cilantro.

Quick and Easy Tip
Grill bananas whole, with peel on, if you prefer, until black. Peel back and serve as outlined above.

The $7 a Meal Quick & Easy Cookbook

Cider-Poached Apples
with Raisins

Serves 6

Prep time: 5 minutes
Cook time: 45 minutes
Total cost: $5.72
Calories: 164
Fat: 4g
Protein: 0g
Cholesterol: 1mg
Sodium: 91mg

6 Granny Smith apples, peeled

1 cup apple cider

¼ cup sweet white wine such as Reisling

Zest and juice of 1 lemon (zest first, then juice)

3 whole cloves or ¼ teaspoon ground cloves

2 cinnamon sticks or ½ teaspoon ground cinnamon

¼ cup golden raisins

When a recipe requires both lemon zest and lemon juice, be sure to zest the lemon first, then roll the lemon on a hard surface to break up the juices inside, and then juice the lemon. Trying to get the zest off a juiced lemon is near to impossible and will most likely result in an injury to your hand.

1. Place apples in a large saucepan with the cider, wine, lemon juice, zest, cloves, and cinnamon. Simmer, covered, on medium heat for 30 to 45 minutes, until apples are fork tender. Remove apples and set aside.
2. Reduce cooking liquid in half. Serve apples sprinkled with raisins and drizzled with remaining liquid.

Quick and Easy Tip
Apple cider is not to be confused with apple cider vinegar. If you can't find apple cider, just use apple juice.

Easy Lime Tart

Serves 8

Prep time: 8 minutes
Cook time: 25 minutes
Total cost: $5.20
Calories: 103
Fat: 4g
Protein: 1g
Cholesterol: 26mg
Sodium: 100mg

3 limes, zested and juiced

3 eggs, beaten

2 tablespoons cornstarch

½ cup granulated sugar

1 cup water

1 ready-made frozen pie crust, baked

For this recipe, prebaking the pie crust is essential to a crispy tart. Placing the filling into an unbaked pie crust will result in an undone or uncooked pie crust bottom.

1. Mix together all ingredients well, except pie crust, and place in a medium-quart boiler over medium heat. Bring to slow simmer and stir mixture constantly so the eggs don't curdle until it becomes thick.
2. Pour lime mixture into pie crust and bake for 15 minutes.

Quick and Easy Tip
Substitute lemons if you prefer.

The $7 a Meal Quick & Easy Cookbook

Zabaglione with Marsala Wine and Peaches

Serves 6

Prep time: 10 minutes
Cook time: 10 minutes
Total cost: $6.97
Calories: 198
Fat: 8g
Protein: 8g
Cholesterol: 159mg
Sodium: 308mg

3 pounds fresh ripe peaches, peeled, halved, pits removed

¼ cup granulated sugar

3 large egg yolks, room temperature

2 tablespoons water

¼ cup Marsala wine

Zabaglione, or sabayon, is a thin custard-like sauce for berries or other fruits. It is delicious when poured into a martini glass and topped with fresh berries. Make the day before and keep in the refrigerator overnight.

1. Slice peaches into ⅛-inch slices and fan out on plate to serve.
2. Combine sugar and yolks in top of double boiler over medium heat. Using an electric mixer, beat mixture until frothy. Add water and wine. Continue to cook over simmering water, beating constantly with mixer at medium speed until mixture thickens, about 8 minutes. When serving, pour sauce over peaches and serve hot.

Quick and Easy Tip

Don't be intimidated by using a double boiler. It is very easy and its whole purpose is to prevent your ingredients from burning! Just be sure that the water underneath is not high enough to touch the top boiler.

Piña Colada Grilled Pineapple

Serves 6

Prep time: 10 minutes
Cook time: 10 minutes
Total cost: $6.12
Calories: 259
Fat: 1g
Protein: 1g
Cholesterol: 2mg
Sodium: 9mg

3 tablespoons dark rum

½ ripe medium pineapple, peeled and cut crosswise into 6 slices, ¾-inch thick

1 tablespoon brown sugar

1 cup frozen whipped topping

¼ cup shredded coconut

Try serving this in the shape of a butterfly for an impressive presentation!

Preheat grill to medium. Drizzle rum over pineapple slices and sprinkle with brown sugar. Grill pineapple, with grill cover down, for 5 minutes per side, turning only once. Serve with whipped topping and shredded coconut.

Quick and Easy Tip
If you are making this for a party, slice the pineapple the day before and then have your friends help with the grilling for fun!

The $7 a Meal Quick & Easy Cookbook

Lemon Drop Cookies

Serves 16

Prep time: 12 minutes
Cook time: 10 minutes
Total cost: $4.75
Calories: 120
Fat: 8g
Protein: 2g
Cholesterol: 1g
Sodium: 33mg

1 cup granulated sugar

2 sticks unsalted butter, softened

3 teaspoons lemon juice

1 large egg

¾ teaspoon baking soda

¼ teaspoon sea salt

2 cups plain flour

⅓ cup powdered sugar

These lemon cookies are a perfect complement to the end of a delicious meal.

1. Preheat oven to 350°F. Line a baking sheet with parchment paper. In a large bowl, combine sugar and butter and cream together until smooth. Add lemon juice and combine. Beat in egg.
2. In a separate bowl, add baking soda, salt, and flour. Stir to blend. Using an electric mixer at low speed, gradually add flour mixture to butter mixture until just blended into a soft dough. Drop by heaping teaspoonfuls onto baking sheet. Place cookies about 1½ inches apart.
3. Bake on middle rack in oven 9 to 10 minutes until a toothpick inserted into center comes out clean. Do not overcook. Dust cookies with powdered sugar while warm. Let cool for 2 minutes and remove from baking sheet.

Quick and Easy Tip
Pay attention not to overmix dough as cookies will become overly flat when baked.

Brownies with **Chopped Pecans**

Serves 16

Prep time: 10 minutes
Cook time: 35 minutes
Total cost: $6.08
Calories: 138
Fat: 7g
Protein: 2g
Cholesterol: 39mg
Sodium: 11mg

¼ teaspoon sea salt

½ teaspoon baking powder

½ teaspoon ground cinnamon

½ cup plain flour

1 stick unsalted butter

4 ounces semisweet choco-
late pieces

2 large eggs

1 teaspoon vanilla extract

¾ cup granulated sugar

1 cup chopped pecans

Even though I am known as The Bikini Chef, sometimes chocolate and ice cream really do the trick! Leave out the pecans if you are allergic to nuts or are bringing these to a party.

1. Preheat oven to 325°F. Grease a 9" x 9" baking pan. In a bowl, combine the salt, baking powder, and cinnamon with the flour until well blended.
2. Fill heavy quart boiler 1½ inches deep with water. Place butter in a metal bowl that fits securely on top of the boiler. Place boiler with bowl on stove over medium heat. Heat until butter is beginning to melt. Add chocolate to butter and melt together, stir only occasionally. Once both butter and chocolate are melted, remove from heat and beat in eggs. Add vanilla extract. Stir in sugar, then blend in flour mixture. Stir in pecans.
3. Spread batter evenly into prepared pan. Bake on the middle rack of oven for 30 minutes or until toothpick inserted comes out nearly clean. Let cool and cut into 16 bars.

The $7 a Meal Quick & Easy Cookbook

Oatmeal Cranberry Chews

Serves 12

Prep time: 10 minutes
Cook time: 12 minutes
Total cost: $4.75
Calories: 345
Fat: 11g
Protein: 3g
Cholesterol: 23mg
Sodium: 103mg

1 cup butter

½ cup granulated sugar

½ cup brown sugar

1 egg, plus 1 extra if needed

½ teaspoon baking soda

½ teaspoon baking powder

¾ teaspoon ground cinnamon

½ teaspoon ground nutmeg

1 cup plain flour

1½ cups quick-cooking oatmeal

½ cup dried cranberries

These little cookies are great as a snack as they are fairly healthy and taste great.

1. Preheat oven to 350°F. Line a baking sheet with parchment paper. In a large bowl, cream together butter and sugars. Beat in 1 egg. In a separate bowl, sift together the baking soda, baking powder, cinnamon, and nutmeg with the flour. Blend well. Add flour mixture to butter mixture and blend thoroughly. Stir in oatmeal and dried cranberries. If dough is too dry, beat in remaining egg.
2. Drop by heaping teaspoonfuls onto baking sheet, placing cookies about 2 inches apart. Bake for 10 to 12 minutes or until done.

Quick and Easy Tip
When making the dough, only use the second egg if the dough mixture feels overly dry. Don't be afraid to use your hands, even if they get a little messy. You can always wash them. Just be sure to start with clean hands first!

APPENDIX

EQUIVALENT CHART

Ingredient	Equivalent
3 teaspoons	1 tablespoon
2 tablespoons	⅛ cup
4 tablespoons	¼ cup
8 tablespoons	½ cup
16 tablespoons	1 cup
5 tablespoons plus 1 teaspoon	⅓ cup
12 tablespoons	¾ cup
4 ounces	½ cup
8 ounces	1 cup
16 ounces	1 pound
1 ounce	2 tablespoons fat or liquid
2 cups	1 pint
2 pints	1 quart
1 quart	4 cups
⅝ cup	½ cup plus 2 tablespoons
⅞ cup	¾ cup plus 2 tablespoons
1 jigger	1½ fluid ounces or 3 tablespoons
8 to 10 egg whites	1 cup
12 to 14 egg yolks	1 cup
1 cup unwhipped cream	2 cups whipped cream
1 lemon	3 tablespoons juice
1 orange	⅓ cup juice
1 pound unshelled walnuts	1½ to 1¾ cup shelled
2 cups fat	1 pound
2 cups granulated sugar	1 pound
3½ to 4 cups unsifted powdered sugar	1 pound
2¼ cup packed brown sugar	1 pound
4 cups sifted flour	1 pound
3½ cups unsifted whole wheat flour	1 pound
4 ounces (1 to 1¼ cups) uncooked macaroni	2¼ cups cooked
7 ounces uncooked spaghetti	4 cups cooked
4 slices bread	1 cup crumbs

INDEX

Butter, 16, 19, 21, 23, 27, 47, 56, 79, 83, 84, 85, 92, 101, 109, 112, 119, 124, 127, 130, 133, 135, 137, 138, 143, 146, 155, 157, 158, 173, 177, 182, 202, 204, 207, 208, 209, 210, 211, 215, 218, 221, 223, 226, 227, 230, 232, 233, 260, 261, 264, 270, 271, 272, 275, 277, 279, 280, 281, 283, 287, 288, 290, 291, 292, 308, 310, 311, 312, 315, 317, 323, 324, 325

Buttermilk, 14, 25, 111, 208, 288

Caesar dressing, 68, 70
Candy bars, 308
Cannellini beans, 99
Capers, 43, 124, 128, 191, 207
Cardamom, 56, 182
Carrots, 64, 65, 71, 86, 126, 136, 155, 164, 166, 221, 268
Cauliflower, 238, 282
Cayenne pepper, 53, 56, 79, 85, 100, 156, 174, 178, 215, 292
Celery, 48, 62, 74, 80, 85, 92, 117, 127, 136, 150, 155, 163, 186, 198
Cheese, 15, 19, 20, 21, 22, 29, 42, 45, 47, 49, 54
American, 231
blue, 14, 171, 284, 298
brie, 236
cheddar, 62, 69, 71, 85, 107, 115, 117, 118, 230, 231, 240, 292, 299
Colby, 304
feta, 66, 67, 72, 167, 220, 254, 301
goat, 81, 300

gorgonzola, 232, 253
Gruyère, 101
jack, 70, 180
mascarpone, 138
Monterey jack, 230
mozzarella, 57, 61, 133, 134, 229, 242, 243, 245, 246, 247, 248, 249, 250, 251, 252, 254, 255, 257
Parmesan, 68, 83, 95, 112, 128, 130, 133, 137, 160, 173, 175, 183, 195, 197, 203, 212, 214, 218, 219, 221, 226, 229, 258, 259, 260, 262, 271, 273, 291, 292
Pecorino Romano, 128, 244
pepper jack, 103, 174, 235, 243
provolone, 63, 243
ricotta, 229, 255
Romano, 137, 208, 291
Swiss, 63, 161, 303
Cherries, 25
Chicken, 79, 86, 116, 117, 297
breast, boneless, 63, 64, 65, 70, 75, 78, 109, 113, 114, 115, 118, 119, 120, 121, 124, 125, 126, 245, 250
broth, 85, 86, 93, 94, 96, 99, 103, 104, 107, 199, 122, 124, 128, 130, 135, 136, 157, 158, 164, 191, 195, 203, 206, 208, 216, 226, 260, 261, 273, 276
ground, 39
tenders, 55, 62, 110
whole, 111, 112, 123
wings, 252
Chili
beans, 100, 234
peppers, 154, 197, 282
powder, 49, 92, 100, 169, 184, 189, 203

sauce, 114, 131, 203
Chinese cabbage, 265
Chives, 46, 49, 92, 109, 210, 211, 226
Chocolate
semi-sweet, 314, 324
syrup, 313
Chutney, 39
Cilantro, 49, 50, 129, 163, 168, 200, 222, 237, 266, 318
Cinnamon, 56, 154, 162, 239, 287, 319, 324, 325
Cloves, 141, 154, 157, 162, 319
Coca-Cola, 170
Coconut, 322
Cod, 204
Coffee powder, 309
Coleslaw, 303
Coriander, 129, 143, 165, 222
Corn, 28, 53, 69, 73, 92, 100, 163, 168, 191, 238, 288
creamed, 103
flour, 111, 229
Cornbread, 110, 140
Cornmeal, 111, 142, 197, 199, 201, 271, 288
Cornstarch, 92, 126, 140, 164, 320
Cottage cheese, 15, 48, 51
Couscous, 276
Crabmeat, 41, 192
Cranberries, dried, 39, 60, 71, 142, 325
Cranberry sauce, 299
Cream, 122, 207, 211, 221, 290, 314, 316, 317
of broccoli soup, 125
cheese, 26, 48, 298, 299, 309, 310
of chicken soup, 118
Creativity, 10